WILTON

NOW AND THEN

IN

HAILE AND WILTON

Produced by the Haile and Wilton Local Heritage Group.

Published by the Haile and Wilton Local Heritage Group
3 Haile Park, Haile, Egremont, CA22 2ND
www.HaileandWilton.co.uk

First published in Great Britain in 2004 by the Haile and Wilton Local Heritage Group

The Haile and Wilton Heritage Group gratefully acknowledges the sponsorship of the Local Heritage Initiative.
The Local Heritage Initiative is a partnership between the Heritage Lottery Fund, Nationwide Building Society and The Countryside Agency.

Local Heritage *initiative*

Typeset 10¹/₂ on 12¹/₂ Adobe Garamond
Designed and printed by Titus Wilson and Son, Kendal.

ISBN: 0-9548550-0-0

Front cover: Haile Village about 1904
Back cover: Haile Village, 2004

The illustration of plants throughout the book are some examples of those
species which indicate an ancient woodland.

Each illustration of items you would find, at one time, on a farm or in a farmhouse has a question.
The answers to the questions can be found in the Appendix at the back of the book.

CONTENTS

Haile Hall.

ACKNOWLEDGEMENTS

We acknowledge the help of the following organisations, without whose assistance so much of the book could not have appeared.

We acknowledge the essential financial help given in the form of a grant by the Countryside Agency's Local Heritage Initiative. The Local Heritage Initiative is a partnership between the Heritage Lottery Fund, Nationwide Building Society and the Countryside Agency.

The staff of Cumbria Record Office and Local Studies Library (Whitehaven) who have given such unstinting help to our volunteers, guiding, finding, translating and generally encouraging our enthusiasm and informing our ignorance.

Illustrations of the Advertisement for the letting of Haile Hall; the Bill for a meal at the Golden Lion; the Title page of the sale catalogue for Haile Hall estate; the Advertisement for the letting of the Buck's Head Inn; and the Notice of Reward for information about stolen geese, appear courtesy of Cumbria Record Office and Local Studies Library (Whitehaven).

The Whitehaven News for permission to use references, extracts and the photographs of 'The stirrup cup' and 'Hounds walking up the village'.

The Beacon Centre, Whitehaven for permission to use the photographs by Norman Roberts.

The Yorkshire Post for permission to use the photograph of Cumberland and Westmorland wrestling at Grasmere Sports.

We would also like to thank the following people.
D. R. Perriam for permission to use the ground floor plan of Haile Hall, drawn by John Robinson, after H. B. Stout.
Lord Egremont for permission to use the map of the Haile Hall estate and the key to field names.

MEMBERS OF THE HERITAGE GROUP AND CONTRIBUTORS TO THE BOOK

Ailsa Butler
David Crayston
Isobel Crayston
Eileen Dixon
Michael Forsdyke
Mavis Gaskell
Eva Graham
Doreen Greening
Mary Gregg
Mary Hogg
Val Holmes
Janet Hunter
Norman Hunter
Nora Hutchins

Jennifer Jackson
Lyndsey Johnson
Phil Johnson
Dave King
Louise King
John Leavens
Tom Milburn
Jean Moore
John Mumberson
Joyce Reed
Penny Thompson
Fiona Van Mourik
Mary Wallace

Bluebells in Haile Wood.

FURTHER ACKNOWLEDGEMENTS

So many people have helped us in so many ways. We earnestly hope that we have included everyone here and offer our sincere apologies if any one has been overlooked.

John Atkinson
Albert Banks
Dave Banks
Teresa Barns
Tom Barns
Robert Baxter
John Benn
Clive Bowd
Ida Bowe
Margaret Bowness
Keith Bradshaw
Joseph Bragg
William Bragg
Mary Brown
Alan Butler
Catherine Clark
Christine Craghill
Henry Crayston
Geoff Dixon
Terry Dixon
Winnie Dobson
Mervyn Dodd
Helen Donaghue
Elsie Farren
Kathleen Fawcett
Jim Fisher
Maureen Fisher
Marian Foster
Mavis Fox
Vic Goodwin
Lawrence Graham
Betty Haile

Muriel Haile
Sheila Hardcastle
Alice Harrington
Russell Harrington
Alistair Herd
Gill Hudson
Peter Hutchins
Myra Hutchinson
Philip Jenkinson
Margaret Jones
William Jones
Edward Kennedy
Margaret Leavens
Vera Lowrey
Henry Manisty
Betty Marshall
John Mawson
Molly Mitchell
Keith Mossop
Jean Nanson
Hubert Nanson
Henry Noblet
Shirley North
William Park
Anthony Phipps
Elizabeth Phipps
Virginia Phipps
John Pritt
Annie Raven
Alan Read
Freda Relph
Julie Relph

John Robley
Andrew Schofield
Dorothy Schofield
John Sears
Ann Sherwen
Penny Smiles
Eric Smith
Betty Spedding
John Thorley
John Todd
Florrie Tyson
Andrea Walker
John Walker
Elsie Wightman
Jack Wightman
Harold Wilson
Jim Wilson
Angus Winchester

2

FOREWORD

When a group of villagers with an interest in their local history meets to discuss the formation of a local heritage group with the possibility of producing a book, there is inevitably much interest and excitement. One such group met in Haile Village Hall on 10th September 2002. Little did they know the journey they were about to embark on.

Twenty-four undaunted explorers began with a WEA ten-week course on the sources of local history, without the encouragement of which this journey might never have begun. We knew where, roughly, we wanted to go but we had only a vague idea how to get there.

So putting together this book has been an expedition entered into without a clear map. Looking back at the whole process we do wonder whether, had we had the map, we would have set off in the first place. But, it is said, the more difficult the journey the more worthwhile the destination.

The reader may need a genuine map to find where the communities of Haile and Wilton are. For it is these two communities which, though some distance from each other, go to make up the larger part of the parish whose peoples, traditions and histories are the subject of this book. We could say, just leave the A595 at Egremont and turn one way or t'other, if you want to find us. But it is rather more picturesque and better reflects the way most of us feel about the place to say that we nestle between the foothills of the Lake District – on the quiet side – and the gentle plains that move the eye towards the Irish Sea. We have the best of two worlds.

So what did our particular journey involve? Of course, it started with an idea which, once funding from the Local Heritage Initiative had been obtained, took off with an enthusiastic group of people prepared to go where no one of them had been before. We listened to visiting speakers who gave guidance on how to tackle this journey and who spread an infectious enthusiasm. We had training on how to research our past, how to look afresh at what we have around us, how to find and interpret old documents, how our landscape has changed and why, and how buildings can tell a story. We organised ourselves: everyone had a task, whether it was collating resources, collecting and organising photographs, providing illustrations, carrying out interviews or embarking on our own research following our personal interest and writing up the results. Editors were chosen to bring it all together.

The work, over months, put in by all the members of the group has been helped enormously by so many others. Friends, near and far, have freely shared their memories, some even being prepared to face the novelty of recorded interviews. People have racked their brains, consulted family members, written and telephoned, sometimes again and again, with information. And they have always been so patient, pointing the way. We know that memories can be a little fallible at times, but we have tried to ensure that the information we have given is accurate, and we do apologise if there are any details that the reader feels are not quite right.

Now we are nearly there. The journey has not been without its frustrations but it has certainly brought its rewards, chief among them, perhaps, is having our eyes opened to just how many of the aspects of past life in the parish and its environs we can still enjoy today – the buildings, the walks, the woods and the wildlife. In some very pleasant respects, our parish has not 'moved with the times'.

We hope that those who read the book will find their awareness and enjoyment similarly expanded.

THE NATURAL WORLD

EARLY BEGINNINGS

Our story of Haile and Wilton starts 500 million years ago. You will immediately ask why we are interested in such ancient history and what we can possibly know about these times. However, the geological processes that have taken place since that time have been immensely important to our area because they have formed our landscape, provided the rocks used in our buildings and created the fertile land and minerals that have given the area its prosperity. So our story would not be complete if we ignored these early beginnings. Of course geologists have studied the area for a long time, but their knowledge was greatly enhanced during the 1990s by the largest geological investigation ever carried out in Britain in preparation for the proposed NIREX nuclear waste repository. Anyone who lived in Haile or Wilton at that time will remember the convoys of huge vibrating trucks on our roads, the lines of markers across the fields and the helicopters flying overhead with instruments suspended underneath. NIREX subsequently abandoned the project, but the information gathered at that time remains and it gives us a knowledge of the geological history of our area that is second to none.

Although Earth had originally been formed some four billion years earlier, the oldest rocks seen in the parish today date from 500 million years ago. Incredibly, the land that is now Haile and Wilton lay well south of the equator at that time and was submerged under the deep waters of the ocean. The mud, silt and sand that formed the ocean floor gave birth to the rocks known to geologists as the Skiddaw Group, the grey, broken rock that appears widely around the parish and is used so extensively to make farm and forest roads.

Around 450 million years ago the rocks known as the Borrowdale Volcanic Group were formed. As their name suggests, these were formed by volcanoes erupting molten lava or hurling ashy and cindery solids on top of the existing Skiddaw Group rocks. These volcanic rocks are much harder and vary in colour between grey and blue-green. During this period of intense volcanic activity an event of great significance for the Lake District took place when a huge mass of molten rock was intruded deep below the centre of the area. This body of rock, known as the Lake District batholith, is roughly in the shape of a cone, some 40 kilometres in diameter and up to nine kilometres thick in places. The effect of this mass can be compared to the foundation of a building and it has allowed the mountains that stand above it to remain intact through hundreds of millions of years. The coastal plain, to the west of the Lake District, has no such support so that it is unable to bear the weight of mountains. Wilton lies about on the edge of the Lake District batholith and so the mountain of Dent is found to the north of the village. Haile, on the other hand, lies in the coastal plain on heavily faulted, or cracked, and lower lying ground.

The next significant period in the development of our area occurred around 300 million years ago. By this time the land had been carried north by the movement of the plates that form the Earth's crust and lay in tropical latitudes, roughly on the equator. On a typical Cumbrian day, with the wind howling and the rain lashing

Uldale valley.

4

down, it is hard to imagine that we once enjoyed a climate similar to the Caribbean, but that is how it was 300 million years ago. In warm, shallow water, which sometimes dried out, limestone was formed from the calcium contained in marine life. At one time limestone covered most of the Lake District but, being an easily dissolved and softer rock, much of it eroded away. The only large body of limestone visible on the surface within the parish is found at Mousegill Quarry, although large amounts exist below the surface.

Not much later, around 250 million years ago, the land had been permanently lifted out of the water. Now somewhat north of the equator, it became a sandy and rocky desert, similar to parts of the northern USA today. Compacted over millions of years, this produced the sandstone that can be seen extensively around the parish, both in the ground and as the obvious material for the construction of most of the older buildings. Geologists have identified several types of sandstone in West Cumbria but Haile and Wilton have the St Bees Sandstone, probably the best known, most easily worked and hardest wearing variety.

By this point in time the basis of all the rocks found today in the parish had been created. Since then, movement of the earth's crust has carried the area to its present mid-northern latitude, lifting the land, distorting and fracturing the strata and compacting the mud, silt and sand into solid rock. Heat generated by this crustal movement also changed the structure of some of the material. Cavities formed, particularly in the easily dissolved limestone, which were filled by other solution-borne materials, notably iron ore in the case of our parish. It is generally accepted that the Lake District mountains were much higher at one time and have been considerably eroded during this period.

The final event in the formation of the landscape, and arguably the most important, occurred much more recently when the area cooled and became covered by permanent ice. There have been several ice ages in this area, starting about 200,000 years ago, interspersed with relatively warm periods when the ice disappeared. However the last ice age, which ended about 10,000 years ago, has been mainly responsible for the landscape as we see it today. At times during the ice ages the Lake District was covered by ice to a depth of

Glacial meltwater channel at Stockbridge.

perhaps 1000 metres. These glaciers, which were no different to the glaciers seen in many parts of the world now, were constantly moving very slowly. This huge weight of ice gouged out any loose material, and much of the underlying rock, carrying it with it, to be ground up and deposited when the ice melted, creating the gravel and clay found in many places in the parish. The ice flowed outward from the centre of the Lake District, predominantly in a westerly direction in our area, deepening and widening valleys that open westward.

A secondary effect of the glaciers occurred when they melted and the enormous volume of water washed away loose material from the higher ground, particularly steeper sloping areas, and deposited it in lower lying areas. The volume of water was much greater than the flow observed in becks and rivers today and it produced the melt water channels that the keen eye can find around the parish, a good example being the valley that the Kirk Beck follows between Stockbridge and Church Bridge. The material washed from the higher ground settled in the bottoms of the valleys and, as they dried out, produced the flat, fertile land that is used for growing crops. The movement of the ice and water, together with the action of rivers in more recent times, rounded blocks of fractured rock into the boulders that later provided valuable building material for houses, barns and walls.

HAILE WOOD

Haile Wood is an ancient wood, a place of special scientific interest, the Best Wood in the Cumbrian lowland and to get all these honours is no mean feat – it's taken hundreds of years!

Haile Wood is in fact made up of various woods, Danielbrow, Meadow, Low Orchard, Pigeonhouse, Grange, Stockbridge, Horse-close and The Great Wood, which have, over the years, combined to form the wood we see today.

From the carpet of bluebells in spring, to the lush ferns in summer, moving to the golden canopy in autumn and the tranquillity and sleepiness of the winter months, Haile Wood always has something of interest.

Haile Wood occupies the sheltered, steep-sided valley of the Kirk Beck and comprises a variety of woodland types, which reflects the complex geology of the area. To the north, hazel, birch and oak have developed where the valley cuts through Skiddaw slates and Borrowdale granites. To

WOOD SORREL

the south the valley narrows as the geology of the valley changes to St Bees sandstone. Here ash, oak and hazel dominate the steep valley sides.

Indeed, what makes Haile Wood so special, is that it has all the features of a former working ancient woodland such as old coppice stools, where poles were cut on a 10 to 12 year rotation, yielding sustainable woodland products for a working rural economy. This practice has helped create the woodland we see today. The rich ground flora is encouraged by hundreds of years of coppicing, which enabled the rays of sunlight to reach the woodland floor by the rotational felling of the poles.

Applications for the coppicing of the woodland would be placed in the local papers as stated in Barbara Ponsonby's letters to her solicitors on the 21 July 1892.

'I will send advice about Coppice Wood to be inserted in local papers next Thursday. Will you see that persons applying about Coppice Wood are taken to see it. The five acres of oak coppice wood is close to Haile Church and extends up Church walk towards the Hall. Enclosed letter from West Cumberland Land Owner says price would not be above £10 an acre. Things have changed; oak was the most valuable on account of the bark, now it is the least valuable. Oak cannot be peeled until the sap runs in April and the whole lot ought to be cleared away and fences, posts and gates made good by Martinmass, wood is given away in our part of the world compared to other places'.

The low price the Ponsonbys put on the coppicing seems due to the fact that, although the oak bark, used in the tanning industry, was removed when the sap was rising in spring when it was most easy to do, the bark had to be removed by hand, which was very labour intensive, and this impacted upon the price.

Studies have found 12 different plants that are indicative of an ancient woodland, flourishing within the wood; the Bluebell is a prime example but not alone. Primroses appear in droves, along with Anemones, Wood Sorrel, Wood Violet, Greater Woodrush, Sweet Woodruff, Barren Strawberry and very large local lichen – Peltigeria horizontalis.

The Kirk Beck nearly runs the entire length but this is not the only beck within the wood; Quicksand Gill, Ragga Beck and Hannah Beck all feed into Kirk Beck contributing to the deposits of nutrient-rich alluvial soil, on which grow Ransoms and Moschatel, both indicators of old woodland. Standing on the banks of the Kirk Beck within the woods is Haile Mill, once a working water mill, where the local farmers from the parish of Haile and Wilton would take their wheat and corn to be milled. On the opposite side of the beck to the mill, high-up on the fringe of the wood, are the partial remains of the Pigeon House now unfortunately derelict and overrun by nature.

It's not just the flora but also the fauna that's worth a mention. Red squirrels, an endangered species, inhabit the woods and sometimes if you're lucky you'll catch a glimpse of a roe deer feeding. Woodpeckers, wrens, and buzzards are just a few of the birds that inhabit the woods. Some parts of the wood, though not all, have public footpath access so if you decide to visit, whatever the time of day or season, Haile Wood always has something to offer and is a place that will live on in your memory.

BLUEBELL

SESSILE OAK

PIGEON HOUSE

The Pigeon House.

7

SOME HISTORY

THE PONSONBY FAMILY OF HAILE HALL

In the 12th Century a family with the Norman name of Ponson or Punzon, came from Picardy in France and held the Manor of Ponsonby. From them the parish was called Ponsonby or Punzun's Place. The first Ponsonby died around 1177 and it was his son John Fitzponson who gave the church at Ponsonby to a Hospital which later became Conishead Priory. It is thought that John may have held the office of Barber to the King from which three combs argent were emblazoned on his shield and are still on the Ponsonby coat-of-arms.

The Ponsonby family crest.

The Manor of Hale granted to Thomas de Multon passed to a family who took the name of Hale. By the time of Henry III (1216-1272) Hale was the property of Alexander de Hale. One of his daughters and co-heiresses, Agnes, married William de Ponsonby presumably beginning the Ponsonbys of Hale.

Later Ponsonbys had connections with the church. A John Ponsonby was Parson of Egremont in 1391 and Richard Ponsonby was the last Abbott of Calder Abbey. William Ponsonby was a 'ballinus monastrie' (bailiff) probably involved in the administration of the Abbey estate, and Roger Ponsonby was a clerk. These were probably lay positions. Matthew Ponsonby was however a monk in holy orders and he was included, among others, in a report on the immoral conduct of some monks!

In 1647 John Ponsonby of Hale Hall was in Dublin at the beginning of the Irish Rebellion. He raised arms and a company of men to serve King Charles I but when the King was beheaded he deserted the Royalist cause. He went to Ireland with Cromwell as a Colonel of a Regiment to help subdue the rebels, was knighted and was given the Kidalton estate in Southern Ireland. He changed the name to Bessieborough (Bessborough) in honour of his second wife Bessie. He had a great reputation as a cavalry leader, and soon regained favour with the Royalists.

Sir John's son John did not go to Ireland but stayed at Hale Hall to run the estate and he did this so effectively that when he died in 1708 he left his wife, formerly Anne Copley of Gosforth, £2,000, a considerable sum in those days. The family connection with the armed forces continued, however. In 1804 Miles, the great great grandson of the John mentioned above, was commissioned by the King,

> 'to be a Captain of a Company in Corps of Whitehaven Volunteers, but not to take rank in the Army except during the time of the said Corps being called out into actual service . . . You are therefore to take the said Company into your care and your best endeavour to keep them in good order and discipline and obey orders from his majesty'.

Miles took the not-unusual step in his will of leaving his Estate 'in trust' to make sure that what had obviously become a valuable inheritance was not 'frittered away', and to make sure it was handed on to his heirs.

In 1814 the male line of the Ponsonby family died out and Dorothy Ponsonby, daughter of Miles and Catherine Clementson inherited Hale Hall. She had married John Fisher of Whitehaven and, in accordance with Miles's wishes, they and their children assumed the name of Ponsonby by Royal licence, so the name continued.

The care in trying to protect the inheritance was evident again (and was by now more necessary) in the will of 1887 of Miles' grandson, Miles, who, while allowing his son, Henry, a legacy of £180 a year, stipulated that if he is 'squandering' his money, payments to him are to cease. It was Miles' daughter, Barbara, who had the task of administering this payment and who was occasionally put under pressure by her brother for an early payment when his money had run out. On 11th June 1892 she writes,

> 'With regard to the £90 my brother Henry wants paid on July 1st, I have written to tell him I will send it to him this time in advance'.

By 20th July a telegram had arrived from the Isle of Man, where Henry was living, saying, 'Remit by wire to the Isle of Man Bank £20 this day to save disaster in the family'. It was Barbara's task also, although she had the 'free use, occupation and enjoyment of my mansion at Hale Hall', to administer the affairs of the Estate since her brother, Miles de Hale Ponsonby, who inherited the Hall, had earlier emigrated to Tasmania.

Haile Hall. An earlier photograph of the Hall which shows it having a front porch.

BARBARA ELLEN PONSONBY

The period during which Barbara supervised the running of the Estate, from 1892 to 1919, were hard times for both the Estate and its tenants. In a letter of 14th May 1892 she says: 'Every shilling counts; so much going out. So little coming in'. Very little seemed to be profitable. Of part of the woodland she writes in 1893:

'I think it would be worth taking into consideration the poverty of Hale Hall Estate . . . I cannot afford to pay £40 or £50 to thin

it late on with no chance of getting that money back from the Estate, nor do I think I am called upon to do it. Let those, I say, who are living at Hale Hall 18 to 20 years hence; perhaps times will be better then'.

But Barbara herself was still there twenty years later and the financial situation did not seem to be any less difficult.

She well understood the difficulties her tenants were facing and asked her solicitor in February 1893 to write to her brother about the problem:

'Will you write to my brother in Tasmania and tell him how rents stand. I hope you will tell him that a reduction in rent has to be made to all farmers at present owing to the depressed times'.

It was at this point, seemingly, that her brother, Henry, who had now returned from the Isle of Man to live at the Hall with his wife, wanted to have his say about the income from the Estate. His attitude to money was very different from that of Barbara and so she was compelled to ask her solicitor:

'I wish you would write a letter to Henry Ponsonby who is at Hale Hall with his wife, giving him an account of the rent payments . . . My brother seems to think no reduction is necessary for the farmers, so I hope you will tell him it will be worse for us if the farms are untenanted'.

This awareness of the plight of her tenants and her shrewdness in recognising that she had to be realistic is reflected in her reply, in that same year, about a tenant who was obviously having problems.

'I have just had Joseph Sharp here, farmer of Side, who wants a reduction in his rent of £10 a year owing to the depressed times. He is a very nice farmer, perhaps you could get him to accept a less reduction, say £7, but I would rather rent was reduced than lose him as a tenant'.

She looked for any way to improve things, appealing against the tax assessment of Hale Hall 'as it is only a small house' and keeping her eye open for any other ways of increasing income. (On one occasion she paid £1,600 off a mortgage from her own funds, in effect subsidising the estate.) In October 1893 a Mr Barnes wished to view land looking for iron ore, and Barbara wrote:

'I have written to Mr Barnes . . . it would be well if a good

Company could be formed to bore for minerals, providing they do not bore too near the Hall'. And in November 1897: 'There has been a rich find of iron ore at Ullcoats and a probability of further explorations. I should like to know what are the royalties in Wilton that belong to the Ponsonby Estate'.

Despite the problems, Barbara was a good landlord and was prepared to spend money on the tenants' property. In August 1892: 'With respect to having new doors for byres and rooms upstairs at Whitehow Head, I will go and see what is required'. And in February 1893 the tenant at Whitehow Head writes: 'Blacksmith has got the gates up at Whitehow Head but has some of the stoops to alter'. He added, however, a complaint:

> 'I mentioned Head of Hale midden running into our water to Mr Helder. I also mentioned about Benson throwing his dead pigs into our water and he said he had done it many times and he would do it again, so I think our water is going to be middling stuff'.

It is not surprising that at times Barbara felt the frustrations of her role as landlord. You can imagine her feeling that she was reaching the limit when she wrote: 'Farmers want two months' grace for payment of their rent. The farmers are never done asking favours'.

Quite a lot of patience and diplomacy was needed in the handling of situations. What do you do when a tenant writes in March:

> 'Moffat came for two trees in Whitehow Head and he left a gap in the hedge you could get a horse and cart through, but I think it is not right to come with their carts where they like without asking liberty',

and then you have the reply from the timber merchant:

> 'The tenant you name must be a very uneasy man and fond of making mountains out of a molehill. I was in the woods last weekend and did not observe any damage done to the fences, in fact was surprised so little had been done considering so many trees near the hedge. I will write to the man who cut the wood'?

Then there were other problems.

> 'I hear that Mr Harrington at Brayshaw is subletting part of the farm. May I have confirmation that the tenancy agreement does not allow this?'

And, of course, accidents will happen. In 1902 Barbara received a letter from Isaac Benson who, now aged 70, had worked for her as a groom and gardener. He was asking for compensation for having had his leg broken. It seems that when they were felling a tree a branch hit him and, as Barbara commented to her solicitor, 'He did not get out of the way fast enough'. Doctor Braithwaite wrote that, 'Benson will not work again but his club will pay 5 shillings a week'. Mr Benson had been advised that he could make a legal claim and so Barbara settled out of court for £50.

During all this time, and despite the energy which Barbara devoted to the Estate, she continued to show her concern for things beyond Estate business. One organisation which benefited greatly from her involvement was the local school, in which she took a great deal of interest. From the school log books and Management Committee records, it is clear that she was a fairly regular visitor to the school between 1886 and 1906. On several occasions she cleared the school debt. On one occasion she presented a harmonium to the school. A letter from Joseph Wilson, a School Manager, states:

> 'At the committee meeting of the Haile and Wilton School held on Monday night it was unanimously resolved that the committee on behalf of the parishioners tender to you their best thanks for the harmonium which you so generously presented to the school and also assure you that they thoroughly appreciate the gift'.

Later it is recorded that the school was used for 'Miss Ponsonby's tea and Xmas tree' which may have been a regular Christmas treat. Another entry in the Managers' minutes tells how Miss Ponsonby 'had in her kindness entertained the scholars at tea'. Another valuable contribution that she made was regular supplies of 'cartloads of sticks' needed to keep the fires going. Despite this generosity shown to them, the youngsters of the village were expected to show their respect to the local gentry. Muriel Haile, who was brought up in Haile and is now living in Bedfordshire, remembers her aunt, who as a girl helped out at the pub, saying that if the carriage passed by, the girls would drop a curtsey. Similarly Joe Noble, born in the village in 1890, remembers as a lad at the beginning of the last century, having to doff his cap or else you would be in trouble.

It is sad that, despite all her concern and her efforts to keep her brother's Estate functioning, in the ten years after Barbara died the Hall and its Estate suffered neglect. Ronsley Ponsonby inherited the Hall but because his home was in Tasmania, he rented the Hall to a string of tenants and eventually it was left empty and neglected. That is until Sir John Ponsonby bought it in 1929.

Major General Sir John Ponsonby
KCB. CMG. DSO. 1866-1952

Sir John Ponsonby was born on the 25th March, 1866, in 6 The Cloisters, Windsor Castle. He was the son of Sir Henry Ponsonby, equerry to Queen Victoria at the time, and Mary, nee Bulteel. He was born with a cleft palate and hare lip, though as we shall see this impediment did not hold him back. He was educated at Eton, within sight of his home. His ambition was always to be a soldier, but Queen Victoria, when approached about this, is reported to have said, 'But poor boy, he can't make himself understood'.

Sir Henry Ponsonby was made Queen Victoria's Private Secretary in 1870, and the family moved into the Norman Tower, a grace and favour residence. Mary set about making a home out of what was described as 'an uncompromising feudal fortress'. Two of the rooms had been state prisons. Mary had to obtain permission from Queen Victoria and the Office of Works to remove the plaster from the walls. They weren't happy about the project but Mary won. When the plaster was removed it was found that some of the inscriptions exposed were medieval and that caused quite a stir. The walls were left bare.

Sir John was brought up in a happy home with loving parents. All the children had their own table for their 'occupations' which could be anything from painting, carpentry, working with metals, etc. His mother was a very practical lady and, in many ways, well ahead of her time. Carpentry was a hobby she had learned from her father. Lady McDonald wrote of her in 1858,

> 'she was impulsive, energetic, with a feverish longing for a wider sphere and action than has been allotted by circumstances'.

She sang, danced, acted in charades and painted in water colours. In Canada she took target practice with a rifle and was a keen pool

Young Sir John Ponsonby.

player. She had the 'image of a daring and bold woman not afraid to rattle the gold-rimmed teacups'.

She supported Girton College, Cambridge (the first college for women) to which she donated money and encouraged her friends to do so. She also supported the Society for Promoting the Employment of Women.

Mary had been Lady-in-waiting to Queen Victoria, so was well used to Court life, and although Henry was deeply involved in his job (he was often away for three months in a year) his letters show he missed his family very much.

Living in the Norman Tower meant the Ponsonby family were in close proximity to the Royal Household. Every day they saw the Queen driving in her carriage with two grey horses and an outrider. No-one had to meet her on these outings so it was a case of diving for cover when she approached, which proved difficult for some of the older courtiers.

The Queen loved her 'performances' which were put on by the Royal Household. Most of the Ponsonby family, including Sir John, took part in these theatricals.

From time to time a member of the Ponsonby family would be asked to dine with the Queen. Apparently she ate very quickly and when she finished that was the signal for everyone's plate to be removed, so it was good policy to waste no time.

Sir John overcame his disability and joined The Derbyshire Militia; he was later commissioned in The Irish Rifles, and transferred to The Coldstream Guards in 1888.

Who's driving? Queen Victoria's daughter (at the front) and Sir John Ponsonby's sister, Maggie, seem to be a little apprehensive at the advice given them by Sir Henry Ponsonby.

He saw active service in Matabeleland, Uganda, and the South African War (Boer War), where he fought against General Smuts. When hostilities ceased, the two men became firm friends, and Jan Smuts became a frequent visitor to Haile in later years when Sir John had taken over Haile Hall.

In the Boer War he served with the Rhodesian Field Force, the 5th New Zealand Regiment and the Guards Mounted Infantry. While serving as an Adjutant with the New Zealanders, who were a 'wild body of men', he was elected to be their Commanding Officer. When their tour of duty was completed they wanted him to go to New Zealand to retire there but it was not to be.

In 1899, Sir John had a bout of Blackwater Fever. His loyal men carried him for miles to safety and he was then sent home to recover. He went back to serve with the 2nd Guards Mounted Infantry who were immortalised in Kipling's poem 'The Mounted Infantry'. He served there until the Armistice.

At the outbreak of World War I, in early August 1914, Sir John took his battalion of the Coldstream Guards over to France. He was in the thick of the fighting at Mons and Cambria and was wounded in the leg on the 14th September. At the Battle of Aisne Sir John narrowly escaped capture. It is said he showed great gallantry and coolness in battle and was loved by his men.

While at the Front Sir John produced a daily typewritten 'news sheet' for the Officers called *The Daily Dump* or *The Unintelligent Report*. This was a light hearted spoof intended to help raise morale.

He had an aversion to tin hats, which were compulsory for the troops, so he had one made out of cardboard and covered with hessian. It looked just like the real thing complete with Coldstream Guard cap badge. When he was on a tour of inspection of the trenches a gust of wind blew his 'hat' into the enemy lines, much to the hilarity of his troops.

He was mentioned seven times in despatches and was awarded the CMG in 1915 and the CB in 1918. He was awarded the French Legion of Honour, Commander of the Order of King Leopold of the Belgians and the Croix de Guerre of both France and Belgium.

For five years between the wars Sir John commanded the Madras District of India, years when he was very happy with plenty of polo (for which he won trophies), racing, hunting and entertaining. He was Hon. Colonel of The Suffolk Regiment from 1924-1939 and retired from the Army in 1928 when he was made a KCB.

Sir John had a brother, Arthur Ponsonby, who was a page to Queen Victoria when he was 11 years old. There was no sign at that time that he would become a Liberal and a pacifist. In 1907 he became a Socialist. He lost favour at court and was struck off the garden party list! In 1914 he spoke out against the war and in the House of Commons, with Keir Hardie, he commanded attention and respect. He followed the pacifist line all through the war, enduring both bodily risk and misunderstanding.

In later years, when he came to visit Sir John, the arguments between the dyed-in-the-wool old soldier and the pacifist were heated and forceful. His brother did not approve of his political views and did not hesitate to tell him.

Sir John was a skilled horseman and horses played a prominent part in his life; he could ride just about any horse, even riding in a

Zebra race in Africa. Only one horse proved too much for him. He had borrowed a horse from his brother Fritz to go riding in Rotten Row and the horse bolted, knocking an elderly rider and his horse over. The following day a newspaper reported:

Molly Robley (Lady Ponsonby). A photograph of Molly as a young woman, taken in the style which was popular at the time.

'The galloping cad who knocked over an old officer in Rotten Row may be glad to hear that there were no bones broken'.

Thereafter the horse was always called 'The Galloping Cad' and there continued to be many more incidents with various riders. One unfortunate horseman chose to visit his aunt on this steed. When they arrived, the horse, instead of moving to a place to be tethered, set off across the lawn and completed thirty laps before it could be brought under control. The resulting state of the lawn convinced the rider that it would perhaps be better if his aunt did not have the benefit of his company on this occasion. The horse was eventually sold for 25 guineas at Tattersalls.

Haile Hall, the home of Sir John's direct ancestors, was put on the market in 1928 by his kinsman, Ronsley Miles Ponsonby but failed to sell. Sir John, who, after his retirement from the army, was looking for a residence in Cumberland, contacted John Robley, Estate Agent who later became his Land Agent, and through him bought the house. John Robley had a sister, Mary, and that is how Sir John met his future wife, Lady Ponsonby. The house was in a dilapidated state. After the death of Miss Barbara Ponsonby in 1919 it had been tenanted for five years and left empty for five years. It had been vandalised, some rooms had no floor boards, and the story goes that while Sir John was talking to someone both his feet went through the floor.

'Conveyance dated 24th January 1929, between Alice Waugh of the Burroughs, Papcastle, near Cockermouth, mortgagee of the one part and Ronsley Miles Ponsonby esq. of Launceston in the

Sir John Ponsonby on St Cloud. This photograph was taken in France during the First World War.

Colony of Tasmania, and Sir John Ponsonby of 40 Chelsea Park Gardens, in the County of London, a Major General retired. The vendor has agreed to sell the property free from incumbrances at the price of £2,800'.

The Ponsonby window in Haile church.

Sir John set about putting the house to rights, including the garden which was mainly under grass, as well as building tennis courts, a golf course, fish pond and croquet lawn. He had a Hillman Wizard car believed to be the first car in Haile. At this time he was courting Mary Ponsonby and there begins another story.

Sir John died in 1952 at the age of 86. A stained glass window was installed in Haile Church in his memory, showing his family motto 'pro rege, lege, grege' (for the king, the law, the people) and St George fighting the Dragon.

In his obituary in *The Household Brigade Magazine,* Sir Charles Lloyd wrote:

> 'He was a unique character, popular with young and old alike with a kindly disposition and human outlook and a great sense of fun. He disliked the cruelties of war but his cheerful spirit got the best out of everyone'.

Lady Mary Ponsonby. 1901-2003

Mary, the daughter of Thomas Robley and Elizabeth Smith, was the first child to be born in their new house, Ingleberg, Beckermet on the 3rd July 1901. With her elder sisters she was educated at Dagfield School, Southport, where the Headmistress was a Miss Clark. She went to school at the age of five years and left at seventeen. Discipline was strict and there was a system of fines for breaches of discipline; 6d per offence was deducted from her £1 allowance for each misdemeanour.

In the early 1920s she accompanied her mother on a grand tour of the Mediterranean and North Africa. Even before her marriage she took a keen interest in social work, the Women's Institute at Beckermet of which her mother was a founder member, and Whitehaven Hospital. After her mother's death she consented to marry Sir John; their engagement was announced on the 19th December 1935 in *The Times* and they were married on the 21st December 1935 in the Church of St Martins-in-the-Fields at 8.30 am. The ceremony was conducted by the Rev. Dick Shepherd. A few hours after the ceremony they embarked on the *SS Oranto* from Tilbury Docks bound for their honeymoon destination of Majorca, Egypt, and Malta. The wedding was a private affair because of the death of Sir John's brother, Frederick, First Lord Sysonby on October 20th 1935.

Because of the great difference in their ages, it was perhaps inevitable that some of Sir John's friends – that is, before they got to know her – speculated on the notion of 'The country girl captures the title'. But in fact it was a marriage full of happiness and humour, so much so that along with his will Sir John left his Molly a letter of thanks for their life together.

Sir John and Lady Ponsonby travelled a great deal, sometimes being away for three months at a time. They kept a flat in London where they spent most summers and on these visits one of the maids usually accompanied them.

At home, one of the events best remembered by the people in the village was the annual party held in the Barn for the children of Haile, when they all received a present. Lady Ponsonby said one year Sir John bought all the boys a sharp penknife which did not meet with all the parents' approval! Mary continued to support her

The Spout House Red Cross group. Lady Ponsonby, who is in this photograph, was a supporter of the Red Cross for many years. 1940.

Sir John and Lady Ponsonby in the garden.

mother's interests in the community, such as the Red Cross (which she had joined in 1919), and served with them during the Second World War as Commandant of the Third Detachment. From 1964 to 1974, she was Divisional President, West Cumberland and held the Red Cross Badge of Honour. She started the Red Cross Shop in Whitehaven Hospital, insisting that the profits were retained to be spent on equipment in the Hospital rather than paid to the Red Cross Headquarters. Collectors of the Red Cross were always assured of a generous donation.

She was a member of Haile Parochial Church Council from 1936 to 1952, and was always interested in Church affairs. She always sat in the pew next to Sir John's stained glass window with her cushion made by Betty Spedding (who incidentally also made all the hassocks in the Church).

She had a keen interest in the Cumberland Nurses' Benevolent Fund and her other interests included the NSPCC and the WRVS. In February 1971 as Divisional President she was awarded her 15 years Long Service Badge; she was President of the Whitehaven and District RNLI for forty years.

Her gardens were her pride and joy and once a year, until about 1970, she opened them to the public in support of charity. Her love of gardening stayed with her all her life and even into her 'old age' she was to be found on her knees tending to her plants. It was fitting that she was the founder President of the Lakeland Horticultural Society and in 1969 the Steering Committee proposed that she should be invited to fill the post of President, which she accepted. A very sound choice. Henry Noblett, writing in the Lakeland Gardener, Autumn 2003, said, 'She was a gracious, charming President who spoke to her audiences with a friendly and sincere authority. She always attended the Annual General Meeting over which she presided most efficiently. A regular visitor to the Annual

Lady Ponsonby. In front of some of her azaleas.

Lady Ponsonby, the gardener. As many people remember her, taken in 1961.

Plant Sale, she took a great interest in both the development of Holebird Gardens and in Society affairs generally'.

Lady Ponsonby had a wide circle of friends who visited her regularly. Those who knew her well will remember her height, her bearing, her voice, and her genuine interest in all around her. In her 90s a little make-up and a spray of perfume set her up for her day. She had a wealth of wonderful stories to tell having led such an interesting life. She had tremendous recall for details and events. She could be straight to the point as in the case of the unfortunate gentleman visitor who was told 'You need a shave and a hair-cut'. But she was always fair.

An anecdote:

At Preston Station, meeting Lady Ponsonby off the London train, the Attendant for the Disabled settles her into a wheelchair and goes at a cracking pace down the steep ramp to the exit. Suddenly he realises her name. 'Ponsonby? They call you Ponsonby? Have you got connections with Waterloo? Did you have somebody at Waterloo?' Despite her reputation for friendliness no answer was there from the Lady as she hung on for dear life.

Lady Ponsonby died on 18th, April 2003 aged 101 years.

The Waterloo Connection

Every year on the anniversary of the Battle of Waterloo, June 18th, 1815, two gentlemen came to see Lady Ponsonby. They were Bill Collins and Ian Lowe and they brought a dozen red roses and usually a picnic hamper which they prepared themselves. Tea was taken on the lawn if the weather was fine.

This tradition began when a deputation from the 12th Lancers took Lady Emily Ponsonby a bouquet of flowers on the anniversary of the Battle and every year afterwards until she died at Hampton Court Palace in 1877. Her husband, Sir Frederick Cavendish Ponsonby, fought in the Battle and was severely wounded. He lay on the battlefield for 18 hours, was robbed twice and was finally rescued.

St Bees Charters – Some Very Early References to Haile

In our searches for early references to Haile we found a sequence of eight 'charters', or deeds, referring to land in Haile, in the St Bees Priory Register. In the published Register the charters are given in the medieval Latin, with some explanatory footnotes in English. We have had the relevant ones translated, and they make an interesting collection worth recounting.

The earliest one is thought to date from about 1210. (Dates aren't given in the documents but some approximate dates, deduced, for example, from names of witnesses, are given in the footnotes.) In it, one Adam, son of Ketell, gives one acre of land in Hale, plus common pasture sufficient for ten cattle, thirty sheep and two horses, to God and St Mary, and St Bega in Copeland (Coupland) and 'the monks in the same place'. The document ends by saying that he is making the gift 'for my salvation and that of my heirs and all of my ancestors'. Witnesses names included Alexandro de Caldra (Calder) and Gilberto de Haverington (Harrington).

The identity of this Adam is a bit obscure, but the editor of the Register notes that he is the first recorded 'owner' of land in Haile and a contemporary of one Yuuain de Hale.

Four further documents concern land in Haile given by another Adam, son of 'Ywan', to William the chaplain of Haile (capellani de Hale), who himself was son of Henry the 'steward' of Haile. The land is described as one acre, half a rood and seven 'virgates' (a variable small land measure), together with the 'liberties' and use of common pastures etc. that went with it.

The gist of these is that the land and associated 'rights' is 'held of' 'St Bega and the Priory and monks there', for a yearly rent of four pence, and that William first gave it to his stepson Peter, who then gave it to his (step) sisters Agnes and Cecilia. After their brother Adam renounced any claim he had to it, the sisters, in a charter thought to date from 1260-70, gave it to one John, another chaplain of Haile. The final document shows this John giving his rights in the land back to 'Blessed Mary of York' (St Mary's Abbey, York) and the monks of the 'cell' of St Bega.

Three other interesting charters relate to a more familiar name, one John (Johannes) de Hale. This is probably the same John de Hale who got into legal disputes about certain offences and rights to the church, and had lands confiscated (for a time) by a Royal 'commission' of 1266.

Two of them are thought to date from no later than 1250 and consist of agreements with the 'prior and his men' of St Bega. In one of these, John undertakes to be bound to the prior and his men to pay 40 shillings to the building of St Peter's (York Minster), 'whenever and however often I or my heirs or anybody of mine makes any trespass against the said prior or his men', provided they can prove it. 'And for the greater security (that) this bond may be faithfully observed', he has bound himself by his 'corporal oath by touch of the relics and on the bracelet of St Bega'.

In the other agreement between the same parties John states that 'if the cattle of the said prior and his men are reasonably seized in my pasture at Hale and impounded' they will pay him one penny for five cattle, in summer, and one penny for ten in winter, and for horses

> 'whatever may be right according to the view of the country (local custom). If however the said cattle are seized in a cornfield or meadow, they will restore damages according to the view of upright and lawful neighbours'.

If horses get into a cornfield or meadow, 'and cannot be captured', and it be proved that 'they have made damages', the prior and his men will pay damages 'according to the custom of the country'.

In the last charter in the series, probably from a similar or slightly earlier date, John de Hale gives, to

> 'God and St Bega of Coupland and to Michael the miller and his heirs . . . a half acre of my land in my lordship in the vill and territory of Hale, namely, that half acre of land which goes from the old dyke (or ditch) of the mill pond to Sourmire, next to the moor of arable land'.

(The Latin word fossato used here, translated as dyke or ditch, could perhaps also be interpreted as meaning a water course, or possibly a dam.)

Some bits of the following text are missing but the charter basically goes on to say that the land is to be 'held of' St Bega for a payment of three pence yearly (by Michael the miller), and that Michael and his heirs will be entitled to all 'service and common easements pertaining to the aforesaid vill' (which would include common pastures), to be shared with their neighbourhood, for 'their own animals, oxen, cows, sheep and a horse'. (Only one horse in this case it seems, for Michael and his heirs and their half acre.)

Mention of a mill is of interest, although we don't know exactly where it was, as we can't identify 'Sourmire'. Reference to the old 'dyke' of the mill pond, i.e. old in the 13th century, suggests that

milling in the parish had been going on since time immemorial. Likewise the first charter and those of John de Hale in particular show similar preoccupations with livestock control and use of common land, to those which we see in our manorial records from much later centuries.

The Pigeon House. Showing the original arched doorway.

Also worth noting are the witnesses' names. In particular some of the charters relating to both William the chaplain's land and to John de Hale's include Roberto de Wilton and Alexandro and Willelmo (William) de Ponsonby (spelt variously as Punchunby, Punzunby, Puncunby and Punsunby). Other common witnesses included

Hugone (Hugo) de Moresby (Moreceby), Ricardo and 'Thoma' de Cleator (Cleter, Cleterk, Cletergh), 'Johanne de Gosford', 'Thoma' de Irton, and some other de Hales. Long established Cumbrian family names such as 'le Fleming' and 'Sevenhous' (Senhouse) also appear.

All in all, these very old documents echo aspects of life in our rural area which persisted for many hundreds of years.

HAILE HALL

Had it not been for Sir John Ponsonby in 1928 looking at Haile Hall and deciding, despite its deteriorating state, to buy the property, it is doubtful whether this ancient, country manor house would be here today. He bought it from a relative, Ronsley Miles Ponsonby of Tasmania, who had inherited the Hall. He was a descendant of the main line Ponsonby family who had owned Haile Hall from its early years. In his book on the family Sir John wrote, 'Haile Hall, referred to sometimes in old histories as Haugh, Heale, and Hale, may be described as the cradle of the family.'

Haile Hall set among trees.

Haile Hall is almost hidden from view, standing in its own grounds, surrounded by woodland. But you can catch a glimpse of it across the valley nestling amongst the trees, when you travel by road from Egremont and descend towards the church. Once through the old, stone gateway you follow a long, imposing, beech-lined driveway which runs under a sixteenth century archway bearing the Ponsonby Coat of Arms and motto, granted to the family in 1647. The archway is part of the old gatehouse. This is described in the 1928 sale catalogue as 'a bothy, with room above, formerly used as Estate Office'. Since Sir John bought the Hall, the gatehouse cottage on the right, cleared of encroaching undergrowth and made habitable, has been home to several of his employees.

On the other side of the archway are a long barn with buildings beneath and other outbuildings, some of which are quite derelict. According to that same document these buildings included:

'8-stall stable with loft over, coach house, harness room, two dog kennels, two loose boxes, two piggeries with enclosed yards, byre and dipping apparatus',

reflecting the fact that it was a working farm in the past. The early Ponsonbys were known to be yeoman farmers. The barn and some of the other outbuildings are still standing. While Sir John lived in the Hall and for a while after, the barn was used as a display area for his collection of old weapons and hunting trophies from his time in India. It was also used for special events in the parish, such as Coronation Day, dances and children's Christmas parties. Unusually, there is an arched stone fireplace halfway along one side which Sir John had put in especially for these occasions. He also put in a new floor, the one which during the war was unable to take the weight of the Government rations stored there, and spectacularly collapsed.

Having passed under the archway, as the Hall comes into full view for the first time, the drive soon sweeps into a large gravelled area in front of the Hall. At first glance, the outside of the Hall looks rather plain but decorative surrounds to the top of the windows, known as 'drip mouldings', and a line above the ground floor windows that runs right across the bay, called a 'moulded string course', offset that plainness of rendered walls. The large Venetian window attractively relieves the plainness on the west front. A virginia creeper helps

THE GATEHOUSE HAILE HALL

Val Holmes 04.

The Gatehouse. The view of the gatehouse from Haile Hall, showing the steps up to what was the estate office.

more beautiful rhododendrons. There remains no physical evidence of it today, but Sir John had a small golf course made, possibly just outside the gardens.

On this side of the Manor House are remains of more outbuildings, which included a coal house, stick house, poultry house, two W.C.s and a store room. It is believed that the outbuilding still standing, that looks like a tiny cottage situated to the east on the way to the kitchen garden was once a laundry. Inside around the walls are stone sconces and at one end an old setpot. In the more recent past it looks as though it has been a gardener's potting shed.

The kitchen garden, once part of a field and cultivated up to about 1995, is found to the east, outside the main grounds on the other side of the track that runs down behind the Hall through the woodland to Mill House. Apart from being large enough to provide the Manor House with lots of fresh produce it once boasted a central feature of a pond with goldfish, one of many ideas of Sir John's. In the centre of the pond stood a stone statue. Leading to this pond from an old decorative iron gate was once a path edged with small box hedging. Further down the track and off to the right in the woodland is evidence of the large fish pond Sir John had created to provide fish for the dining table at the Hall.

enhance the appearance of the Hall for much of the year and the decorative Oriental-style chimney pots provide an interesting feature. The gravelled area in front was once a walled courtyard, the walls of which were demolished about 1840. From this standpoint you begin to appreciate the attractive gardens, a perfect backdrop to the Hall, created by Sir John and Lady Ponsonby. On what was 'an old grassy bank' they planted a colourful array of azaleas, rhododendrons and hydrangeas. On the opposite side of the Hall are lawn, borders and a grassy slope planted with daffodils. To the north are a second lawn which used to be a tennis court and another driveway flanked by yet

Haile Hall itself does not belong to any one period since different parts of it were built at different times. It is quite possible that the present Hall, comprising four gables, had its foundations in medieval times, starting its life as a pele tower in the 14th century. This is a debatable point amongst historians as pele towers were more usually found nearer to the Scottish border. Sir John, in his book published in 1929, wrote that,

'The manor came into the possession of the Ponsonby family about 1300, so that it has been the home of the Ponsonbys for over six hundred years'.

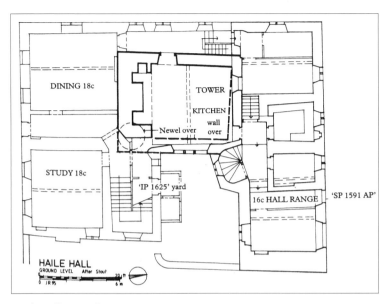

Haile Hall room plan.

The de Hale family were living here by the 13th century so presumably there was a building of some sort here then. According to the pele tower theory, as you can see from the plan, the present kitchen was the base of the tower, the walls of which are particularly thick, as outer walls would have been. Leading from this area is a pointed doorway, showing masons' marks. This doorway now leads into a passage at the west end which was probably built on in the eighteenth century at the same time as the symmetrical front gable at the south end. The gable at what is now the back (the north end) was built in the sixteenth century with irregular mullion and transomed windows. At the top of the north wall, standing out just above the roof is a small stone arch (possibly *c.*1700) which used to hold a bell for calling the workforce in at mealtimes.

The earlier of two date stones, 'SP 1591 AP', referring to Simon Ponsonby and his wife, Anne Eaglesfield, appears over the present back door, which has an ornamented Tudor arch. This could have been the original front door. The later stone, carved with a cross fleury and 'IP 1625', is found above the pointed door, by the main staircase, which now leads into a cloakroom but used to lead outside into a yard. These initials probably refer to a Sir John Ponsonby, Simon's son, born in 1608. The date stones do not necessarily refer to the date of building but could refer to a special event; for example the earlier date could refer to the marriage of Simon and Anne.

At the front door, once covered by a porch, there now proudly stand, one on each side as if on guard duty, two ornately carved, wooden Victorian bedposts – another of Sir John's ideas. On entering, you feel you are stepping back in time and wonder what secrets from

Haile Hall doorway. The present back door to Haile Hall, which may have been the original front door.

21

the past lie hidden here. Dr C. A. Parker's description of 1904 seems most apt:

'. . . a quaint old mansion full of narrow passages, sudden turns, and small unexpected doors, the kind of place where one might expect a first-class ghost story'.

The dining room on the ground floor is therefore unexpectedly light in spite of its low wooden ceiling. However, it is a large room, well lit with three good windows and it has an interesting wooden, fluted fire surround dating from the eighteenth century. For a long time the 'study', as shown on the plan, has been referred to as the smoking room and before that it was the library. A well proportioned moulding, more ornate than that in the dining room, contrasts well with its plain ceiling. In the centre of the ground floor is the kitchen with its original chimney arch and supports above the fireplace. The '16th century Hall Range' on the plan housed the domestic offices, including, from west to east, the lamp room, butler's pantry, larder, scullery and servants' hall. Here a wooden partition wall to create a passage was erected very much later than the 16th Century. Below were a store and wine cellars.

Between the study and the kitchen a wide, wooden staircase of 'easy gradient', where once there lurked figures in armour, one in plate armour and another in chain mail, leads to the first floor. This floor can also be reached at the back of the house by the newel (spiral) stairs (*c*.1500s), one of the most notable features of the Hall, built out into the yard as a turret like the ones at Orchard Brow Cottage in the village and at Gosforth Hall. Wooden treads cover the well-worn red sandstone steps.

On this floor above the dining room is the most attractive room of the Hall, the Library – once the Drawing Room – created by Sir John (having inherited a love of books from his father) and Lady Ponsonby. It already had the splendid Venetian window, which probably dates from a later period than the gable itself, and a beautifully carved, white marble mantelpiece, both dating from the late eighteenth century. Opposite, on the other side of the Victorian wood-panelled partition wall across the passage, is a small sitting room, again created by Sir John and Lady Ponsonby from a bedroom, and used by them during World War II to save on heating. Lady Ponsonby, later on in her life, used it a great deal. Intriguingly, at the back of the firegrate is a moulding of the Royal Coat of Arms. Above the Victorian fireplace is a Mathias Read mural painted directly onto the wooden panels of the wall. There is another similar mural in one of the bedrooms. These date from 1710 and are of distant views of the Hall set in the surrounding landscape. Also on this floor are bedrooms and bathrooms, including the principal bedroom complete with four-poster bed. It is in this room in particular that some of the broad floorboards are loose, perhaps because they have become so over the years. But it is known that from around the fifteenth century floor-boards were purposely left insecure so that they could be taken up easily and moved, along with the windows, when the owners moved house.

The newel stairs in Haile Hall.

The newel stairs at the back of the Hall continue up to the second floor. Opposite the top of the main staircase at the front and hidden by a door is another, wooden, newel stairway that connects the first and second floor, where there are more bedrooms and a bathroom. Presumably, this is where the servants slept. At the front are an attic space and what used to be a billiard room with smoke room attached, but that has long since been made into a bedroom.

From two different rooms on the top floor there are two different fire escapes. The older is a substantial rope tied to an iron ring firmly fixed to the floor. The later, more sophisticated but easier to use, is a metal ladder with chains between the metal steps allowing it to be folded up and kept in its metal box securely attached to the floor. Lady Ponsonby remembered that when it was first installed they asked the butler to be the first to try it out. It seems his descent was accomplished quite efficiently until he was almost down, when he put his foot through the pantry window.

Haile Hall in winter.

Before Sir John came to the Hall, the Ponsonbys rented it out from time to time. The 1851 Census Return reveals that a family of eight with a nephew and five servants were living there. Apart from that occasion the Returns between 1841 and 1891 show that Miles Ponsonby was in residence and as his family increased and decreased so the number of servants altered accordingly. After Miles' daughter, Barbara Ellen Ponsonby, died in 1919 the Hall was rented out for about five years to several different tenants, after which it stood empty for another five. During those years nothing seems to have been done in the way of maintenance and indeed it fell foul of vandals who took up floorboards and did other damage.

So, it was generally in a very poor state when Sir John bought it in

1929. He was newly retired from the Coldstream Guards and, the story goes, was looking for a property to buy in the Ponsonby area because of the family connection. His ancestors had lived at Haile Hall but in the mid-seventeenth century his branch of the family had moved to Ireland. Through the estate agent, John Robley, he discovered that Haile Hall was for sale and took a 'fancy' to it. John Robley introduced Sir John to his family including his sister, Mary, who was later to become Sir John's wife. Not only did the agent provide Sir John with a home but he found him a wife as well! They married in 1935 after which Lady Ponsonby helped Sir John with the renovations of the Hall, though they made no major alterations as they wished to preserve its history. He was responsible for putting electricity in and having the first telephone in Haile, the number being Beckermet 57. He named the bedrooms after the early female Ponsonbys e.g. Agnes de Hale, Dorothy Sandys and Anne Copley.

The Robley family, 1899. The family into which Molly was born two years later.

In her interview for the local radio in 1994 when she was 93, Lady Ponsonby said how Sir John had never lived in the north before, but enjoyed it and loved Haile Hall. They kept a flat in London which they visited regularly but they enjoyed coming back and always returned for any village function. They used to have three men helping in the garden and about five people in the house. When Sir John and Lady Ponsonby were away the staff remaining at the Hall could use such things as the garden, golf course and tennis court.

After Sir John died in 1952, Lady Ponsonby remained at the Hall, continuing her charity work, and the work she was involved in with different organisations. Of course, she continued to work in her beloved garden with the unstinting help of Lizzie and Nora, both of whom worked for Lady Ponsonby for well over sixty years.

In the Lady's words, 'It's been a very happy home.'

HAILE HALL ESTATE

An early record of the Haile Hall Estate dates from 1739 when a plan then drawn up reveals that the Estate covered some 415 acres encircling the Hall, including two farms (Whitey Head and Tortolacate) rented out, a corn mill, arable and pasture land and woodland. The Ponsonby family also owned other lands and properties outside the parish. It is clear, though, that from then on the development and maintenance of the Estate was at times no easy matter.

The Hall itself was no doubt a pleasant place to have as a home and as is suggested by this quotation from Jollie's *Cumberland Guide and Directory* of 1811 – 'It is, notwithstanding, a commodius mansion, and well situated for a sporting seat' – there was hunting, shooting and fishing on the Estate. It is thought that there was a Gamekeeper's Cottage, what is now known as the Pigeon House. This same building has also been referred to as the Dove Cote though there is some question that it ever housed doves as there was a dove cote among the outbuildings at the Hall.

When there were to be no members of the family in residence for a time the Hall on occasions was let out as seen in the advertisement in

The Cumberland Pacquet of 28th September 1819. See p. 27.

Running the Estate had its unpleasant side as Miles Ponsonby (1745-1814) discovered in June 1791 when he wrote to Joseph Benn, his tenant farmer at 'Tortola' since 1st April, 1789, giving him notice to quit the farm on 25th March, 1792. The reason as stated in the legal declaration to The King's Bench, was that Joseph Benn did 'wilfully wrongfully and maliciously make and permit waste spoil and destruction in and upon the said messuage'. It was alleged that all buildings – two stables, two barns, two cowhouses, ten other buildings and two limekilns at Mousegill Quarry – were,

> 'uncovered open and exposed to the weather so that main Timbers Roofs and Ceilings were and are rotted spoiled and damaged by the Rain descending thereupon . . . whereby Buildings, Barns . . . became and are ruinous and in great decay'.

He was accused of 'pulling down removing and carrying away' doors and windows and

> 'cutting up breaking down, prostrating and destroying Pales Gates Stiles Hedges and Fences . . . whereby the said premises were and are very much damaged and injured and the said Reversion of the said Plaintiff (Miles Ponsonby) was much diminished and lessened in value'.

Miles Ponsonby, in his declaration, claimed damages of £1,000, a considerable sum in those days.

By the time claims were to be submitted in 1811 for the Parish Award, the Estate had acquired a further 65 acres. With the Award in 1814 a further 120 acres, mainly on Wilton Fell, some on Haile Moor and a very small amount on Brayshaw Moor were allotted to the Estate. It is interesting to note that in his claim to the Commissioners in 1811, Miles Ponsonby, who died in the year of the Award, pointed out that he had built a lime kiln at Mousegill the site of the quarry, and that if the Commissioners were going to make this public he would ask for recompense. As it happened, the quarry was made public and, although the people were awarded the right to build lime kilns for themselves it is possible that the Ponsonby kiln was widely used by members of the parish who would pay for the use of it.

It was not only the Estate itself that occupied the attention of the resident family. As Lord of the Manor of Haile and Wilton the owner

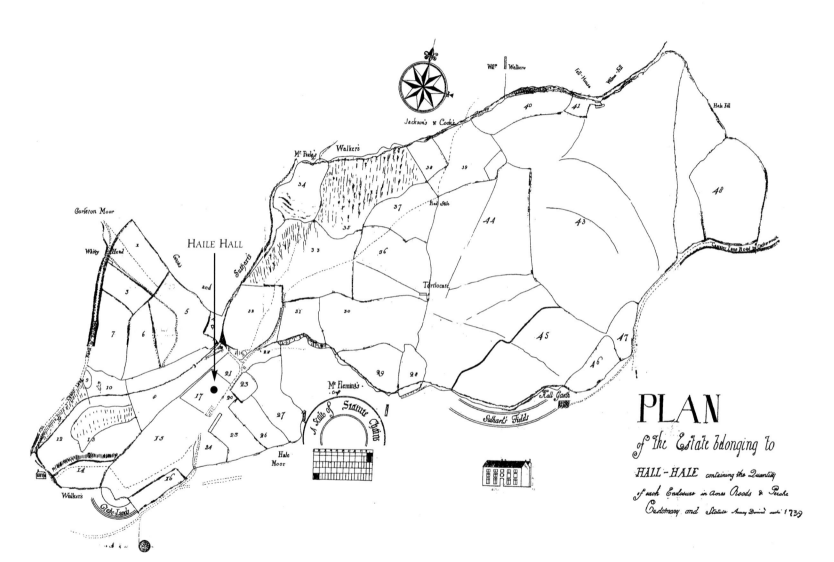

Haile Hall Estate map.

Key to field names.

of Haile Hall would need to keep his eye on manorial affairs as well as on those of the Haile Hall Estate. Miles Ponsonby took seriously his responsibility to the parish, as, for example, when in 1801 he agreed to take on a young apprentice, 12 years of age, by the name of Henry Haile, a pauper child of the parish to 'teach and instruct in husbandry' until he reached the age of 21.

The tenancy agreements which were an essential part of the administration of the Estate sometimes went into surprising detail. One such agreement with the farmer tenant of Tortolacate and the enclosed land on Hail Fell in 1817, illustrates how detailed the agreement could be. Little was overlooked: John Braithwaite was

'to keep in good and sufficient repair Buildings, Walls, Roofs, Windows, Hedges, Ditches, Gates, Stiles, Posts, Rails, Bridges, Water courses, Roadways, and other things belonging to said premises (This last statement was included, presumably, on the slight chance that something may have been missed out.) . . . except walls of houses and outhouses and principal timbers . . .'

The rules went so far as to insist on how the land itself was used. While the instructions in the agreement were obviously based on good farming practice, no risk was taken that the tenant farmer might be ignorant of accepted methods of rotational cropping or might even have his own ideas as to how it should be done. The farmer shall

'not take more than two successive white crops (oats and other cereals) from off any part of the premises after breaking the same out of Ley but shall the next succeeding year after the first white or corn crop give the same land a clean fallow and have thereon a crop of turnips and some other green plants and shall lay spread and bestow a sufficient quantity of well-rotted dung or compost upon the lands . . . Where any land is so laid down the same shall be sown with a sufficient quantity of clover and grass seeds. These lands shall not be again plowed for three succeeding years at least. Not to be cut down or mown for hay any of the grass land sown with clover and grass seeds for more than two years in succession without laying and spreading thereon a sufficient quantity of manure or compost upon the grounds so to be mown . . .' etc.

The rent at that time was £230 per year payable in two instalments. Presumably the advice was free.

Advertisement from The Cumberland Pacquet. *September 1819.*

Fifty years later the tenancy agreements were just as detailed and sometimes included a 'Sheep Bond' to which the farmer was bound to the sum of £250. He was instructed to 'enjoy the fleeces and other products' but neither the number of sheep nor their value was to be lessened.

Side Farm, on the fell outside the parish, and Brayshaw, once owned by Calder Abbey, both became part of the Estate at some time as it expanded, but from about 1850 onwards it appears that the Estate was running into financial difficulties. Petersburgh, Beckermet, a property belonging to the Ponsonbys, was sold and a number of mortgage deals over several years was set up, including ones concerning Tortolacate, Whitey Head, Manesty Cottage and land at Head of Haile, reaching a total of £7,000. Even during these difficult times, though, it seems the tradition of giving the tenant farmers dinner on rent day was retained, at least in the times of Dorothy Ponsonby and Barbara Ellen Ponsonby.

Miles Ponsonby (1808-1892), grandson of the earlier Miles, aware of the industrial developments of the time, promoted mining for iron ore, copper and lead in the area, under his own lands and where the mineral rights had been reserved when properties of the Manor had been enfranchised. It was reported that around 1873 'Mr. Miles Ponsonby of Hale Hall drove a mine shaft into a Hillside near Beckermet but had no success in finding ore'. However, he did have success in the mining industry. Discussion and even dispute (involving solicitors and leading, in at least one instance, to Court) arose over ownership of minerals and non-payment of dead rent (i.e. when the mine was not actually working). The Court established that the surface of the land had been purchased but not the minerals underneath.

After her father, Miles, died in 1892 Barbara Ellen, a trustee with her nephew Henry Staveley Hill, took over the day-to-day running of the Estate. Although living on her own at the Hall, she had her nephew's support and advice when necessary and was also in frequent contact with her solicitors. Nevertheless she seemed to have a constant struggle to make ends meet, referring to 'the poverty of Hale Hall Estate'; 'a lot of expenses coming all at once'; and 'what privileges and benefit may I have' from paying rates on 66 acres of woodland. She remarked that 'wood was given away in our part of the world compared to other places.' She was even on the look-out for further opportunities in mining. This, despite the fact that by this time the Estate was receiving rent from Mill House, Pigeon House, Manesty Cottage, four farms, 50 acres of pasture land and rents and royalties from mining.

In response to tenant farmers' demands that their hedges be kept in order she suggested they each either be given £2 out of their rents to do their own fencing – since she was not keeping outside men-servants at Haile Hall – or be given 500 yards of park wire which will last for years if 'properly put up'. On the inspection in 1917 of the small Carleton Moor Plantation, valued at £285, Barbara Ellen thought that mines requiring wood may push up the value of timber. After a good response to an advertisement for the sale of wood by a number of timber merchants, Barbara recommended her solicitors accept the tender of £485 from a firm of boat builders in Coniston and Ulverston. The same company offered to buy more but government restrictions in those times would allow only £300 worth of timber to be sold every three months.

F. IRWIN,

Golden Lion Inn, Market Place,
WHITEHAVEN.

	£	s.	D.
Breakfast,			
Dinner,		10	
Share of Dinner Bill,			
Crackers and Fruit,			
Bucellas, Claret,			
Champaigne,			
Supper,			
Eating,			
Wine and Negus,		10	
Brandy and Rum,			
Gin and Whiskey,			
Ale and Porter,		1	
Tea and Coffee,			
Chocolate,			
Tobacco,			
Cigars,			
Post Chaise,			
Coach Fare,			
Gigs,			
Omnibus,			
Horse Hire,			
Hay and Corn,			
Saddler's Account,			
Blacksmith's Account,			
Carriage Greasing,			
Tailor's Bill			
Shoemaker's Bill,			
Postage and Paper,			
Servants' Eating and Ale,			
Beds,			
Fire in Bed Room,			
Washing,			
Ginger Beer,			
Soda Water,			
Waiter,			
Chambermaid,			
Ostler,			
Boots,			

J. GIBSON AND SON, PRINTERS.

The cost of eating out. The bill for a meal provided by Dorothy Ponsonby for her tenant farmers on the occasion of the annual payment of rent in August 1850.

Apart from dealing with the financial side of the Estate there were other matters to be dealt with, such as: repairs to buildings; a complaint from a tenant farmer that woodcutters had damaged fences; Isaac Benson's claim for compensation (described elsewhere); a farmer sub-letting; 'seven or eight larch trees "cut down by some unknown person"'; and the unsuitable tenant in the Pigeon House who came and went with his family and allowed his dog to run all over the woodland and Haile Hall grounds. Barbara Ellen thought that by putting up the rent, which she felt justified in doing because of the scarcity of homes at this time (1913) owing to the expanding mining industry, she would force him to leave. However, they reached a compromise over the rent increase and he got rid of the dog!

Other problems included negotiations over the possibility of a water supply from Castley Hill being piped across the Estate to certain dwellings, and repair of the Estate's section of the Winscales road. The responsibility for this Barbara Ellen reluctantly accepted but she wanted it done as cheaply as possible and she asked to be forewarned of the cost. She had a request for some land from the West Cumberland Fishery who wanted to create a hatchery on the left side of the 'Kerbeck stream', passing through the wood about 100 yards from the Hall. The hatchery would consist of a wooden hut containing four boxes of ova with a constant supply of water piped from the stream flowing over the boxes. The water would then return a little further downstream. Writing to her solicitors, Barbara Ellen suggested a sum of £15 to £20 as a possible charge. A reply from the Board indicated they were willing to pay 20 shillings a year for a portion of land for the hatchery and for four ponds into which the fry would be placed after hatching out if this should be desirable. The Board did have an offer elsewhere, free of charge, but preferred the seclusion of the Haile site. Local farmers downstream were concerned that the hatchery might result in a lack of water for them. As far as we know, there is no evidence that this venture went ahead.

Repairs to the farms and the Hall had to be dealt with and when the Hall was assessed for taxes in 1893, Barbara Ellen wanted to appeal. The annual payment had been £185 since 1881. She felt she could let the Hall for only £40 or £50 a year since it was only 'a small house'. In July 1912 the following draft account had been drawn up

The Pigeon House when it was still inhabited. 1986.

for income tax purposes assessed on letting the Hall furnished:

Rent for ten weeks @ £10. 10s. a week *(note this)*		£126 0 0	
<u>Less</u> Auctioneer's commission @ 5%	£6. 6. 0		
Proportion of cost of agreement stamp on same	1. 6. 0		
Auctioneer checking inventory on furniture	2. 2. 0		
Man's wages £1. 1. 0 for week	10. 10. 0		
Part Rent and Rates	10. 0. 0		
Wear and Tear of structure	6. 0. 0		
Say £36 0 0		36 0 0	
		£ 90 0 0	

In 1913 the mortgagee called in monies owing to be paid on 2nd February 1914 but she agreed to a request to extend the mortgages to a year later as the Estate of the deceased Miles Ponsonby was not fully administered. It was not until May 1937, however, that the various mortgages were discharged.

Not long before she died Barbara Ellen, still in regular touch with her solicitors and nephew, was discussing with them the government valuations of different parts of the Estate for insurance purposes. Of course, the Hall was included, being insured for £8,000, a figure that Barbara Ellen thought much too high. 'The House is very old, out of date in every way.' It could not be let for more than £50 or £60 a year. From an insurance point of view, she felt that the cost of rebuilding would be out of all proportion to what it would sell for. Therefore, she suggested the value be reduced to £6,000 but her solicitors thought £3,000 or £4,000 to be a more realistic figure.

> 'In the case of farm houses and buildings we think these might be increased somewhat having regard to present cost of building and the cost in these particular cases would be greater than average because the buildings are so remotely situated and material would have to be carted for some miles particularly in the case of Brayshaw and Side Farms which are situated at a considerable height, almost on the fells'.

With the death of Barbara Ellen Ponsonby in 1919 the Estate passed to Ronsley Miles Ponsonby from Tasmania. He was the son of Miles de Hale, Barbara's older brother who emigrated to Tasmania when he was a young man. In 1928 after no real success in renting out the Hall, Ronsley Ponsonby decided to sell the Estate which then covered, in spite of earlier difficulties, some 1,134 acres.

By this time the 1739 map of the Estate would have been extended to include: to the East – Brayshaw and Side Farm; to the West – extra land at Whitehow Head, a plot of woodland known as Carleton Moor and a mixed plantation also known as Carleton Moor; and to the North – an allotment known as Whitehow Head Park next to Mousegill quarry.

Then the break-up of the Estate began. Among the introductory remarks in the 1928 catalogue of sale are:

> 'The Estate has been and could again be made a very fine

sporting property, there being several well-placed woods and covers with high and low ground shooting over an area of more than 1,100 acres.'

'There is Trout fishing on the Estate, and good Salmon and Trout fishing can be obtained in the neighbourhood.'

'The whole of Cumberland and Westmorland Lakes are within the limits of a day's motor tour.'

According to *The Whitehaven News* of 2nd August, 1928, the only Lot to be sold on the day of the auction was the disused cottage, Manesty, in the village but the date on the draft Conveyance for the sale of Brayshaw is 26th September, 1928. However, the late Sir John Ponsonby, related to the direct line of the Ponsonbys of Haile Hall, bought the Hall in 1929 for £2,800, along with the gatehouse, grounds, woodlands and parkland, the Mill House and the Pigeon House. The latter was rented out until it became uninhabitable and is now quite derelict. The Mill House continued to be rented out until the late Lady Ponsonby sold it in 1989 to David Crayston who is restoring the old mill. The parkland was and still is rented out to local farmers.

Whitehow Head 'a valuable mixed farm' continued to be rented out to the Wightman family until it was bought by them in 1972. After a period of semi-retirement towards the end of the 1900s, the family retired fully in 2001, selling the remainder of the land. They still live in the farmhouse but the farm buildings are being converted into four separate dwellings.

Brayshaw 'an excellent mixed farm', the only farm to be bought at the time of the auction, was sold to J. R. Harrington who had been renting it from 1921. After changing hands several times since, Brayshaw is now farmed in partnerhsip with Head of Haile by the Moore family.

Tortolacate 'a capital mixed farm with a flock of 117 Herdwick sheep heafed on Lankrigg' continued to be rented by J. Wilson whose family had farmed the holding for more than 60 years at the time of the auction. From 1944 A. Mawson took over the tenancy and finally his sons, John and Atkinson, bought the farm in the early 1960s. It was sold on in 1976 to N. Graham, who now runs the farm in partnership with his son, David.

Side Farm 'a desirable fell farm with a flock of 230 Herdwick sheep heafed on Town Bank' continued to be rented by J. Sharpe whose family had farmed there for 50 years at the time of the auction. D. Robinson took over from J. Sharpe but the farm was sold to the Cowman family in 1958 who farmed the land but did not live in the farmhouse. The land is still farmed but, sadly, the farmhouse and buildings are now derelict.

With the death of Lady Ponsonby in April, 2003, we have reached the end of an era. There are no longer Ponsonbys living in Haile Hall but the connection with the village remains, since woodland and approximately 45 acres of pasture, the Mary Longmire Land, have been retained by the main branch of the Ponsonbys living in Tasmania.

WEST CUMBERLAND.

Particulars, Plan and Conditions of Sale
— OF —

The Valuable Freehold, Residential, Sporting and Agricultural Estate
KNOWN AS

"HAILE HALL"

Extending to about 1,134 Acres,
— COMPRISING —

THE OLD MANOR HOUSE

With GROUNDS, WOODLANDS, GATEHOUSE, COTTAGES and PARK LAND,

Four Capital Agricultural Holdings

ACCOMMODATION LAND,

SMALL HOLDING & ALLOTMENT,

The whole producing a Rental of approximately £664 per annum (exclusive of the Hall, Grounds and Woodlands, which are now in hand),

WHICH WILL BE OFFERED FOR

SALE BY AUCTION

(as a whole and in suitable Lots) by

Messrs. THORNBORROW & CO.

— AT —

THE MASONIC HALL, DUKE STREET, WHITEHAVEN,
On THURSDAY, the 26th day of JULY, 1928, at 2 p.m.
(Unless previously sold by Private Treaty).

The Tenants have kindly consented to show their respective Holdings and the remaining portion of the Estate may be viewed by arrangement with the Agent.

Orders to view may be obtained from any of the undermentioned:—
SOLICITORS: Messrs. BROCKBANK, HELDER & ORMROD, Whitehaven.
LAND AGENT: J. ROBLEY, Esq., F.S.I., 48, New Lowther Street, Whitehaven.
AUCTIONEERS: Messrs. THORNBORROW & CO., Penrith and Keswick.

The sale of Haile Hall Estate. Title page of the sale document for the sale of the Haile Hall Estate, 1928.

THE CHURCH

VICARS OF HAILE CHURCH

- 1658 William Wilson
- 1705 John Parker
- 1715 Joseph Thompson
- 1722 George Connel
- 1757 Stephen Reay
- 1761 William Stockdale
- 1763 Daniel Myers
- 1767 Thomas Tyson
- 1773 William Greers
- 1777 Joshua Southward
- 1779 John Clark Gillbank – 1783
- 1785 Isaac Grayson
- 1791 John Lindow – 1794
- 1799 Thomas Jameson
- 1802 Henry Bragg
- 1813 Richard Poole
- 1814 Isaac Kitchen
- 1817 Graham Brown
- 1822 William D. Grice
- 1837 William Bellas
- 1839 John Vicars
- 1861 William Sidney Pratton
- 1878 Robert Webster
- 1884 J. A. Bateman
- 1887 Arthur Harry Cooper
- 1910 J. Steele
- 1912 Victor H. Scallon
- 1926 J. A. Lightfoot
- 1928 Arthur Taylor
- 1932 J. S. Woof
- 1935 F. R. Berry

Haile Church. From a painting by J. Adair in 1884

- 1944 G. W. Burnside
- 1947 A. E. Gibson
- 1952 W. Breay
- 1962 B. S. W. Simpson
- 1970 A. G. Hardie (Archdeacon of West Cumberland)
- 1980 Tom Hall
- 1981 Graham Hartley
- 1990 David Wood
- 1995 Norman Hayton
- 1999 Gavin Walker

We are indebted to the Rev. Lightfoot who listed the clergy who had officiated at Haile from 1658 up to his own time of 1926-28.

A HISTORY OF HAILE CHURCH

Before retiring from the parish, Rev. Graham Hartley left a small notebook, compiled by a former vicar of Haile, Rev. J. A. Lightfoot, which contains some historical notes of the Parish from other published editions. I am indebted to Rev. Lightfoot and Rev. Ben Simpson for information I have been able to use in this article.

The Rev. Simpson, during his ministry at Haile (1962-70), took a special interest in the parish's history, noting that there are three places with that name in the north of England, with three different spellings, namely Hale, Haile, and Hayle, its meaning in old English being 'nook or corner'. There is no record of the church having been dedicated to a particular saint, and there was recently no desire to make amends, the church council preferring to adopt 'Haile' as a place of welcome to all seekers of spiritual reunion. The Norman Lords of the Manor also adopted the name, in recognition of their entitlement, by adding the suffix 'de Hale'.

A distant view of the church.

The appointment of the first Archbishop of Carlisle was in 1122, though covering only the area to the north of the Derwent. From *Bulmer's Directory (1829)* we learn that the church at Haile was of 'plain fabric', with a small tower and a spire, belonging to the Diocese of York in 1345 and that it 'occupies a beautiful situation in a secluded spot, through which runs a small beck'. It was appropriated to the Archdeacon of Richmond, and earned him a yearly pension of £6. 8s. 0d. Haile was attached to Conishead Priory *(Rural Deanery of Gosforth, 1889)*, while also the earlier church was a chapel of ease for the Monks of St Bees.

It is interesting to note that in 1385 Haile had not had a sermon for 5 years. Perhaps history is repeating itself, as now in the 21st century the future pattern of services is uncertain, owing to financial problems within the Carlise diocese. As late as the 1950s four services could take place in a day, while now in 2004, we normally have only the one Sunday service.

The earliest written reference to Haile is in a 'Pipe Roll' (tax list) of 1226, though an article named 'Copeland Chronicle -5' in a cutting from *The Whitehaven News* dates it back to 1180. However, its history as a place of worship can be traced to a much earlier period, through archaeological remains of Roman, Celtic and Viking origin. 8,000 bodies were supposedly buried between the Kirk Beck and the church, and a spiral and trefoil interlaced carving on a quoin built into the main building of the church would appear to confirm open-air worship in Celtic times. The church's exterior walls are of medieval construction, with part of a Saxon cross-shaft dating back to 10-11th century being re-used as a quoin in the southeast corner. The whiteness of this sandstone led to the theory that the stone had been brought from across the Solway at Whithorn but, more recently, a report describes it as medium-grained yellow sandstone, possibly bleached and from St Bees, with hand carving relating it to work in St John's Church, Beckermet. In a letter sent to Rev. Lightfoot, Collingwood suggests that the small altar cross, possibly a grave cross, dates back to the 14th century, while the hood moulding from a square headed window is more ancient than the cross. There is a corresponding stone in the Saxon work of Hexham Abbey. However, the investigation in 1988 did not give this stone a mention.

A small entry in *Old Parish Churches of Cumbria* mentions that larger, Georgian, plain arched, windows have replaced the previous windows which pierced the medieval walls, an initiative of Ferguson, (Architect from Carlisle). Perhaps the ornate window mullion, which appears to have been of a more ornate design and which is now built into the vestry, is from the earlier church, when it boasted a tower and a spire. Ferguson also designed the porch, vestry and bell tower for two bells.

It says in Mrs Webster's book, *The Life of a Country Clergyman*, that the present vicarage (now in private occupation), was built in 1875, replacing one at the top of the hill which was obviously not habitable as the vicar had to reside elsewhere for a year. Canon Loftie mentions,

A Saxon carved stone.

'ruins of ancient dwelling house, said to have been the residence of clergy, standing upon the hill between the village and the church, remains of mullioned windows point to at least the 17th century, if not much older'.

The new vicarage was built on land donated by a Mrs Walker of Silecroft, and cost £1,000, raised by subscription, plus a grant from the diocese of £180. However, the Church of England must have overlooked this matter as they pocketed all the proceeds from its sale.

The church fell into disrepair and a massive programme of restoration took place in 1883, under the caring ministry of the Websters, Mrs Webster seemingly playing an influential role and her husband ministering in Haile from 1878-84. Funds were raised at a large-scale fête.

Not that this was the first time large funds had to be raised to keep the church going. There is evidence that there was fund raising at a much earlier period, as disclosed in some records kept by the Benn family who occupied Brackenthwaite during the 19th century. William Benn having been churchwarden of Haile Church in 1842-3, listed:

'Donations from 1843 – Subscriptions for erecting vestry room and Gallery in the Church, William Benn being a warden: 52 subscriptions from £2 – 2/6d plus donations 11/6d and including £13. 12s. 6d. collected from a rate for painting the church. Total £36. 10s. 0d spent thus:

To 130 foot of Fir Wood at 1/4d per ft	£8. 13. 9
To 4 bushels of lime 3/11d, Riddling 1/6d	5. 4
To Laths, Nails, Haire, etc. Plasterers work	£1. 15. 7
To iron work	10
To joiners work	£12. 0. 0
To flags at Mason Work	7. 6
To painting the parish part of church	£12. 12. 0
To one table for vestry room	10. 0
To pulpit trimmings etc.	5. 0
Total	£36. 10. 0d.'

It would appear that the work on Haile church in 1883 reflects the increasing prosperity of the nation which led to a wide movement of church restoration, as John Betjeman's poem, 'Hymn', reads:

*'The Church's restoration
In eighteen-eighty-three
Has left for contemplation
Not what there used to be.'

The total cost of the restoration was £826, this sum being raised by the public subscriptions mentioned, and a grant of £50 awarded by the Diocesan Church Extension Society. At this time a carved screen was erected 'To the Glory of God and in memory of a faithful wife and loving mother', enclosing the chancel from the wider nave. Betjeman continues:-

'Of marble brown and veined
He did the pulpit make;

He order'd windows stained
Light red and crimson lake'.

Haile's pulpit, another anonymous gift, was not of marble, but of carved oak, given as 'A Thanksgiving for recovering from sickness'. The Victorian stained glass window was made by Wales of Newcastle, and cost £35. Depicting the crucifixion, it was installed above the altar, resulting in Mrs Webster's description of the church as resembling a little cathedral. A second stained glass window, dated 1898, depicts the distribution of bread by St Bega, while a third window with its metaphoric depiction of good over evil in St George slaying the dragon, provides a befitting memory of a soldier and the last in the Ponsonby line, Sir John who died in 1952. Another reminder of Ponsonby ties is found in a carved screen behind the entrance door, depicting the Ponsonby Coat of Arms and the Tower of London. It is a memorial to Henry and Mary Ponsonby, the former having been private secretary to Queen Victoria.

It is interesting to read in a deed for Town End Farm, Wilton, that when the farm was sold in the 1840s, the new owner was entitled to sit in the sixth pew on the left hand side of the church. Presumably this right would be forfeited when the enclosed box and bench fitments were taken out and replaced by simple carved oak pews.

It was during this upheaval that various antiquities came to light, uncovering a Roman altar, a small grave cross and sandstone window mullion from an earlier building, these being built into the internal walls of the newly constructed vestry. The grave cross, minus its base, is very small (28 cm by 16 cm) of pink-gray sandstone, dated by Bailey and Cramp as 12th century, bearing the relief design of a straight-arm cross, enclosed in a circle. The Rev. J. A. Lightfoot, recorded these historical findings in his notebook during his short ministry at Haile, between 1926-8, and must have written to R. G. Collingwood about them also. A letter of reply, dated 1927, answers his query regarding the inscription on the Roman altar. This, it appears, was dedicated to the gods Hercules and Sylvanus. Collingwood suggested that the former god referred to

'civilising labours' while the latter to 'wild country', inferring engagement in some work such as road- or bridge-building, perhaps in constructing the road from Ravenglass to Moresby. He suggests the inscription was connected with the successful fulfilment of a promise, noting that a custodian of either the armory at Ravenglass or Moresby Fort had been sent off with a detachment for some special duty. He adds that there is no real ground for giving the altar any particular date. There can be no certainty as to what century it belonged, though a reference to the altar by Dr C. A. Parker suggests around 220 A.D.

The Viking Grave Cover or Sarcophagus Lid was initially mentioned in a lecture given by Canon Knowles in 1876, when, it appears, 6 fragments were known, all having disappeared by 1899. They could possibly have been built into the boundary wall which was extended to include more land for burial. Four pieces were

Early grave cross.

Roman altar.

34

Inside Haile church.

grave cover and Bailey notes that it is the only example of this form of grave cover west of the Pennines, there being plenty of examples from the east side in the Durham Library Collection.

Possibly the most interesting feature rests against the exterior wall of the porch – described aptly in *The Whitehaven News* article mentioned earlier as:

'Crudely lettered, with all the 'Ns' cut the wrong way, poorly spelt and often with a word divided and written on two lines, it makes a delightful, honest memorial'.

Haile is one of the few parishes to have preserved a complete list of records of births, marriages and deaths almost back to the date 1544, from when Thomas Cromwell made the order that they should be kept.

Tombstone of John Ponsonby. The inscription reads: 'Learn reader under this stone doth lye a rare example cald John Ponsonbye. If I said any lese I am sure I lyd. He was a faithful friend and soe he dyd. November 25 in the year 1670'.

Window mullion. The mullion was probably from an earlier, more ornate, church on the same site.

rediscovered in 1926 by Parker, which, he writes, were fixed to the west wall, but in 1966 these were uprooted and brought into the church by Rev. Simpson. Richard Bailey identified these as being from the Viking period of the 10th-11th century, made from medium grained red St Bees sandstone and dated by the characteristics of the ornament of three strands of interlacing cords, employing the Stafford knot. Bailey suggests there is evidence of a local sculptural school, similar patterns having been found at Beckermet, Brigham and Workington. Reconstruction of the pieces forms a large bowed-shape

In 1861 a large chalice and paten were provided as presents, from St Nicholas' chapel in Whitehaven, when the custom of serving Holy Communion with a chalice in each hand was discontinued. Before that, Haile appears to have been able to comply at the time with Queen Elizabeth I's order of 1571, to restore communion to the laity, with 'a communion cup and cover of silver', not in 'any profane cup or glass'.

There are many records of rents and tithes, of quarrels long forgotten, of lads apprenticed and of poor being relieved. Haile people seem to have cared for those less fortunate: a Poor Money Fund, distributed by the Lord of the Manor on St Thomas's Day, came to light only recently.

Perhaps we can thank Rev. Simpson also for the fact that we were able to transfer the deeds of the former Church School over to village hall trustees, as he was the one who first suggested the possibility. He discloses that it was the Walker family from Orchard Brow who in fact had donated the land and some of the materials – a deed being drawn up between Henry Walker on the one part, and the vicar and churchwardens on the other – making the purpose plain. It was to

'Use and control the building on Sundays and weekdays as a place of education and recreation for the benefit of the parish'.

While other church schools became the property of the education committee, this deed protected villagers' rights. So a modernisation plan was pursued, and eventually the Church School was handed over to a village hall committee, in order to claim council grants.

Rev. Simpson retired before he had wished, in promise of a secure seat for Haile Church as the future seat for the Archdeacon of West Cumberland. A decade later this promise was broken through a diocesan change of direction. Still the little church goes on.

* The extracts from John Betjeman's poem 'Hymn' are reproduced by permission of John Murray Publishers, from his 'Collected Poems'.

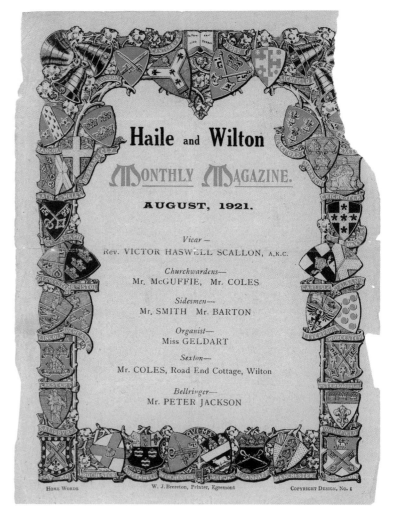

Church magazine cover. The church magazine for a time was presented with a particularly attractive cover. This example was kept by Annie Raven as it announced her baptism.

Memories of Haile Church

From 1950s to 2003

One of my earlier memories from childhood, of Haile Church, is the sound of the church bells following up the valley of the Kirk Beck and resounding very clearly in Wilton on a calm summer evening, one bright clang followed by a more subdued one. Another is of a small party of Wilton children walking together, teasing and playing games on the way to Sunday School, despite being dressed in our Sunday best coats and matching felt-brimmed hats, the latter serving also as a football. Rev. Breay and his wife treated the children of the parish as their family, though the main attraction was to qualify for an invitation to their Sunday School Christmas party held annually in the vicarage – a wonderful spread for approximately 20 children, followed by traditional party games including postman's knock, gathering nuts in May and the Grand old Duke of York. On one special occasion we all sat and watched an animated television production, in black and white, of 'Wind in the Willows'. This was a special treat for the Wilton children as electricity only arrived there in 1956. Lastly, a present was handed to every child – I particularly treasured, and still have, a small book named *Rhymes for Young Nature Lovers* including a poem about a swan which I learnt off by heart.

Church giving has always been an issue and has remained a problem in recent years. I remember putting a sum equivalent to a day's school dinner money, as a weekly donation. A school dinner would now cost about £1.50 pence.

Later memories are of being sent to church as representative member for the family, and having to answer questions on my return about who was there, what they wore, what the sermon was about and being ticked off for not providing the answers. Unfortunately I spent the very long hour daydreaming, completely switched off by repetitive prayers, dreary hymns and monotonous psalms. Happily, Jimmy Fisher decided when enough was more than enough and a bout of coughing soon brought the sermon to an end. Only later did I learn that this was pre-arranged. Looking back I realise that my

Sunday Services—10-30 a.m. and 6-30 p.m.
Holy Communion—First Sunday of the month, at 8 a.m.
        Third Sunday, at midday.   Fourth Sunday, in the Evening.
Churchings & Baptisms—Any Sunday, at 3-45 p.m., on notice being given to the Vicar.
Sunday School—In Church, at 2 p.m.
Choir Practice—Wednesday Evening at 7-0 p.m.

LETTER FROM THE VICAR.

My Dear Friends—The days of June were marked, in our village life, by four events which occurred too late for last month's issue of the magazine. 1. The members of our Choir, to whose regular service we are much indebted, had their annual outing on Saturday, June 18th. Last year's outing was so much enjoyed, that with one consent the Choir voted for another visit to Blackpool; and again they brought back glowing accounts of a happy and successful day. 2. Four days later, on June 22nd, Miss S. C. Noble was married in our Church to Mr. Harold Wright, of Southport. In my absence, the Rev. H. M. Fairlie officiated. We shall be united in wishing much happiness to the bridal couple. God bless them. 3. The third event which caused some stir amongst us was the visit of the Prince of Wales to Cumberland, on June 29th. Haile could not claim even a passing salutation from the Heir to the Throne; but through the kind gifts of friends all the children of our school were motored into Egremont, where they had a good sight of the Prince, and afterwards had tea in the Town Hall. 4. The last of the four note-worthy events is the success of Grace Noble in the Minor Scholarship Examination for our County. This means that Grace will have four years' free education at the Whitehaven Secondary School, with books provided free of charge, and also the cost of travelling to and fro. We congratulate Grace, who thus places her foot on the rung of an educational ladder by which through diligence and character she may rise to useful womanhood. We rejoice with Mr. and Mrs J. S. Noble, who have in their daughter's success an experience of great joy; and we heartily congratulate Miss Turner, who has a task of no small difficulty in a School in which " Standards " cannot be separately taught. This success of one of her pupils reflects great credit on our Head Mistress.

The storm of Sunday afternoon, July 10th, will long be remembered in Haile; for our Village was then the centre of a violent cloud-burst, and in a few minutes the floods were out indeed. Some of our friends suffered severely, but we may be thankful that the damage done was not more serious. The Vicar of Irton, who had kindly come to take an afternoon Service in our Church, had a very small congregation.

You may have noticed that the East End of our Church has been greatly brightened by a thick coating of fresh white paint. We owe this to the kindness of Miss Turner who supplied the paint, and of Mr. J. S. Noble, who applied it. We cordially thank them both.

I am hoping to be able to continue the Services regularly, though my bruised shoulder does not give promise of speedy recovery, and is not favourable to my general health. But I have much to be thankful for.

J. A. LIGHTFOOT.

The vicar's newsletter. August 1927.

mother's curiosity was her only way of keeping in contact with the outside world. Such were the limitations of country life. There was no daily delivery of newspapers, no public transport and few women could drive. Mobile vans delivered groceries, meat, fish and bread to the door. Farmers' wives were virtually imprisoned.

While Rev. Breay had a particularly bad stammer, our next Vicar Ben Simpson, spoke so quietly, it was difficult to catch all his words

Approaching Haile church from the village.

burial plots, but a note in a magazine during his last year of ministry asked for help in completing these blanks, a task later completed by Rev. Tom Hall's devoted efforts.

Rev. Graham Hartley is best remembered for leading his parishioners astray! introducing them to his love of mountaineering by taking a party on a very exposed scramble on the Gable Girdle – an experience never to be forgotten. Angel's Leap, a very exposed move, followed, with a sheer drop down the mountain if one failed to find and access with the left foot, a cleft in the rock's surface. (He explained that the cleft had been there in 1945!) Horror struck the party when Jim Hall dropped his walking stick, and they watched it descend the mountain at a tremendous pace. This is a day many of us will never forget but it led to several parishioners pursuing scrambling on the mountains!

and when he visited us, he ate cheese with apple pie – quite unheard of at Wilton! However, his biggest surprise was announcing, at his retirement party, that he had married his longstanding housekeeper. This was no surprise to an exceptional worker for the church, Nora Dixon, who, having bought some bedroom furniture from the vicarage, had taken note of the sleeping arrangements, and dryly responded to everyone's amusement, 'Ay, ah thought sumat was ga'an on. There's nout but ya' bed med up up thear'.

The incumbency of Archdeacon Hardie followed – a breath of fresh air with his unconventional services, particularly his 'Family Services' which lasted little longer than half an hour but which were packed with life. Invitations to these were regularly despatched to families within the parish, delivered personally by the vicar or his wife. Devoting his ministry to his parishioners, while renouncing bureaucracy – including keeping up to date church records – Mr Hardie regularly popped in to talk to mums and tots in the newly-developed Mother and Toddler Group. After his ministry there were no records of 'hatched, matched or despatched' or a plan of filled

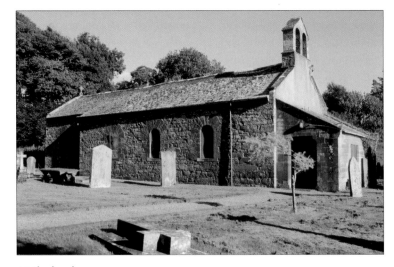

Haile church.

Rev. David Wood provided a different approach in meditation and spiritual renewal, and awakening the awareness of poverty in the inner cities. As well as always showing a sensitive response to those parishioners in need of comfort, he and his wife Sheila extended a warm welcome in their home and regularly offered the vicarage as a meeting place.

Then, Norman Hayton, a man in tune with human beings, wearing a different *hat* for every occasion, and as well as ministering keeping all his congregation up to date with the latest football scores. Norman also had a great talent for entertaining and for inspiring the congregation to discover their own talents. He is remembered by many for playing the part of 'Old Spice' in a concert act mimicking the Spice Girls and helping to raise funds for the village hall improvements by acting as auctioneer at a 'promise auction'.

Rev. Gavin Walker continues the spiritual dimension in a fast-changing world when there are diocesan financial problems, changing world values and too few people in the ministry. He also has a great talent for entertaining in his double act with his wife, Jo. It may be, though, that he is the last vicar to have particular responsibilities for Haile people.

Having been threatened many times with lack of money, amalgamation, and the possibility of part-time ministering, Haile has shown its independent spirit, fighting to retain its individuality in the face of all adversities – a united effort by church and non-church members to retain independence, even though we are now part of the Egremont team. Two Flower Festivals in the latter part of the twentieth century helped to safeguard our finances, financing also an overhaul of the electronic organ which had, in the 1950s, replaced a double-pedal harmonium.

Despite lack of attendance, and a different attitude to religious worship, the people of Haile and Wilton still have a spiritual faith, shown in their determination to fight for, preserve and cherish their church, a very special place, bringing together both heart and soul.

An Organist Remembers

Mrs Hutchinson was organist at Haile Church in the 1970s until she left in 1980. She remembers fondly the place and the people.

Whenever she played at Haile, which was usually twice every Sunday, it was her habit quietly and unobtrusively to help herself to a

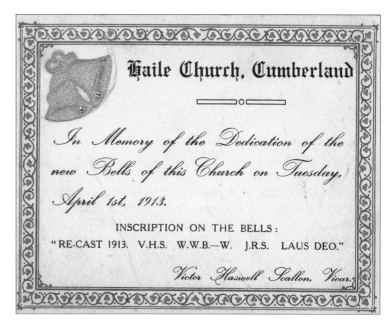

An unusual memorial card.

few wild daisies on her way home.

When the time came for her to leave Haile church, there was a presentation ceremony, during which she noticed a little girl leave the church on her own. She remembers thinking 'I hope they know that she's gone out'. The ceremony continued and Mrs Hutchinson was presented with a lovely cut-glass vase and a bouquet. And then the little girl returned with a bunch of newly picked daisies. Mrs Hutchinson says she treasures the vase and loves bouquets, but the thing that meant most to her was that small bunch of daisies.

POPULATION

HEARTH TAX RETURN FOR 1664

The hearth taxes for 1664 relate to a levy of two shillings on every hearth in the occupation of each person whose house was worth more than 20 shillings. Aimed at the better off, it was introduced at a time of serious fiscal emergency by Charles II and was for the period of 1662-1674. Whilst this tax return cannot be used as a total census of population, as there were always exemptions and evasions (nothing, it seems, has changed) it does give the names of those in the parish who lived in the 'better' houses. But it is no indication of the total number of properties in the parish at the time.

The return lists John Ponsonby as having three hearths and a further 26 names with one hearth each. The tax return does not indicate where each of the properties was situated, but cross referencing these names in other documents (e.g. Probate of Wills) shows that twelve of these were in Wilton/Uldale and the remaining fifteen in Haile/Blackbeck. As with so many of the old documents, it is interesting to see in this one the appearance of names that are still common in the area today.

John Punsonby (3 hearths)	John Punsonby
John Bragg	Henry Punsonby
Richard Sudhert	Richard Gunson
Clement Parke	Henry Jackson
Richard Jackson	Richard Walker
Richard Bragg	Christofer Haile
John Punsonby	Richard Punsonbie
Robert Punsabye	Henrie Vicars
William Baiteman	John Dale
Anthonye Steele	Wm Piele
John Kirkbye	Henrie Walker
George Fleminge	Robert Sharpe
Nicolas Brownrigg	John Browne
Thomas Shipheard	

A STUDY OF THE POPULATION OF THE PARISH OF HAILE AND WILTON 1841-2003/4

In the 1841 Census Haile Parish had 50 dwellings of which 26 were farms. Haile – 14 farms; Black Beck – 2 farms; Tail End (now part of St Bridget's, Beckermet) – 1 farm; and Wilton – 9 farms. This was a farming community and most of the people who lived and worked here were totally involved in it for their livelihoods. By the end of the 19th century new industries were being developed and we see evidence of that in the changes of some of the occupations listed in the census returns such as iron ore miner or postman. When the 20th century drew to a close the land was still being farmed but on a far larger scale and the Parish had slowly evolved into something quite different.

Many changes began in the 1960s with the first modern bungalow in Haile being built on the site of Manesty/Mary Longmire Cottages. Since then a small housing estate in 1974 and numerous houses in all parts of the Parish have almost trebled the number of dwellings. The majority of people, as in most villages in the country, are no longer connected with farming but are employed elsewhere and in this instance many probably having some connection with Sellafield. Farm houses and buildings have been sold separately from the land

and converted into homes and in some cases businesses. Hall Garth and Tilery Cottages have completely gone and nothing has been built in their place.

Some of the seven farms that exist now in the Parish have grown considerably in size by amalgamating with smaller farms or acquiring extra fields when farms have been sold. Beck Brow, the last farm in the centre of Haile village, was sold in 1997 with parcels of land going to separate buyers, and the farmhouse, buildings and adjacent land are now home to five families.

PEOPLE'S OCCUPATIONS – PARISH OF HAILE 1841 TO 1901

The first Census in 1841 is very simple and gives for each dwelling the occupation of the head of the household and also the occupation of any employee e.g. farmer and agricultural labourer. Although it would be probable that the members of the farmer's family who were of working age would work on the farm, this is not acknowledged.

Thai Mumberson with the bull. Most farms, before the days of AI, had their own bull in residence. They were mostly shorthorns.

Later Census Returns become more detailed so that almost everyone is shown as having some occupation such as 'farmer's daughter employed at home' and school age children listed as 'scholars'. In 1901 the Census shows when sons are employed on the family farm and lists them as 'workers'. Women of working age are given occupation titles when they are widowed and head of the household or have a specified occupation such as 'dressmaker' or 'servant'. At other times they are classed as somebody's wife/daughter.

It is interesting to note how new developing industries begin to be seen as some people in the Parish are employed in them rather than in farmwork, such as a 'Railway Clerk' in 1881.

Main Occupations	1841	1851	1861	1871	1881	1891	1901
Farmer	26	28	26	26	24	24	23
Ag. Labourer	26	45	11	10	9	6	6
Farm Servant M	24	–	22	21	21	–	–
Farm Servant F	18	–	15	3	7	–	–
Dom. Servant F	–	18	9	21	10	10	12
Blacksmith/Apprentices	3	4	2	3	6	2	4
Miller/Millwright	1	3	2	3	2	1	–
Carpenter/Joiner/ Wheelwright/Apprs.	2	6	5	3	4	–	–
Shoemaker/Apprentices	2	3	3	–	–	–	5
Dressmaker/Seamstress/ Apprentices	–	1	4	7	6	5	–
Stonemason	1	–	–	1	–	–	–
Schoolteacher – Haile	1	–	1	2	1	1	1
Schoolteacher – Wilton	–	1	1	–	–	–	–
Pub/Innkeepr	2	2	2	2	1	1	2
Nurse/Monthly Nurse	1	2	1	4	1	1	–
Vicar	–	–	–	1	1	1	1

OTHER OCCUPATIONS

These are only listed occasionally or just once during the years 1841-1901.

1841

Hawker, Fishmonger, Grocer/Wine & Spirit Merchant, Woodcutter, Independent Means (4).

1851

Gardener/Coachman, Governess, Sicklemaker, Proprietor of Houses, Wine Merchant (visitor), Surgeon (visitor), Pauper/Agricultural Labourer, Errand Boy, Annuitant (8).

1861

Housekeeper (3), Magistrate, Tailor, Builder + 2 Apprentices, Letter Carrier, Gardener, Rate Collector, Hide and Leather Tanner, Road Labourer (2), Undergraduate at London University, Farrier, Sailor (Merchant Service), Cook, Landed Proprietor. .

1871

Woodcutter, JP, Tilemaker (2), Post Servant, Banksman/Iron Ore Mine, Railway Labourer, Coachman, Rate and Tax Collector, Laundress, Husbandman, Milliner, Cook, Landed Proprietor (6), Teacher/acted also as Organist and Parish Clerk.

1881

Annuitant (2), Housekeeper (5), Magistrate, Tailor, Iron Ore Worker, Railway Clerk, Gardener, Coachman/Gardener, Retired Ship Owner, Commercial Traveller, Cook.

1891

Woodcutter, Independent Means (5), Postman (3), Iron Ore Miner, Gardener, Coachman, Drainer, Engineering Student, Law Student, Coal Merchant, Shepherd, Vet Practitioner/Farmer, Millwright, Traveller (farm machinery), School Sewing Mistress.

1901

Independent Means (7), Housekeeper (2), Tailor, Iron Ore Miner (5) and Labourer (2), Collector – Rated Poor Law, Gardener (2), Farm Manager, Newsagent, Baker, Land Agent, Shopkeeper, Machine Maker, Draper's Apprentice, Farmer's Son Working on Farm (15), Cowman (5) + 1 boy, Horseman (10), Cook, Confectioner.

H.Haile's account book. No ordinary taxi service this. There was a wide range of transportation to choose from.

Farm Workers (Male and Female) Haile Parish 1841 to 1901

	1841	1851	1861	1871	1881	1891	1901
No. of Farms	26	28	26	26	24	24	23
Farm Workers	60	64	57	55	47	28	34
Total Adult Population	198	233	220	211	190	172	164

It will be noticed that the number of farm workers in 1901 is only half of what it was in 1851. Towards the end of the 19th Century farm mechanisation started to be introduced and agricultural workers were leaving the land. In 1901 farm workers were given titles and the census shows 10 horsemen, 5 cowmen and 1 boy included in the total of 34 farm workers. Farmers' sons were described as 'working on the farm'. In the list above, 'Farm Workers' are people who work on the farm but are not family members.

The Mumberson family and helpers have a tea break.

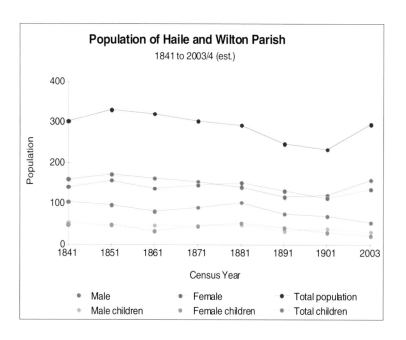

POPULATION: PARISH OF HAILE AND WILTON 1841 TO 2003/4*

Census Year	Total Population	Male	Female	Children Male	Children Female	Children Total	No. Farms	Other Dwellings	Uninhabited Dwellings
1841	303	160	143	55	50	105	26	24	
1851	330	172	158	48	49	97	28	26	
1861	321	163	139	48	34	82	26	37	5
1871	302	155	147	46	45	91	26	36	4
1881	293	141	152	49	54	103	24	36	3
1891	248	116	132	34	42	76	24	35	7
1901	234	120	114	40	30	70	23	33	5
2003	295	159	136	32	22	54	7	89	2

*Estimated. Census material is only available after 100 years; thus the large gap between 1901 and 2003/4.
Children 1841-1901 up to 14 years of age.
Children 2003/4 up to 16 years of age.
In the nineteenth century most children were working by 14 years of age but occasionally there are some instances of children younger than this being employed. Margaret Britson, aged 12 and born in the Isle of Man, was employed at that age as a farm servant, and James Brown, also at 12 found gainful employment as a postman. Now, of course, children are 16 before they can be employed full time.

WHERE WERE PEOPLE BORN?

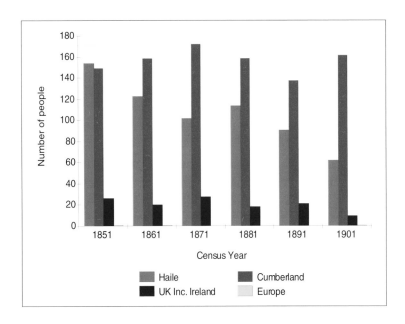

Haile village in the early twentieth century. It is thought that the people standing outside were some of the Noble family. It could be that the person in the horse and trap is Barbara Ponsonby.

The 1841 census asks only whether 'born in the same county?' There appears to be only one inhabitant who was not born in Cumberland.

It would appear that people from other local villages have always moved into the parish to live and work, and as the 19th century progressed so the movement increased.

People who came from outside Cumberland were mostly from North Lancashire or Westmorland and only a very few came from further afield such as Scotland or Ireland.

THE HAILES

There have over the years been many people associated with the village who have carried the name Haile. The handsome young man of this photograph, Moses Haile born in 1833, was the grandson of

the earliest recorded Haile publican, Moses Haile, born in 1772. It looks as though being the village publican was not enough to provide a living, for he seemed to be something of a handyman. In the years around the beginning of the nineteenth century, along with a Jacob Dickinson, Moses had a lot to do with maintaining the old village school. In 1804 he was fixing windows in the school. In 1807 he and Jacob were paid five shillings each for thatching the school, and the straw for the job cost one pound. He was still working in 1840 when, for

Moses Haile.

44

the sum of a pound, he was employed to whitewash the school.

An interesting fact about the cousin of Moses in the photograph came to light, which illustrates the different life a child might expect in the early nineteenth century. This cousin, Henry, was apprenticed in 1813 to William Russell of Sheepfields presumably to do farm work, at the tender age of eight. The fact that, instead of going to school, young Henry was apprenticed, in no way prevented the family in future from developing its skills: it was Henry's son, Isaac in the photograph, whose nephew Henry (are you following this?) wrote the well-crafted and beautifully written letter. It was written to his brother, George, who was at The Stanley Arms, Calderbridge. At the time Henry would be twelve years old and living with his grand-parents whilst attending Ghyll Bank school, Whitehaven. Give a child a chance and just see what he can make of himself.

Mr and Mrs Isaac Haile.

Henry Haile's letter.

FARMS, SETTLEMENTS AND BUILDINGS

FARM BUILDINGS OF HAILE AND WILTON

Hut circle at Tongue How. This circle of stones, just to the west of the parish, is part of an extensive scheduled ancient monument. The remains of dwellings, stock enclosures and field systems show evidence of habitation and farming from around 3000 B.C. to 1000 A.D.

When we think of old farm buildings we tend to go no further back than the evidence now visible in our parish. But in fact, if we take a short step just outside our parish we can go back several thousand years to Neolithic times, and see the remains of farm buildings. Neolithic times were a period traditionally associated with the origins of farming when the hunter-gatherers first began to settle. On Kinniside Common there are prehistoric stone settlements that are

acknowledged as a well-preserved Ancient National Monument No. 27822. An archeological survey undertaken by Lancaster University in 1989 at Town Bank, found crop growing evidence of cereal seed and weed pollen from the third millennium B.C., indicating woodland clearance and settlement.

Beyond the River Calder by the track leading to the Worm Gill waterworks at Tongue How, prehistoric stone hut circle settlements, field systems, funerary cairns, cemetery and cairnfield, Romano-British farmstead, Medieval shieling and lynchets can be seen, evidence of long-term management and exploitation of land in this area. There is little evidence of farm buildings after this time till we get to the 16th century. In the meantime the Vikings (Scandinavians) have made their presence felt by leaving behind their place-names and

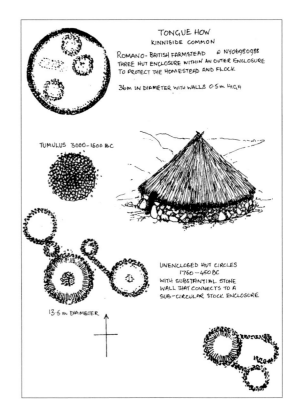

language, such as fell – mountain; beck – stream; dale – valley; gill – ravine; and thwaite – clearing, so we have Brackenthwaite, Uldale and Quicksand Gill.

It is not until the late seventeenth and eighteenth centuries that the present farmhouses of Haile and Wilton start appearing in their present form. This was a very backward area agriculturally, and remained backward till the late eighteenth century and early nineteenth century. During this period Whitehaven was enjoying a boom in ship building, a large merchant fleet, the coal trade to Ireland and a considerable trade in tobacco with Virginia and Maryland. All this activity as well as mining, rope-making, pottery and the development of the town itself demanded a larger work force. Some of the profits were invested in farmland. A census of 1762 stated that the population had quadrupled by the end of the seventeenth century. Improving roads and communications to markets coupled with the food demands of a growing population, encouraged better methods and techniques in agriculture and animal husbandry. All this brought new wealth to the yeomen farmers, who set about improving their farm buildings.

The farm buildings that we can see evolved from humbler beginnings over a long period of time. The changes in their construction have often been uncovered in their renovations. There has been a long tradition where the farmer, his family and livestock dwelt under the same roof, the barn and outbuildings being a continuation of the farmhouse under the one roof, making it a 'long house'.

Early farm-houses consisted of two rooms. The larger, more public room, reached through the only entrance door, contained the principal or only hearth and served as the room for living, dining and cooking; the smaller room opened off it and served as the only bedroom. This kind of house could be attached to farm buildings or extended with additional service rooms, or stand alone. Town End (Wilton),

Brackenthwaite, Uldale, Beck Brow (Wilton), Whitehow and Tortolocate all show evidence of this.

As the income of the farmers grew, so did the quality of their housing. The two-room living space was increased gradually. At first a

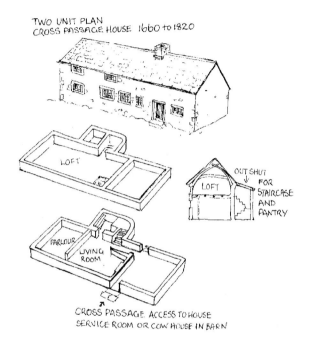

TWO UNIT PLAN
CROSS PASSAGE HOUSE 1660 to 1820

LOFT

OUTSHUT FOR STAIRCASE AND PANTRY

LOFT

PARLOUR LIVING ROOM

CROSS PASSAGE ACCESS TO HOUSE
SERVICE ROOM OR COW HOUSE IN BARN

ladder was used inside at one end to get up into the roof space where the children could sleep, or it could be used for storage. Then a stone staircase was added at the middle of the back of the house extending beyond the existing back wall as a semicircular extension; the roof was extended over it at that point. It has been labelled an 'outshut'. Such a feature is still easily visible at Orchard Brow Cottage in Haile, and was possibly part of the development of Brackenthwaite.

The next improvement came when the roof was lifted. The cramped loft space became a full height upper storey and contained the principal bedroom as well as three other bedrooms, all reached by an adequate stone staircase. Now there were four rooms upstairs and four rooms downstairs. The downstairs rooms consisted of the front door opening straight into the living room, off which is the parlour. Behind are the kitchen, staircase and dairy, with variations in arrangement. This doubling up of floor space has been labelled a 'double pile plan'. In older buildings two parallel gables could be found showing this development. Brackenthwaite's two pitched roofs have now been replaced by one larger roof.

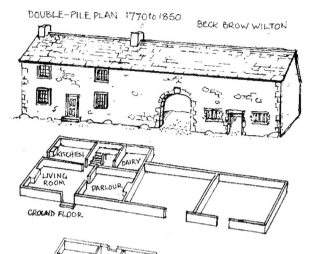

Aerial view of Brackenthwaite showing the two roofs.

Beck Brow (Wilton) was a humble yeoman's dwelling. The existing house is an extension of the original two-roomed house. The attached barn was burnt down in 1971, revealing a gable end of the old two-roomed house. It had been built over and out to raise the height, and depth of the house, creating a 'double pile' construction as described above. The house sits on foundations on top of the ground; foundations consisting of large granite boulders, impervious to damp. They have not moved in over two hundred years.

The house, like many others, was sited without an outlook, with small windows and dark inside. The position of this house was sheltered by the barn in front and the one to the side. The walls are made of a great mixture of sandstone, limestone and glacial boulders.

All these are available locally – a limestone quarry just up the hill, a sandstone quarry just down the hill and a wealth of glacial granite type boulders from over the hill (Ennerdale, in fact) to be found lying all around in field and beck.

Granite type boulders were deposited here by the action and movement of ice in the different ice ages, as the ice receded towards the Irish Sea. The pinkish coloured granite boulders were part of intrusive igneous rock that cooled very slowly deep inside the earth's crust, and called Granophyre, which is to be found in Ennerdale.

The farmhouses were built with any easily available local building material. (Removing some old hair lime plaster from an internal wall at Beck Brow (Wilton) revealed a boulder with some beck-type moss still on it.) The outer wall was built on top of the granite boulder foundations and is approximately 25 inches wide. Its construction was of two walls built side by side with a gap in between filled with small stones called heartings. The inner walls are twenty inches wide. They are made of unevenly sized and shaped stones where much care and ingenuity has been exercised in their placing. The transverse bonding has been obtained with liberal use of headers – stones, which reach from the face to beyond the middle of the wall, overlapping in the centre. Through-stones that extend to the full thickness of the wall were used every so often to bind it together.

An interesting feature at Beck Brow was at the top of the stone staircase. On either side of the stairwell were rectangular openings 22 inches by 28 inches through the walls and into the bedrooms,

BANK BARN TOWN END
BANK BARNS: PERIOD OF USE FROM 1730 ONWARDS

possibly put there to house a lamp or lamps that would illuminate both the stairs and the adjoining bedroom at the same time.

In contrast to the available common materials used in the construction of Beck Brow (Wilton), Town End (Wilton), was built with ample dressed sandstone, suggesting a wealthier owner. Town End was built in the style of the 'long house' with the pitch of the roof continuing uniformly across the house and the barn. The roof timbers were of oak and covered with Lake District slate. Like many farms in Wilton, it has a bank barn. Very few examples of bank barns can be found outside the Lake District, some in Scotland and Devonshire and a few in Yorkshire and Lancashire. They can also be found in the mountainous parts of Europe – South Germany, Switzerland and parts of central France and Norway. Whether there are any points of similarity stemming from a common origin has yet to be proved. These bank barns follow the traditional pattern with warm quarters underneath for cow sheds, stable, loosebox and cart shed. The conventional threshing floor is above with storage for hay, straw and grain. This upper level is approached by a ramp on the higher side of the slope to allow carts to be driven into the barn. The winnowing door is in the wall opposite the ramp, opening inwards and situated high above the farmyard level. The bank barn is an economical construction that covers many activities under one roof with one set of foundations.

The house itself is of double pile construction, four rooms downstairs and four rooms upstairs, an inner wall of the house being built up to bear the weight of the roof. It is this 'double pile' form that is common to most of the farmhouses in Haile and Wilton. Woodlands, dated 1668, is one of the earliest farmsteads still existing. It is a three-storey dwelling with original living quarters above the byre. The windows are of 2-light type with flat faced mullions and small-panel glazing. Woodlands Cottage, dated 1736, the year that it was renovated, has original stone mullion windows.

By the end of the eighteenth century, although the farmhouse kept the same four down, four up form, it was built detached from the barn and byre, as can be seen, for example, at Beck Brow (Haile) and Orchard Brow (Haile).

Tortolacate in the early twentieth century.

49

Few farmhouses have been built in the parish since then. It was the end of vernacular architecture. In the following period agricultural practices changed little, and the enclosures created a more settled field system. Then came the twentieth century with rapid changes, upheavals and new farming methods. Small farms gave way to fewer, bigger farms requiring bigger buildings. The old barns have lost their intended use, many have been converted in such a way as to hide their original shape and purpose. Most of the old farmhouses are no longer lived in by farmers.

BRACKENTHWAITE AND HIGH HOUSE

Brackenthwaite farm, on the northern fringe of Wilton village, is typical in layout and construction of most of the farms in Haile and Wilton and is one of the oldest farms in the area. It was built to meet the requirements of the mixed farming economy of cattle and corn that flourished in the 18th and 19th centuries. Although the present farmhouse and buildings date from the late 18th century, there is evidence of a much earlier settlement. The name 'Brackenthwaite' comes from the Norse word 'thwaite' meaning clearing and, of course, clearing was what early farmers had to do to develop new land for cultivation. Brackenthwaite is also one of the closest farmsteads to the prehistoric settlements, the old drove road and the packhorse bridge just over the hill on Cold Fell. The only certain evidence of the age of the farm are old deeds which go back to 1633 and the discovery of a date stone, or more correctly, half a date stone reading '16..'.

The family for generations associated with Brackenthwaite were the Benns. Indeed, the packhorse bridge close by, originally called 'Monks' Bridge', became known locally as 'Matty Benn's Bridge' after Martha Benn who regularly used the bridge from 1860 onwards when driving her sheep up on to the fell where she had grazing rights.

The first Benns to move to Wilton were Joseph and Sarah in 1747, when they took over the tenancy of Huecroft, then in the possession of the Lord of Egremont. Much of the land in Wilton then was part of the Percy Estates and was administered by the court of Egremont but some was part of the Ponsonby Estate and administered by their own Manorial Court. When Joseph died his son John took over Huecroft (now known as Yewcroft) as well as, in 1765, The Croft which was next door. The Benn family lived in The Croft until 1830 but nothing of the building exists today apart from the daffodils and primroses that appear each spring to remind us of what was once there.

Brackenthwaite itself was acquired in 1777 but two years later John died, aged 55, leaving a wife to look after their four children and three farms. At this point Huecroft was given up. John's son married Jane Dixon from Townend, who was at least four months pregnant when they married. This was not unusual in those days as it guaranteed that children were possible.

A similar tragedy struck the next generation when John's son, also John, died aged 46, leaving his young widow Jane to bring up seven children and run two farms. This did not hold back the family, however, as two years later, in 1814, when the moorland near Brackenthwaite was enclosed, the Benns were awarded two plots of land and bought a third. They now owned a total of 76 acres and this, together with the

Matty Benn's Bridge

demand for food brought about by the Napoleonic wars, led to a boom time for farming generally and Brackenthwaite in particular. The need for an extra barn at this time is suggested by the fact that a date of 1818 and the initials W. B. are inscribed on the beam over the main barn door.

However, tragedy struck again in 1820 when the eldest son, John, was killed when he fell from the horse and cart as it turned into the yard. As a consequence William took over the farm and changed from farm labourer to yeoman farmer overnight.

Later William took on the important role of churchwarden at Haile, collecting taxes and administering to the poor. As the person responsible for keeping the church accounts, it was probably William who, in 1843, organised a special collection for erecting a vestry and gallery in the church.

Unfortunately, William died aged 61 when he choked to death whilst intoxicated at home. A further tragedy followed a few years later in 1864, when his grandson, Wilton, aged only two, was killed by a tree being felled by his father, John, in the yard at Brackenthwaite.

Throughout this time, as the periods of prosperity and the needs for more accommodation became evident, the house and farm expanded, as did so many others in the area, from the original two-roomed house, to becoming eventually a five up and five down house.

The farm stayed in the Benn family for two more generations but they sold it in the early 1880s after feeling the effects of a big slump in British farming in the 1870s. The Sumptons and Wilsons farmed it until 1983 when the present owners, Terry and Eileen Dixon, took it on adding it to their

existing farm, High House. The early farmers of Brackenthwaite would perhaps be more familiar with what is now happening at the farm than they would with many of the developments of the twentieth century, because the farm, under the Dixons, has moved to organic status. This involves the reversion to the use of farm yard manure instead of artificial fertilizers, and the use of crop rotation and clover pastures to build up fertility. The farm, like many in the parish, has joined the 'Environmentally Sensitive Area' scheme which has involved, amongst other things, the completion of a ten mile hedgerow restoration scheme. The aim of this scheme is to establish

The winnowing door at Town End, Wilton. Once the door was opened, the draught helped blow away the chaff.

The old thresher at Brackenthwaite. The doors on the right gave access to the drive belts within the thresher. The main drive shaft went through the wall to the pulley wheel which was driven originally by a horse-driven gin-ring and later by petrol engine. The straw came out of the gap on the left and the grain collected inside at the back.

an old-style hedgerow, mainly to bring back the benefits of a wildlife that we seem to have forgotten is also a part of our agricultural heritage, and maybe a more important part than we have sometimes realised.

William Suddart of High House. This photograph was taken in about 1908 when William, his wife Jane, and his daughter Hannah lived in Frizington. The vehicle is a Rexette 6HP Tricar, first registered in 1907.

High House

High House followed the pattern of Brackenthwaite and many other farms in the area in that it started as a two room affair with a traditional barn adjoining the house, built in the late 18th century, and expanded over the years. Older deeds have not been traced but from the Manorial Court Records, it is clear that the Suddart family was associated with it in the 18th century and kept it until 1931. The Dixons bought it in 1977 and expanded it – as became necessary in the 20th century for reasons other than increasing prosperity or large families – with land from Yewtree, followed by the inclusion of

Brackenthwaite and then Moss Dalts. This farm also has become part of the return, in effect, to many of the ways of the old-style farming which we now call 'organic'.

Memories of Farming at Town End, Wilton

My earliest memories of farming practice relate back to my pre-school years in the late 1940s, waiting with my two sisters on the steps descending to the low, wooded-stalled byre at Town End for my father to fill our beakers with warm milk, freshly hand-drawn from our favourite cow, Clara. My younger sister, Irene, had difficulty pronouncing its name, so it became known to us all as 'Swearer'.

Each of our eighteen dairy shorthorn cows had a name as did our two carthorses, Robin and Phyllis, which were regarded as family pets. While my father was harnessing them to the plough, or while they were being fitted with new horse shoes, we would decorate their head-collars with briar roses. I remember our excitement when the first tractor came in the 1940s, probably little realising what that would mean for our Clydesdales.

Increased demand for milk after the war and stricter dairy hygiene regulations meant that we had to modernise the old system of steamy low-ceilinged byres of the long houses, and replace them with modern concrete and sheeted milking parlours with wider stalls, lower floors and more ventilation. Milking machines were also introduced at about this time driven by electricity, though we had to use a generator to power our machines as mains electricity did not come to Wilton until 1956. The arrival of electricity meant also that we could have light at the flick of a switch instead of the old Tilley paraffin lamps which we slid along a wire stretched the length of the byre to illuminate the area where we were working.

Because of the new standards required of us for cooling the milk, we could no longer rely on the amount of water available from the ancient reservoir and had to make another move forward in the 1950s, joining to the mains supply which ran past the farm.

Haytime tea-break at Town End farm, Wilton. About 1950. Mrs Eleanor Bowes works with the fork while the men have their break. It looks as though the horse, also, is taking a break.

Sheep farming has always been an important activity in these parts and my family has been involved in it no less than any other. My great grandfather's name, James Martin Wallace, appears in the first edition of *Wilson's Shepherds' Guide* as he was a shepherd as well as a publican at Ennerdale. So his sheep had the Ennerdale sheep mark. The Guide stated in its introduction;

> 'The need for such a guide arises from the greater part of the mountain grasslands being unenclosed, so that sheep stray from their proper heaths and may be miles away from their owner'.

When my grandfather bought Town End farm in 1918-1919 there was no sheep mark registered for the farm and so it appears he adapted the Ennerdale sheep mark. My grandmother had a hard time after my grandfather had died in an accident but still worked the farm until my mother took on the tenancy when she married John Bowes. They expanded, taking on the tenancy of Uldale farm and eventually purchasing 78 acres, developing a fell flock using the Uldale sheep mark.

Town End was, however, a mixed farm and as such grew corn and

barley as part of the traditional rotational farming. My memories are still vivid of thrashing days in the 50s when all the neighbouring farms lent a helping hand and I was allowed a day off school to help mother prepare food for at least a dozen workers. This meant an early start as a huge fire had to be lit and dampers drawn to heat the oven, and then two very large meat and potato pies were prepared while gingerbread and apple pies were already cooking.

The stacks in the adjacent field were quickly eaten up by Sutton's huge, orange-coloured, noisy thrashing machine. Loose corn or barley was bagged up from a hopper and taken to the granary, to await crushing later, and loose straw tied into 'bottles' and led by horse and cart into the barn. In the meantime, dust and chaff flew everywhere and one of the helpers, 'Sock' Graham, always used to put a knotted handkerchief on his head to keep out the chaff from his mop of curly hair.

The Ennerdale sheep mark.

There was no disputing when dinner time arrived as the pit horn from Ullcoats mine sounded at twelve noon and very soon an army of dusty-faced men filled the huge kitchen table, and were waited on by the womenfolk.

During and after the war, pigs were a valuable commodity because of food shortages, so much so that they had a value on the 'black market', a practice countered by the authorities with a system of permits and checks. I remember butching the pig as another eventful day in the life of the farm, not that we children were allowed to see the actual killing, but we were involved in cleaning the intestines, reversing and washing them before they were filled with minced pork. Trays of blood were cooked with barley to make black pudding and potted meat was made from the pickings of the pig's head. The neighbours were given handouts of these perishable products as there were no freezers in those days. The flanks of bacon, preserved in saltpetre and draped in muslin to keep the flies off, were hung from ceiling hooks until needed. But there is no doubt that the highlight for us children was being presented with the blown-up pig's bladder to use as a giant football.

Herding sheep in Lowther forest.

My Aunt Agnes recalled that in the 1930s cattle were transported to market by Ratcliffe's cattle truck, but she remembered bullocks being walked to Beckermet for sale and then transported by train from the station. It was the arrival of the trains that allowed new cattle and sheep markets to develop and so people were not as dependent on the fairs that had traditionally been held at places like Boonwood and Arlecdon. Until the 1920s, however, farmers and drovers walked dairy cows to Whitehaven. One of the drovers at that

time, Joe Hewitson from Moss Dalts, she remembers, used a dog called 'Shot' who accompanied Joe to Whitehaven auction every Thursday morning. After the cattle were safely delivered Shot had got into the habit of turning up at the bus stop where, because he was well known by everyone including the bus conductor, he was allowed to travel back to Egremont. When Joe retired, Shot was sold to someone in Whitehaven but on Wednesday evenings he would evade his owner and arrive back at Moss Dalts, (presumably travelling in the way to which he was accustomed!) ready for work the next morning.

Nowadays you might expect, with modern methods of production and better methods of husbandry, that stock levels would be so much higher than in the past. Town End still has ancient rights, going back to 1583, to graze on the common, but the rise of the E.E.C. with its Common Agricultural Policy – the new power in farming – has resulted in stock numbers on the Common being reduced by 40%. It is, and will remain, a contentious issue, but it is certainly threatening the livelihood of the fell farmer. With cows also, there are regulations: while in 1547 a dwelling at Wilton could be described as 'A messuage,

The children at Town End sit on the new 'Fergie' tractor. (Left to right: Eric Slater, Irene Bowes, Jean Bowes, Joyce Bowes.)

5 acres of land with appurtenances and pasture for 4 beasts', today's Ministry figures, dictating the necessity of 2.5 acres for each cow, would render the original farm overstocked.

Furthermore, farms have developed independently to be more self-contained, but this at the expense of the interdependence and community spirit that was once so evident. The modern farmer can be a very isolated figure.

Town End, like all other farms, has always had to contend with the weather, the market and the problems that arise from working with living things, whether crops or animals. Now it has to contend also with what at times seems to overshadow all the rest – a large dose of bureaucracy.

Sheep dipping at Uldale.

BLACKBECK: A CORNER OF THE PARISH

Blackbeck has always been a small community tucked away from the main population centres of the parish. And, in that it has had very little new building since the nineteenth century, it remains small and self-contained. In old Blackbeck (and references to Blackbeck go back to the eighteenth century) there were two farms, Blackbeck House which has since been developed into the Hotel, and Blackbeck Farm which, with its adjacent cottage, granary and barn, has now been converted into housing. Another, separate, barn has recently been converted for residential use. The last farmers in Blackbeck House, in the 1930s, were Mr Stephenson and his sister. The building was later owned by a contracting company at Sellafield and then by Brian Barwise who first turned it into a hotel.

View of Blackbeck.

These farms and a mill appear to go back at least to 1769. The mill had a cottage alongside it, now known as Mill Holme, and both are now residential properties. The building which was the Mill itself has a date of 1916 on it and, as it is constructed of brick rather than the sandstone of all the other early buildings in the settlement, it suggests that it has been rebuilt at some time after it ceased to be a mill. The mill race began further upstream towards Godderthwaite, went by the mill, under the road, down alongside the left hand side of the road, back under the road and then into the beck before it went under the main road. It is a beck that, although of no great size, never runs dry and so was very suitable for a mill.

A cottage which stands on the right as you enter Blackbeck used to be called Isle Cottage, perhaps because it stood between the beck and the mill race.

A building which is no longer there was the wooden chapel or mission, converted in the 1920s into a cottage, which stood on a piece of land alongside where the lay-by is on the main road.

Behind and attached to Blackbeck House was Blackbeck Cottage, home in the 1930s of Jack Raven, and attached to this cottage was a barn. This again had attached to its other end White Cottage which was originally a smallholding This is where Isaac and Elizabeth Moffatt moved to in 1939 and lived with their children John and Georgina. It was taken down in 1970.

The settlement in its early days was essentially a country settlement based mainly on the two farms and the mill. It appears to have been the home later of a millwright and a joiner. Only gradually, during the last century has it lost this feeling of being a settlement based on country industries and become, like so many other small communities, a settlement of people involved in a much wider range of professions. It maintains, though, its sense of community.

Of the people we know of who lived there in the twentieth century, two, largely because of their jobs, were particularly well known.

George 'Geordie' Edwards who lived at Blackbeck in the years before and during the war, was well known because he was the lengthman for the Haile area, and in this job of maintaining the local roads he would meet many people.

Isaac Moffatt who lived with his wife Elizabeth and children was another very well-known character in the area because his main job was draining on local farms. He also caught fish and rabbits to sell in the locality and to local shops, making his own nets for the purpose. As his work was mainly in some of the quieter reaches of the local countryside, he developed a great love of the surrounding country,

especially the Calder valley. He wrote poems reflecting his attachment to the fells and rivers of this area. Unfortunately, Isaac died of Tuberculosis at the relatively young age of 53 but his poems are still here to remember him by.

I WENT A-COURTING

> I went a-courting up sweet Calderdale
> And sat many an hour with my sweet Mary Jane.
> I gathered sweet flowers to adorn her fair form:
> Spring flowers were blooming,
> The birds in full song.
> Worm Beck was joining where we sat on the bank –
> Lovers they are for centuries past,
> They join together whispering their love,
> Then prancing and dancing and throwing of spray
> Both joined together they now wend their way.
> > I then told my sweetheart,
> > My sweet Mary Jane,
> > Just like the Calder we'd go down the dale.

Because Blackbeck was in the parish, even though in the far reaches of it, children from there were invited to the popular Christmas parties at Haile Hall. Georgina Broadbent remembers as a child going to these parties held in the large barn with shooting trophies round the walls and a large blazing log fire. She remembers, also, the generosity of Sir John, not only in providing such parties for the children of the village, but in the presents he gave each one of them. Her last present, and this was at the beginning of the war, was a child's tea set. John Robley, nephew to Lady Ponsonby, who also as a boy went to those parties, remembers also that they had an entertainer, and that the parties stopped sometime during the war, at which time, he reports:

> 'The barn was taken over by the government and used as an emergency food store. I think they had to reinforce the floor to take the extra weight!'

One small footnote. When the main road was widened in 1939 and the parapets of the bridge were rebuilt, the stones indicating the boundary between the parish of St Bridget Beckermet and Haile parish were set in the walls either side of the main road which is the boundary between the parishes. Only when the job was complete was it realised that the stones were on the wrong sides. And they remain so to this day.

MANESTY

An example of a vernacular 'small-house' cottage.

Manesty or 'The Old Thack', as it was affectionately called, was the beautiful, whitewashed thatched-roof cottage which once stood in its own grounds in the centre of Haile village. A tenancy named Manesty features in the Manor Court Book as early as 1690. At that time the annual rent was 6s. 8d. but on the death of John Ponsonby, the Lord of the Manor, the tenant, in keeping with the tradition of the time, suddenly found that he had to pay a Fine (a lump sum) of £11. 10s. 0d. Compared with the annual rents these Fines must have seemed huge sums of money.

Manesty appears an unusual name for a cottage or house, compared with names of other dwellings of similar age in the village, e.g. Orchard Brow, Beck Brow. Could the name Manesty be a derivative of 'manes', the latin word meaning 'the deified souls of departed ancestors' or 'the good'? There were people by the name of Manesty in Egremont in the 17th and 18th centuries. Before and after the dissolution of Calder Abbey there were Manestys farming in and around the Calder. The registers of their baptisms, marriages and burials at Haile Church survive from the reign of Henry VIII. Robert de Manesty, one of the evicted monks, became vicar of St. John's, Beckermet. Is this where the name of the cottage originated?

Thatched roofs were unusual in this part of Cumbria but there is evidence that they were widely used on the Solway plain and in the north-east of the county. Straw was the main material but ling and heather were often used, depending on what was available. Reeds and bracken might have been used for temporary thatching. Correspondence in 1898 between Barbara Ellen Ponsonby, one of the Trustees of Haile Hall Estate, to which Manesty belonged, and her agent reveals that new thatching was being put on at that time. The job had come to a halt for a while because of insufficient straw and then unfavourable weather. But, as soon as the weather was suitable presumably the thatcher returned, as promised, with straw that was now available again. In a 1914 document concerning the Estate, the cottage is described as 'an old thatched dwelling which has been roofed with corrugated iron sheeting'.

Manesty cottage. From a painting by J. Adair in 1884.

The cottage was one room deep, which was common in Cumbria in the 1700s, with sandstone flags as flooring and a wooden staircase to the upper floor. There was a well in the bank opposite Manesty just through the gateway in the painting where the two ladies are standing. Horses were taken down the track to drink from the beck.

For a while, in the later half of the nineteenth century, Manesty was two cottages which were given several different names either by whoever lived there or by whoever completed the various Census Returns. In 1861 the two cottages are referred to by the obvious name of Long Thatch Cottage, in 1871 by the name of Mary Longmire Cottage (the fields directly behind being called Mary Longmire Land), and finally in 1881 by the name of Croft Foot being situated at the foot of the field which might have been called The Croft. You can see from the painting where the division that separated the dwellings was probably made, making one cottage rather larger than the other, though neither would appear big enough nowadays for the size of families living there. The larger one was home to two parents and four children in 1861, and then, in 1881 it was home to an even larger family of two parents with seven children.

By 1891 Manesty had become one cottage and was now referred to in the Census Return by its original name. It was lived in by a widow and four children. The same widow was still living there in 1901 with two married daughters and their husbands! There could never have been a lot of room to spare in Manesty.

In 1855 with other properties belonging to Haile Hall Estate Manesty became part of a mortgage deal. Miss Ponsonby, in that same 1898 correspondence with her agent mentioned earlier, also requested that the annual rent of the cottage be increased to £10. If the tenant, though a 'good tenant', refused to pay this amount, then he would have to leave.

Still rented out at £10 a year, Manesty, in the 1914 document mentioned earlier, is reported as being condemned by the Sanitary Inspector as:

'unfit for habitation but the tenant being unable to obtain another house on account of the scarcity of homes in the neighbourhood and a big demand owing to the proximity of the mines it is still occupied'.

Manesty. The deteriorating cottage before it had to be taken down, brightened up by the daffodils planted over the years by Annie and Joe Noble.

By 1918 it was unoccupied and by 1928 the only inhabitants were hens and pigs owned by the landlord of The Buck's Head who was paying a small annual rent. This was the year when Haile Hall and its Estate (including the cottage) was put up for auction by Ronsley Miles Ponsonby of Tasmania, who had inherited the Hall. Manesty made headlines in *The Whitehaven News* – 'Only Disused Cottage Sold at Whitehaven'. Haile Hall (with the Mill House and Pigeon House) and four farms were withdrawn or no offers made. 'After spirited bidding' Manesty was bought for £35 by an estate agent who sold it on only a few months after the sale to him was completed, making a profit of £15!

With the help of a government grant, the new owners, Joe and Annie Noble of Gravel Bank, planned to renovate the cottage and in the meantime Joe, a joiner, used it as his wood store. But, with the outbreak of war, the grant was no longer available and so, sadly Manesty fell further and further into disrepair until, when it was sold on in 1968, it was so derelict and unsafe it had to be demolished. The land, however, during the Nobles' ownership flourished by their planting over the years of dozens of daffodil bulbs, many of which still flower either in the garden where they were first planted or on either side of the road going down the hill towards the church.

WHITEHOW HEAD

Just outside the north west edge of the Haile and Wilton parish, on the fringe of the Carlton Moor woods lies Whitehow Head.

There has been a settlement on the site for hundreds of years. Some say one of the first buildings on the site was a Roman pay house, which was developed into a strong house for the storage of documents during the War of the Roses and then into a tollhouse for the Ponsonby estate.

Whitehow Head farm used to form part of the Ponsonby estate and records can be traced back to the 1700s when the Dickinson family were tenants. In the 1829 *Directory & Gazetteer of Cumberland* John Hasty is named as farming Whitehow Head and he is still there in the 1851 census along with his wife Elizabeth, their two sons John and Frances, two farm labourers, William Lowry and Samuel Sewell, and servant Sarah Wales.

Mr and Mrs Wightman. Charles and Elsie Wightman with their first two children, Sarah and Samuel, 1925.

White How farm from the yard.

However, by 1883 the occupancy had changed to a John Davy according to the *History Topography & Directory of West Cumbria*. The present day Wightman family took up tenancy of the farm from Willy Willis in 1926 and subsequently went on to purchase the farm from the Ponsonby family in 1972.

The second development at Whitehow Head was the construction of Wood Lea by Tom Wightman in the mid-1970s followed by the first barn conversion, Woodside in 1991, also for the Wightman family. In the new millennium things are changing again, Whitehow Head has ceased being a working farm and the barns and out-buildings are being converted into four new dwellings.

YEWCROFT

Yewcroft is at first sight a modernised house that has been converted from a nineteenth century farm cottage and barn with the roofline at right angles to the lane. This arrangement is also shown on the first ordnance survey map of 1861 and also shows a barn on the bank and other buildings between the two gateways. These have long since gone.

The house as it stands has two interesting features. The first is the sandstone lined well some distance in front of the house and the second is the 12/13th century Celtic-style stone head carving on the gable end of the house.

The well at Yewcroft.

Clive Bowd, a local heritage consultant, and John Billingsley, an accepted authority on sculptured Celtic stone heads and author of *A Stony Gaze – Investigating Celtic and other Stone Heads* have looked into this carving. They conclude that it is a 12/13th century corbel or bracket from a highish position, as the head is angled downwards –

once perhaps supporting a vaulting or something of the sort or maybe a door arch. They believe it to be from an ecclesiastical building and it is a lovely and quite typical example of an archaic head in its features.

From features in the house and from research of historical documents, the house in some form dates back to the 1500s. The earliest record that we have for this house is from the 20th Elizabethan survey of 1578 where it states 'Nicholas Towerson holdeth a tenement a barn and other buildings environed with a hedge . . .'. This property along with five others was part of the Lord of Egremont estate.

Various tax and census records show the property to have been occupied by:
Richard Gunson from 1641-1670 who originated from Gosforth.
James Nicholson
Elizabeth Jackson 1679-
Thomas Cook 1750-
William Haile (occupier) Thomas Cook (owner) 1780
Peter Fisher (Occupier) Thomas Cook (owner) 1785-1791
Jane Pattinson 1806 (enfranchised to her for £120 in 1807)
Isaac Dixon and Richard Thompson (occupiers) Jane Pattinson claimant at the time of the Hail Inclosure
Mr Johnston 1831
Isaac Rennie (occupier) Mrs Johnston (owner) 1837
James Tyson 1851
Isaac Pearson Benson 1861-1880
Joseph & Ann Steel 1881 (possible ancestors of current owners)

The stone head.

It has also been possible from the architectural evidence left to surmise that the property was originally a two-storey building with the roofline parallel to the lane, the upper floor not being as high as the lower level. It is thought that in the 1700-1800s the house was altered by raising the front of the house by the addition of a new gable end and running the roofline the other direction. It may have been at this time that the barn and byre were also added. The rear of the cottage was then left as a single storey building.

The house was modernised to its current shape after Walter Muncaster and his family had bought it. According to a handwritten note on a wall found under some wallpaper, uncovered during some recent work, he bought the house in March 1973 for £3,164. The property was derelict but with the help of a grant from the council it was renovated.

WEDDINGSHAW

Weddingshaw is another of the old properties of Wilton that date back to at least the late 1500s. It was made up of a dwelling and buildings that were part of the Haile Manor, while adjoining land was

Weddingshaw farm. The three ladies leaning on the wall were probably Hannah and Sarah with their mother, Mary.

part of the Lord of Egremont estate. They were eventually brought together when they were enfranchised to Isaac Viccars from the Earl of Egremont on 20th May 1777 for £66. 5s. and from Miles Ponsonby on 4th June 1777 for £100.

According to the Manor Court records and the tax records from the mid-1600s to 1758 the house belonged to a succession of Henry Viccars. On the barn wall there is an interesting date-stone bearing three initials, a heart and the date 1685.

The date stone at Weddingshaw.

This would usually indicate the celebration of a marriage. However, the letters on the stone are not in the order expected if the H and the V stand for Henry Viccars. The top letter is usually the surname while the lower two letters are the Christian names of the betrothed. From the Haile church records (and the Bishop's Transcripts) there does not appear to be a marriage in Haile that matches that date or initials. So whether this was celebrating a marriage that occurred outside this parish, and to whom the initials relate, are questions still to be answered.

The barn, having the date-stone, is probably the original dwelling that has been converted to a barn with a new house being built opposite. When this was done is not known but the house seems to date from the late 1700s.

William Tyson with his horse.

The Tyson family. Father, John. Mother, Mary. Daughters, Hannah and Sarah. Sons, William and Jonathan. Taken in the 1890s.

Although Isaac Viccars inherited the property in 1758 it is unlikely that he resided there but lived in Broughton in Furness. On his death in 1783 he instructed his executors to divide the property equally amongst his five children after the death of his wife.

The youngest son John eventually inherited from his siblings the remaining shares in the property and although he moved back to this area he did not reside at Weddingshaw but ended up living at Ullcoats. The property then passed to William Caddy but again he was only the owner as the Tyson family had been occupiers of the farm from about 1835.

The property had therefore not been owner-occupied from 1758 to the 1950s. The present owners, Mr and Mrs Middleton, bought the property in 1969.

DRUIDS NEAR YEWCROFT

While researching the enfranchisements of the Leconfield estate properties in Wilton a map, from the documents sent over from Cockermouth Castle, came to light. The map was drawn up at the end of the 1700s and located the properties and land being enfranchised with the names of the owners of each. It was then that, not so much as X marks the spot, but a dotted circle with the words 'Druids Temple' was noticed.

The location was in a field between Yewcroft and Brackenthwaite. This site is not shown on the Parish enclosure map of 1811 or on the first Ordnance Survey map of 1860 and it does not appear in the records of the Cumbria Sites and Monuments office in Kendal. This makes this re-discovery of the site very exciting.

This Temple is not going to be a Stonehenge of the North nor contain any passage graves as in New Grange in Ireland but like one of many small stone circles found in this area it suggests that local, tribal or familial religious rites were carried out. Like the tomb-shrines that preceded them, the circles show wide variations in design and alignment.

Inspection of the site at ground level does not give any indication

The stone which may have been part of the Druid circle.

of there being a circle of stones present or signs of post holes. However, in the hedge banking of the field are several very large stones that may have come from the breaking up of the stones from the circle.

These stones have an orange/red hue to them compared to the grey shale and limestone rocks in the rest of the walls and nearby stone outcrops. The area of land is also relatively level with a natural amphitheatre of land behind and to the front, which faces west, to a panoramic view of the sea and the Isle of Man. It is not hard to imagine a circle of these stones being bathed in the setting sunlight highlighting their orange/red colour and making them look magical.

The aerial photographs recently taken of the village unfortunately do not indicate anything unusual, although the photograph available on the *getmapping* website does show some circular shape to that area. Further research will have to be done to pursue this subject further and hopefully prove that Druids were indeed living in Wilton.

FARM WORK

HISTORY OF MAN AND FARMING

You don't have to walk far from the parish to find yourself 5000 years back in history. Set off from Cold Fell gate down the track to the Calder and soon on your right you can see on Friars Moor a small 'hill' about 40 yards around its base, about 9 feet high and with a depression in the top. This is a Neolithic burial mound or 'tumulus' reminding us of our link with a people who hunted and gathered fruits in this area as a way of survival. An analysis done in 1989 of soil samples on Town Bank on the other side of the Calder provided evidence of seed and cereal pollen suggesting rudimentary efforts at cultivation, scratching the earth and planting seed

Stockdale Moor, a little further south, has many cairns and tumuli and was the centre of a large Stone Age settlement stretching from Wasdale to Haile.

Perhaps rather later, in the Bronze Age, there was some kind of ploughing. Evidence for this is shown in ridged areas and linchets. Further fascinating evidence of these earlier peoples and the hunting that they still pursued was the discovery in about 1910 of an early Bronze Age flint arrow head, which was found by Hannah Suddart at

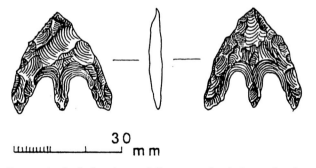

Early Bronze Age barbed and tanged flint arrow head. It was found in about 1910 by Hannah Suddart at High House, Wilton.

High House farm.

There are in the parish two examples still existing of the querns which were used to grind the corn produced in the fields of the Iron Age. It is thought that about now horses were domesticated, perhaps for pulling carts, perhaps for riding but not yet for ploughing. Certainly agriculture was taking more of a hold and there is evidence on Tongue How of the need for enclosures to protect the homesteads and the flock, and shepherds' huts or shielings.

Each group of invaders and settlers seems to have left some trace in our district. Again on Cold Fell there is evidence of a farmstead from Roman times though there is some dispute as to how far towards the fell the Romans can be traced. There is a suggestion that there was a Roman road between Ravenglass and Moresby forts that crossed the river Kirk Beck at the point where the church stands.

The social organisation, of which farming was a part, was perhaps much more recognisable in Anglo-Saxon times. Villages consisted of a number of homesteads built around a larger Hall where the chief lived. Below him there were the free land-holders, and the serfs who were tied to the land. The more isolated farmsteads consisted of wood-framed buildings with a stockade to keep the herds safe at night. Here again there is some local evidence of this generation of peoples: at one corner of the church you will find built-in the remnants of an Anglo-Saxon cross; and the very name Haile is from the Anglo-Saxon word for 'nook' or 'corner'.

We are on ground that is a little more certain when we come to the Vikings, the Norsemen who settled in the north and west of the country and who cleared more and more woodland for cultivation, as the frequency of the suffix 'thwaite' to place names indicates. They lived in groups in farmsteads and left us a legacy both of names and carved stones, both of which are very evident in our parish. To move from, say, the South of England to Cumbria is to meet up with a language whose differences often stem from the Norse words we inherited. Try finding around here a 'stream', 'hill' or a 'valley'! Visit Haile church and you can see a Viking grave cover, but to find the church you'll have to go down to the 'dale bottom' by the 'beck'.

The Norman Conquest brought with it not only a further development of the feudal system of farming where serfdom was the lot of most who worked the land, but it also brought our very own Lord of the Manor. Much of the land, which was still being extended and enclosed, was owned by the Lord who had powerful rights over those who worked for him. Haile became a typical feudal village having a Hall, a church, a mill and home farm. Farming for most people was based on the strip system of ploughing and strict rotation of crops, all overseen and closely controlled by the Lord of the Manor. The main crops grown were oats with some barley, crops which better suited the cooler, wetter climate of the north.

Farmers, who had the rights to it, shared the common land on the nearby Cold Fell – as they still do – for the summer grazing of their cattle and sheep. In winter they shared pasture land for the feeding of the stock that wasn't slaughtered. Shepherds' meets would be held when stray sheep would be returned to their right heaths. Come September all the sheep were brought down from the fells, and fairs were held, where surplus stock could be sold and new stock bought in, though new stock could not be let loose on the fells. Such a fair was our local Crab Fair in Egremont, still going, but with a rather different emphasis. Another interesting method of stock management that was practised then was 'salving': in October sheep were smeared with a mixture of stockholm tar and molten tallow to protect them from lice and scab and to 'waterproof' the fleece over winter. All this had to be washed off again in the following July and several of these sheep 'washes', dammed areas, are still evident in local rivers and streams.

Coppicing of woodland was allowed for domestic use, and was essential for the production of items such as hurdles to pen herds at night or to manure selected areas of land. Among the main uses of woodland was the feeding of some animals in autumn and winter, such as acorns for swine and holly leaves for sheep. And, of course, woodland was a source of fuel. The Lord's pleasure of hunting featured high on the list of priorities. And all these activities were strictly regulated.

Another influence on farming at this time, and up to the dissolution of the monasteries, was the church, and Haile did not escape this influence, being as near as it was to Calder Abbey. The church had built up its own estates, frequently from gifts from Lords of the Manor, and thus wielded powers temporal as well as spiritual. Each tenant farmer was expected to give a tenth of his produce or income to the church: don't let that little word 'tenth' roll off the tongue; just imagine giving a tenth of what you earn now to the church and in those days you could be struggling to make ends meet anyway. This 'tithe' was to be used for 'the priests' maintenance and for giving alms to the poor' and it might just help secure your place in the hereafter. The small farms that the church set up in what were then more outlying places were called 'granges' and examples of these can still been seen in some of the names in the parish. We no longer use the name 'glebe' land for those fields allotted to the church; we give ours, or part of them, the less resounding name of Haile Park. We do, however, retain Friar Gill, Friar Well and Monks' Bridge.

Medicine chest. Why 'universal'?[1]

Not that the church merely took from people. On the feast day of St Luke, it seems, roasted oxen was fed to 'the people of Beckarmet, Ponsaby, and Hale, including the distant farm of Brashaw'. By the way, the monks were some of the few people who could write and spell!

There were many ups and downs in farming in the period 1300 to 1600. Food shortages at times resulted in the reclaiming, enclosing and cultivating of waste ground. The drastic fall in population resulting from the Black Death reduced the number of people able to work the land, and this in turn resulted in tenants having rather more security, and being able to transfer land between themselves. This happened in the 1500s between three Wilton farms, Stockbridge, Ewe Tree and Town End. What was grown on these farms, however, remained much the same. The farms retained rights to cut peat on the fell (turbary) as wood was becoming more scarce and the woods that did remain were the property of the Lord. They also retained the right to pannage and the grazing of swine in the woods.

It may be described as a sideline to farming, but tenants, as part of their duties to the Lord, were also expected to be prepared to fight in the regular border raids which were common in the 1300s. Not only that, but they had to pay increased taxes to pay for extra defences.

The 17th and 18th centuries showed a growth in prosperity in West Cumberland, with a growing population and with better communications allowing the development of markets for trade. The yeoman farmers, of course, were part of this increased prosperity and it was reflected in better and necessarily bigger farm buildings and larger farm houses. Sheep became an even more important source of income as the demand for cloth increased. The building of the harbour at Whitehaven had an effect both on local trade and on land ownership because of the fact that land in the locality became an attractive investment for successful industrialists. For example, a shipping family, the Woods, invested in land at Town End and used it as collateral in their dealings.

Cow horn. Obviously, but why was it cut to this shape?[2]

The end of the 18th century and the 19th century saw the beginning of what in agriculture, as in industry, was one of the biggest changes in history, though it was not a story of constantly increasing prosperity for the farmer. In the late 1700s Agricultural Societies were set up which, with their annual shows, did much to spread selective breeding and new methods of agriculture. These new methods and ideas were promoted locally by John Christian Curwen of Workington Hall. New crops such as clover, roots and turnips allowed the over-wintering of cattle, thus encouraging new breeding programmes for better animals which could be kept from year to year. Shorthorns became very popular. Even so, there was not enough natural organic manure available, and phosphates and nitrates from crushed rocks began to be used. Mousegill quarry produced the limestone that was used to redress the balance of the soil, especially the acid soil common in Wilton, as well as the lime for making field tiles. It was John Curwen who had

introduced draining to make fields more productive, using horse-shoe field tiles. In our parish there is evidence that these tiles were made at Tortolacate Park, and there was once a cottage called Tilery Cottage.

By the middle of the twentieth century mechanical milking was introduced and that was an indication of what was to come: the increasing mechanisation that was to be one of the main features of farming in the 20th century.

Since we have some first-hand memories and accounts of farming in the 20th century elsewhere in this book perhaps it will suffice here to add a few comments and quotations from those who have lived through part, if not most, of that century.

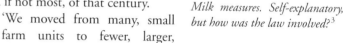

Milk measures. Self-explanatory, but how was the law involved?[3]

'We moved from many, small farm units to fewer, larger, factory-type units. Wilton has changed from 13 small mixed farms all under 100 acres, to one main farm of 600 acres, with 300 cattle and 300 sheep. The same trend has taken place in Haile.'

'Well, we just had your single furrow horse plough and stitching plough just for two hosses to pull and there would be grubbers and suchlike for stitch work and a one horse mowing machine.'

'Oh, no, there were thousands o' birds. When you went into fields to weed kale an turnips. There was droves o' them we used to get out. Ooh, aye, an starlings, sky used to be black wid 'em. An' there isn't hardly any now. An' sparras. When you 'ad cows in byre, you couldn't hear yer own ears for them shoutin. Oh, aye, up in pit yard they were terrible. Oh, there were thousands of them. An all round t'edges of t'fields they'd gone with all ears of corn, you know, 'ad sparras . . . We used to open fields out with scythe an' tie them and set them at back of dyke an' you may as well of burned 'em or threw them away 'cos there wus nowt in them when sparras 'ad eat them off.'

'Oh they could still be ploughing and suchlike at twenty year old. The hoss that had the spring cart had the hardest job really. It was running the roads, you see, going to market and back. It wasn't just walking; it was trotting and took more feed. It was a lighter bred hoss for that job.'

'The thrashing machine was converted to be run by a paraffin engine instead of the horses. Then came the mobile machines.'

'Spring of the year when the men was busy putting the crops in you were coming home from school and you'd git a wheelbarrow and load turnips on til it, and give cows their turnips and that was all done. And then they would land with their horses and you'd maybe start milking and feeding calves. In them days milk was fed only to the calves to rear them.'

'Odd days when it was a fine day after we had been down home for our dinner, father would say, "We could do with you at home this afternoon", so we stopped at home and helped with haytiming and harvest and suchlike. Yeah. The more hands you

Mary Wilson of Tortolacate with some of her family. About 1894.
Mary Wilson, mother of eleven children, whose husband died in 1891 when the youngest child, James, was only six years old, had then to run Tortolacate – where they had moved as newly-weds – on her own. Life was hard. The story goes that the eleven children, the maid and the labourer would sit around the kitchen table together for a meal. When they had finished their main course and thoroughly cleaned the plate, Mary would serve the pudding – on the same plate. She would walk around the table putting a spoonful of rice pudding on each plate, carefully judging it so that everyone had some. She would end the round of plates with the words: 'Right. I've just made enough'. A combination of careful calculation and optimism!

Tortolacate farm. About 1894. Mary Wilson stands outside with four of her children. The butter churn can be seen in front of the barn.

had the better. It all had to be done with hand rakes and pitch forks.'

'You washed on the Monday. If you were lucky and they got dried on the Monday, you may have got them ironed on the Monday, if not the Tuesday. Tuesday was room day. Wednesday was churning day of the cream from the milk. Thursday was a market day and shopping day. Friday was the cleaning-up day – black lead your grate and rub your steel top fender and wash your freestone floor on hands and knees . . . Baking was done on a Friday, with probably more bread made on the Tuesday.'

'Monday was washing day and Tuesday was churning day.'

'But it was hard work was haytime. If you were up on that moo when they were putting, well it wasn't bales then, just ordinary loose hay. It was hard work . . . up in them lofts, you know, with this hay coming at you. Then, you see, we got bales . . . and we had an elevator thing.'

'That dog of ours was a good thing, you know, when you set off to market with sheep and that, driving them along the road. Once they'd been on the road and coming again next week, we'll say, they knew as soon as they were out of the gates. You hadn't to tell them. They knew.'

Cows wait to be milked. After they have been milked the gates will open and the cows move on to make way for the next ones who come in from the far end of the parlour and take their place.

A modern milking parlour at High House.

'It was a hard life when you were having to hand rake and pitchfork your hay and such as that when the weather was bad. We used to get it dried up, ready for to come home and then it rained on it again and all that work was to do over again, but the present-day machinery – well you can do as much in an hour as you did all day in them days.'

'Well, the biggest change was when the tractors come. I think our first tractor come about 1942, but we still hed two draughts of horses then.'

'During the war we put electricity in just for the milking. We got a milking machine. Before that it was just milking by hand, but there again, during the war you were encouraged to have more cows, produce more of everything you see.'

'Electricity was the best thing that ivver come. You just had to put your switch down and the electric motor was working for your milking machine. All your lights and ivverything in the buildings, house and that was all there, otherwise you were just carrying your lamp about with you. Many a time you had to strike a match to see if the lamp was lit.'

'I think our milk would first go to the Milk Marketing Board in 1942, when butter went on ration and you weren't allowed to sell it at home. I think that's what happened then and then milk got to be a decent price. It used to go away on the railway wagons in the morning to Whitehaven, was put on the train to Aspatria or maybe Carlisle or other spots.'

'When you got finished threshing that day, you'd go to another farm and you all just followed on and set up there again and helped them out like and they come to help you.'

So you followed the machine?

'Followed the machine for a week or ten days. Many a time. I

Beck Brow, Haile.

think best thing that ivver did come was combine harvester. Ivverything gets done at once.'

'Yes, the water was – in 1957 they were still using the well which was in the scullery . . . They had no electricity. Of course, it was just a traditional Cumbrian farmhouse.'

'In the 1960s we went round all these farm sales in the Autumn, dispersal sales, and we kitted up. In those days it was possible to

start farming, to buy up all your equipment for something like . . . I suppose I wouldn't have spent more than three or four hundred pounds.'

'Hedges were removed to enable the larger machinery to work in them.'

'Well, one method was silage. That's one thing we nivver done much with. We nivver made it at Townend, but, as I've said many times lately, this last few years back, if all that grass was med into hay it never will be got 'cos the summers isn't there to dry it.'

Markets and Auctions

'Sometimes at auction, if a buyer wanted to change his mind, he would cough – and make out it was the horse.'

'You'd to remember to ask if the horse was used to traffic. Some of them came from so far out that they didn't know traffic.'

'On Whitehaven market day they ran two buses. The first was the 'basket bus' which took all the baskets of butter, eggs, dressed fowls and flowers. It was the second bus that was for the passengers.'

VALUABLE
Farming Stock and Crop,
FOR SALE.

To be Sold,

IN PUBLIC SALE,

On Friday the 8th of March, 1839,

At the House of Mr. THOMAS BELL, of Brayshaw, in the Parish of Haile,

THE WHOLE OF HIS

FARMING STOCK.

CONSISTING OF

Thirty-six Head of Cattle, Three of which are newly Calved, One with Calf at Foot, Fourteen Present and Spring Calvers, Four Back-end Calvers, and the rest Gelt Cows and Heifers of different Ages; One Bull, Three Years old, and One Yearling, both of the pure Short-horned breed; Five Horses, One of which is Seven Years old, Fifteen and a Half Hands High, One Mare, Seven Years old, Fifteen and a Half Hands High, powerful and quiet to work, One Foal Mare, One Filly, rising Three Years old, well adapted for either Saddle or Harness, and One Colt, rising Two Years old; Forty White-faced Sheep, of the Leicester breed, Twenty of which are Ewes in Lamb, Ten Hogs in Lamb, and Ten suitable for Grazing; Thirty Heath-going Sheep, which will be put into Lots suitable to Purchasers; One Sow and Pigs, and Three Shots.

The CROP consists of Four Stacks of Oats, One Stack of Barley, One Stack of Wheat, and about Two Thousand Stones of Ley and Meadow Hay, all secured in good Condition; about Four Hundred Stones of Black Potatoes, suitable for Seed, with all the Carts, Ploughs, Harrows, Potatoe Harrows, Roller, Straw Cutter, Barrel Churn, Two Milch Leads, Cheese Press, and the whole of the Husbandry Gear and Dairy Utensils. The HOUSEHOLD FURNITURE consists of Chairs, Tables, Beds, Bedsteads, Fenders, Fire Irons, and the whole of the

Kitchen Requisites.

All Sums at or under Forty Shillings, Ready Money; and all above, Six Months' Credit on approved Security before leaving the Sale.

☞ *The whole to be Sold without Reserve.*

The Sale to commence at Ten o'Clock in the Forenoon, and as all will be Sold in One Day, an early attendance is requested.

JOHN MOSSOP, Auctioneer.

R. GIBSON, PRINTER, KING STREET, WHITEHAVEN.

Brayshaw sale advertisement. 1839.

Twentieth Century Farming at Town End, Haile

Until about the middle of the twentieth century, the village of Haile was essentially a farming community with four farms within the boundary of the village itself, small as it was, and one just outside. That one, Town End Farm, is the only one of the five still a working farm, the only one which, after it passed from the Mumberson family, who had farmed it from 1894 until 1991, did not find itself split up and sold in its separate parts. So often nowadays the farmhouse is sold as a purely residential property, the buildings sold for conversion to houses or sometimes remaining as farm buildings, and the fields bought by other farmers. The small farms, it seems – and ours have very probably been here since the eighteenth century or before – are gone for ever.

Until the beginning of the second world war, all the farms were farmed the same way, and much as they had been for generations, to make a living for their families, growing their own food such as turnips, cabbage and potatoes (which, by the way, were first introduced into West Cumberland in about the middle of the seventeenth century and were sometimes written as 'potetis'). And, of course, oats which were used to make oatmeal for porridge and as feed for the cattle, sheep, pigs and poultry. As part of the crop rotation hay was grown, ley hay for horses and meadow hay for cattle.

The work was done by the farmer himself, often with the help of a hired man and a boy.

'. . . six months they were hired for. I can remember Dad giving the nipper thirty bob, which was one pound, fifty pence now, for his six months' wage, and the hired man three pounds ten bob. Which is three pounds, fifty pence now, for his wage for the six month. And yet they came back again. Came back with new clogs on, new boots and new clothes, to start another six months' work . . . And then we used to get tramps coming round, as well as wanting a night's lodging. And they used to go into the barn and sleep overnight and they'd get a bit of bait the next day to carry on with.'

Horses played a big part in the farm work, Clydesdales, ploughing through winter, and harrowing and sowing of seeds in the spring. In the summer came the hay-making with two horses to draw the mowing machine, cutting hay. The farmer and men then had to work the hay by hand, using rakes. When the hay was ready to be brought into the barn, pitchforks would be used to lift the hay on to a horse-drawn cart. But times progressed. Came the hay turner, drawn by a horse, which did away with the hand rake. And the new hay-rake was drawn by a horse, as well, to rake over the field to pick up the remaining bits of hay after all the hay had been lifted.

Harvesting oats at Town End, Haile.

Harvest was the time of the oats. Oats are not grown around here now. In the early 1900s the oats were cut with a reaper, again drawn by horses. The reaper only cut the oats, which then had to be hand-bound, making a 'band' out of straw, to make one sheaf. After the sheaves were made they were stood up in stooks of six or eight sheaves to dry out for six to ten days, depending on the weather, before being carted into the stackyard and made into stacks. There they waited until it was time for thrashing. At first each farm had its own thrashing machine in the barn, and it was driven by two horses pulling a gin-ring linked up to it.

Time progressed again and the horse-drawn binder came. This

implement was drawn by three horses.

> 'The binder would come on about then . . . but you had to have three good hosses to pull it. A hard job was the binder. Aye.'

The binder cut the oats, bound it into sheaves with twine and distributed the sheaves along the field. The sheaves were stooked in the same way as before to dry out, before being led into the barn. By now there was a steam-driven thrasher to separate the straw from the oats, ready to feed the cattle, pigs, sheep, poultry and horses during the winter months. When it came to thrashing time, every farm had a visit from the thrasher and all the neighbours went to help each other. As was always the case on such occasions, the helpers were fed by the farmer's wife.

The stock, of cattle and sheep, when they were ready for sale, were taken to the local auction mart at Whitehaven. Local farms sometimes walked their sheep and fat beasts to an auction which existed at Beckermet from where they were transported by train from Beckermet railway station.

Milking the old way. Alf Farley, who worked at Town End, milks a cow outside while the rest were indoors. At this time there was no problem with bringing your cup and having a drink of warm milk straight from the cow.

> 'All the stock was walked. We set off in the morning and walked to Whitehaven auction. One would set off from down this area, maybe git to about Egremont and there would be two or three more with their dairy cows, and they'd join in and drove them on to Whitehaven.'

For a dairy cow in the early 1900s you were lucky if you got £5 and the price of a sheep would be one pound ten shillings.

In the middle thirties came the depression, affecting every industry, including the local iron and coal pits. The men from these pits in Whitehaven, Egremont and Cleator Moor, would cycle round to farms to see if they could find a job, casual labour. They would happily accept potatoes, vegetables or eggs as pay in order to feed their families.

A major change in farming life came in the late 30s when the tractor began to appear on farms. When the war began in 1939 farms were made to plough extra land to grow more food to help Britain

'Forking on' the oats. Dick Sanderson of New Houses, 'forks' oats up to Joe Mumberson, the 'loader' on the cart.

survive. Again, farmers helped each other by taking their tractors round to speed the work. The combine harvester was a further big improvement, which again helped the farmers produce more efficiently. From the mid-nineteen forties the prices of implements and stock began to rise dramatically.

Milk production went through similar great changes in the first part of the twentieth century. Farmers at the beginning of the century had few cows, hand-milked, producing enough milk for the family's needs and for feeding calves. Any remaining milk was made into butter or cheese for sale to regular customers or to local markets.

Joe and John Mumberson at shearing time.

1933 saw the establishment of the Milk Marketing Board and our area depot was at Aspatria. By 1943 all the local farms sent their milk to the Board in churns collected by lorries and taken to Whitehaven to go by train to Aspatria. Farms began to produce so much milk that a milk depot was built alongside Egremont railway station where it was collected before being despatched by rail to Aspatria. Then came the bulk tank collection of milk, which meant the farm had to have a cooling tank, with all the expense that involved, and the milk had to be collected from each farm by the Milk Board tankers.

'When the war was on, they wanted more milk . . . we did have a milking machine . . . And then it got to bulk milk tankers and one thing and another, and then you couldn't do right.'

From about the late forties farmers started making silage from grass to feed cattle. Some feel that this was introduced because the weather was becoming so wet during the summer months. It meant yet more expensive implements, with powerful tractors, cutters and choppers. It takes much less time to get in and is done three or four times during the summer months.

Strange that, as we move into a new century, when much of the hard, time-consuming physical slog of farming has gone, the parish has few farms left. But we are, however, a community which, if no longer a farming one, is still one surrounded by farms.

STARTING FARMING

'The farmers – you couldn't do plenty for them. They were nivver satisfied at the end of the day. I know this particular farmer, the farm that I went on, they must have had about 4 or 5 staff and I was just the young one and it was turnip thinning time and t'crack was it was going to clash with hay-making and one thing and another so the boss would decide after 6 o'clock that he would put us on so much a 100 yards. Through the day I worked with the man, you know, and kept with him and all that sort of thing, and soon as 6 o'clock came I just left him standing. Mind you I was only getting £2. 10s. a week. I was in the picture house at 8 o'clock and I had made sixteen shillings!'

'I would be about oh probably 15 or 16, something like that.

Before I got a start on that particular farm, well this farmer, he farmed at Ponsonby and he wanted a lad and I was a bit cheeky really but me uncle had offered me £3 a week and he give me half a crown luck. You know, when they hired you they used to give you a luck penny, so he give me half a crown. He was a bit of a bad-tempered bloke, so I went away and I thought about it and I thought "Well I'm not going to work for him" so I sent the half a crown back with my sister. So I went again up to this farmer at Ponsonby to get hired and he asked me how much I wanted. I said I wanted £3. He said, "I'll give you 30s". So I was a bit cheeky and said summat to him and left but I ended up getting £2. 10s. at this other place but I only stuck it for 12 months and that was it. That was the finish of farming.'

'And the Fishers of course would never actually tell you what you should be doing or what mistakes you were making but after you'd had a crack with them in the road, you'd go away thinking, "Now I

Peggy, Darling and Royal pull the binder. Always a job for three horses.

John Fisher of Beck Brow finishes feeding the lamb.

wonder what he meant". And you'd slowly get the message. But Jack Fisher was an absolute dear, right up to the end.'

'They were having a dispersal sale up near Ulpha, on the fells above Ulpha, and there was a shepherd there called Stables and part of the dispersal sale was his dog, an old pensioner . . . So I brought it back and Jack Fisher said, "Now, you've got to be really careful. This is an old pensioner, it'll go back, it won't stay with you but I'll give you a secret – a way of . . . stopping it straying. Keep it on a string for three weeks and don't let it out of your sight. Keep it on the string and then put a bit of cheese in your armpit and get up a real sweat, go into the garden and get up a real sweat digging or something and then give it to the dog and it'll never stray after that." So I did this because I believed Jack and I'm sure Jack, in fact, was serious.

'He had all sorts of peculiar remedies like this, family remedies . . . But let me get on with this dog. I did all this, gave it this cheese and it immediately streaked off. This was in June, you know, when it's half past four in the morning when it's getting light . . . They said it will go right back to Ulpha. Well, I went between here and Ulpha day after day, week after week. It must have been before June. This must have been in April, it must have been earlier because there was lambing going on and the dog was probably making a living off eating cleansings in the fields. And in the end, the Hartleys at Prior Scales rang up. They said, "We've got a dog here in our foxtrap". And there was this dog. It had become quite feral, three weeks on the run and we couldn't handle it. It was really fierce and Hartley put a noose on the end of a broomstick and put it round its neck. It was the only way he could handle it. We had to put that one down. That's so much for Jack's remedy.'

'Jack Fisher was very fond of horses, he was very fond of horses. So, he used to come and have a chat, watch me making a fool of myself, trying to catch the pony.

Did he give you any helpful tips, can you remember?

'I don't know if he did exactly, except he was very sympathetic, you know. He couldn't catch him either and the swear words which he came out with, which he would hurl at his horse . . . I asked him, "Well, what was her real name?" And he went all sort of gooey and he said, "I called her Darling"'.

Dick Sanderson (L) and Syd Gregg (R) fork hay up to Joe Mumberson.

And getting the hang of the language.

''E come to have a holiday with them, y'see. An 'e come up t'farm. We were – what you call – 'mowing' at the time. I said to 'im, "Come on an" (help) with 'aytime. Will thou moo for us?" He says, "No, I'm sorry, I'm not a cow"'.

'The other thing quite amusing, I suppose. You see, I'd never worked in farming . . . but it was essential to have a working dog and actually the first one we got was a wonderful dog . . . we got her off a farm on the side of Skiddaw, the Ashburners at Chapel House, and we'd gone over there and brought her back. Then I had to go back because of learning the commands. This dog didn't understand my accent and I had to go back to the Ashburners and be taught phrases like 'Ga 'way back'. But any road, that was our first.'

JIM FISHER 'WALKS THE ENTIRE'

First, perhaps an explanation is owing. 'Walking the entire' did not refer to the distance walked or to any boundaries set, but to the horse itself. Suffice it to say that working horses were castrated and the horse in this account, a stallion, was not.

Jim Fisher was asked to do this job in the early 1940s. It took place from about April to July, a period of some twelve weeks when the mares were likely to be in season. Jim's job was to walk, groom and look after the stallion as he went from farm to farm to see if there was a mare ready for service. He was responsible for the feeding and shoeing of the horse and for its general safety throughout the weeks that they were on the road.

The horse belonged to John Kerr, farmer, of Wigton, one of several keepers of 'entires' in Cumbria who, with them, would join an 'entire' parade in April at which farmers could see the quality of the horses that were available in the coming season. Normally Jim, known as the groom, would have a set round of farms to visit, but that would not prevent him from calling on other farms in case he could pick up some trade there. Competition was fierce. The owner of the horse would have arranged where the groom was to stay overnight and where he was to have his dinner the next day.

Tom Burns with the 'entire'. Tom, who worked for Kilpatricks of Wigton, was part of the competition Jim Fisher faced. When he was walking his rounds during the season, he and his well-groomed horse stayed at Town End farm every Monday night.

The horse had to be kept smart. Raffia was bound in its mane and tail, perhaps it would wear a rosette, and its bridle and girth would have a red stripe to help improve its appearance.

Thus prepared, Jim would set off from Calderbridge on a Monday visiting farms at Haile, Bigrigg and Arlecdon and then staying at Rowrah overnight. On the Tuesday he would be at Ullock in time for his dinner and would have arrived at High Clifton by the night. Wednesday he would stay at Moresby, having visited Branthwaite and Workington. His journey towards home, however, was by no means direct, as by Saturday night he had been to Sandwith, St Bees, Pickett Howe at Egremont, Braystones, Sellafield and was staying at Fleming Hall, Gosforth. On Sunday he had to visit Drigg and Holmrook and, if he was lucky, he might have some time at home to do his washing before he was off again. He must have walked, on average, about twelve miles a day in control of a horse which, because it was 'entire', was rather more frisky than your average steed.

The cost in those days for a service was £3. 0s. 0d. with half a crown for the groom. A further £4. 0s. 0d. became due when the mare was proved to be in foal. The cost of the regular shoeing that had to be done was met by his employer, as was the cost of his keep at the farms where he stayed.

Such a life was rarely boring, despite all the walking. Jim would meet many people, he would have to try to persuade new customers and above all he would have to take very good care of the horse. And there were occasional incidents. One such was when Jim and the horse were passing through Egremont and the animal was caught by a passing bus that came too close. The horse was dragged some way but fortunately was little harmed apart from needing a new shoe. But tempers rose, of course, resulting in the following exchange. Jim said

Jim Fisher.

to the bus conductor, 'You wanted plenty of road'. To which the conductor replied, forcefully but not unreasonably, 'I wasn't driving the b . . . bus'. Which prompted the reply from Jim – never a one to be slow with his retorts – 'It looks as though t'other bloke wasn't either'.

OTHER WORK

HAILE MILL

Situated slightly north-east of the village, nestling in a small valley by Kirk Beck you will find Haile Mill. The location was dictated in the past by its need for a plentiful water supply, as once it was the sole provider of milled grain products for both Haile and Wilton. The house and buildings now stand as a reminder of life long ago, when villages were very self-contained.

What you see is very much as it was a hundred or more years ago, the only major difference being that currently there is no water wheel in place. The basic layout remains intact, including the 'tail' race or water return to the beck.

The mill has many unusual features, including the above-mentioned tail race, which runs underground for quite some distance, wending its way beneath the house and garden, until once again it

Haile Mill.

emerges before rejoining Kirk Beck. The water to operate the mill was fed from three mill ponds, which were immediately behind the buildings. Two of these have all but disappeared, but one higher up is still evident. This one was dual-purpose, being also used to breed trout for Haile Hall kitchens. The original Ordnance Survey maps clearly show the original layout. The buildings are partly below ground level to accommodate the need to get a better head of water to drive the wheel. Because this had the potential to cause severe problems with damp, a tunnel or 'giant cavity' wall was built around the outside of the main building. This is so large a person can walk through it!

Evidence suggests that there have been many 'modifications' over the years, including a total re-working of the drive system when a new and bigger building was constructed. The original mill would have most likely had one pair of stones, producing a fairly coarse milled product. Before milling, the grain would have been dried in the mill's kiln. This was a room with a suspended clay tile floor with a heat source (fire) below. The clay tiles had a pattern of holes on their surface to let the hot air circulate and thus reduce the moisture content of the grain. In latter days these tiles were replaced with cast iron grids as these were becoming cheaper to produce. However, they were not as durable for two reasons: firstly, they were brittle and broke and secondly, they suffered from corrosion. The kiln continued in use throughout the mill's life, being accessed after the new building was erected by a walkway across the top of the waterwheel. The new mill building was much roomier and looks like it probably had three pairs of millstones and other machinery installed.

Exactly when this major extension of milling at Haile occurred is not clear, but presumably it was at a time when the villages of Haile and Wilton were experiencing expansion and a growing population. An interesting feature is the access lane to the mill. It arrives from two directions, one way from Haile village and the other from Wilton in the opposite direction. Rumour has it that residents of Haile came down their lane and returned the same way and the villagers from Wilton did the same thing. This, it is said, was to prevent the lane becoming a 'through' road or shortcut from one village to the other. How much truth is in that remains to be proved, but it is worthy of a brief mention here.

The last century saw the Mill being used mainly as a domestic residence, with occupants having varied occupations outside milling. Some of these were connected to Haile Hall, as until 1989 the Mill was part of the Estate. In the early 1900s Peter Campbell and his family were the tenants and Peter had the occupation of gamekeeper for the Hall. One of his five children, Bella, left her mark by inscribing her name on a stone in one of the walls, along with that of one of her friends. The tenant before the Campbells also left his name for all to see on a corner stone in one of the buildings: this was one George Jeffery, who was a miner.

The last recorded miller was William Shepherd, who left around the late 1800s. He also carved his name into a stone in one of the buildings. As he was not an educated man, it takes a little effort to decipher his writing. He dated his work incorrectly as 1910, but it should be 1901. Milling on a small scale was at this time in decline due to the railways bringing in flour from the big mills. Presumably this is why William was also recorded as a farmer. As the big mills took over, small village mills were dismantled and the machinery re-used elsewhere.

Prior to this the miller was Isaac Dickinson, who was the miller for quite some time at Haile. He died in 1875 and there is a stone in Haile Churchyard in memory of him and his family. It is interesting to note that his daughter, Ann, was married to William Shepherd who became miller after Isaac and his widow, Bridget, lived at the mill with her daughter and son-in-law. It can also be seen from the stone that Isaac had a granddaughter from Ann and William, who was also called Bridget. Sadly, she died only six months after her grandfather, when she was 14 years old. Isaac most likely was kept very busy in his time milling at Haile, as the railways had not yet begun to force their modern revolution upon the people of rural Cumberland. During his time he would be running probably three pairs of millstones, producing milled products and also a machine for making pot or pearl barley.

Going back further, we find one Stephen Hartley at the mill who is recorded in the directory of 1829. According to records he was there until around 1845, when it appears he moved to Tortolacate, a

The Campbell family of Haile Mill.

farm above the mill and at the time also owned by Haile Hall. Exactly how long he was miller is not known, as records concerning the mill before the 1829 date seem almost impossible to trace.

Some very early records have been located which suggest a mill had been on the site since the sixteenth century. How accurate these are remains to be seen, further research being required. It is safe to say there has been a mill in the village for a very long time and it was only due to the transport revolution and mass mechanisation that its decline came about. A very sad end to a small industry that once would have been the life-blood of the village, providing milled grain products for both human and animal consumption.

MINES AND QUARRIES

The ground of West Cumbria has been endowed with a rich variety of useful materials and mining and quarrying to extract these have been major industries for several centuries. Just to the west of Haile parish there are several large iron ore mines, Florence One and Two, the numerous Ullcoats Mine shafts and Beckermet One and Two, the spoil heap from the Beckermet mine dominating the Haile skyline in that direction. All of these are now disused although Florence Mine continues, on a very small scale, as a Heritage Centre. High quality sandstone has been extracted from Grange Quarry for a long time and, although the quarry was disused for many years, it is now back in production and even exporting abroad. Within Haile parish, however, mining and quarrying activities have, for the most part, been confined to providing materials for local needs, the exception being Haile Moor Mine which, for a short while, produced iron ore on a large scale and we will return to this enterprise later.

The development of mining and quarrying has been closely linked to developments in mechanisation, both in the extraction and the transport of material. In the early days extraction was by pick and shovel, so material was only worked from the surface. Later, short horizontal tunnels, known as levels, adits or drifts, were driven into the rock until veins of useful material were reached. The arrival of explosives allowed longer and larger levels to be driven but the holes

The lime kiln at Mousegill Quarry.

Grange Quarry.

for the charges still had to be made by hand. It was not until steam, electricity and compressed air became available, in comparatively recent times, that it became much easier to drive vertical shafts to extract material deep below the surface. Power also made it possible to drill bore holes to establish where the materials were located, so that shafts and levels could be driven with a greater confidence of success.

In earlier times transport was limited to packhorses and, later, the horse and cart, so that movement of heavy materials over any distance was impracticable, unless they were of high value. Consequently materials were extracted as near as possible to the point at which they were to be used. With the arrival of mechanical transport, at first on railways and later on roads, it became much easier to bring materials from greater distances, but equally it opened up more distant markets for materials that could be extracted locally.

For these reasons Haile parish has traditionally extracted its extensive resources mainly for its own use. However, the early operations were small-time and few records were kept, so what little we know about them has to be deduced from passing references in unrelated documents. The Parish Award of 1814, which is discussed elsewhere, recorded that there were four public quarries, producing limestone at Mousegill Quarry, gravel at two quarries near Wilton, one near Cold Fell Gate and the other at the site that is now Wilton Reservoir, and sandstone at Kells Moor. The Parish Award gave these quarries '. . . for the Common Use and Benefit of the Lord or Lords of the said Manor and other the Owners and Occupiers of Messuages Lands and Tenements within the said Manor . . .'. The Award only allowed the material to be used on lands within the Manor '. . . and not to sell or otherwise dispose of the same', so commercial extraction was not possible.

Mousegill Quarry.

In our area the land is quite acidic and requires regular treatment with lime to produce soil that is more neutral and, therefore, more suitable for growing crops. Today lime arrives in large lorries, but in earlier times the presence of limestone made local production very beneficial. Within the parish limestone is only found on the surface at Mousegill Quarry, so this facility has been very important. As quarried, limestone is in the form of calcium carbonate and it has to be heated in a kiln to form the powdery calcium oxide before it is spread on the land. Limekilns have been built near Mousegill Quarry

for a very long time, the Parish Award giving the '. . . Liberty power and authority of Erecting Kilns . . . and burning the stone into Lime . . .'. However Miles Ponsonby, the Lord of the Manor at the time, was unhappy because he had built a limekiln and felt that he should derive some benefit from his investment. It seems that the commissioners were unimpressed and made no provision for this in the Award. Although the plan attached to the Award shows buildings in a similar position to the fine kiln that stands today on Limekiln Lonning, it is unlikely that this is Miles Ponsonby's kiln. The Ordnance Survey map of 1860 shows the kiln to be nearer to the road from Wilton to Cold Fell, which was the site of the quarry at that time. By 1899, however, the map marked this as 'Old Limekiln' and showed a new kiln in its present position. By the time the map was revised in 1925 the quarry was marked as 'Disused', no doubt falling victim to improved road transport and hence the ability to bring lime from commercial quarries further afield.

Drilling Rig. On this occasion, in 1937, the rig was at Town End, Haile, but bores were drilled in dozens of places around the parish and on each occasion the rig and hut had to be dismantled and re-erected.

While the main use of the lime from Mousegill Quarry was on the land, the material was also a constituent of lime mortar and the stone is also seen, to a limited extent, in local buildings, so it is probable that Mousegill Quarry provided material for these purposes also.

The sand and gravel quarries were located in two of the many heaps of glacial and water-borne material found in the parish, making use of the well ground up rocks that were carried by glaciers and melt-water during the Ice Age. The sandstone quarry is located adjacent to the Black Beck where the stream has exposed the stone. All these quarries were also marked as 'Disused' by 1925.

In addition to these public facilities a number of small quarries can be seen around the parish and these were probably privately operated, providing small amounts of materials for local use, some being still in operation to this day. Skiddaw Slate is also found extensively and is quarried to provide an excellent hardwearing material for surfacing farm and forest roads. It is not easy to extract and crush, which is why it was not used in earlier times.

Haile Moor mine when it was working.

Although the common land passed into private ownership under the Award, the Lord of the Manor was confirmed as the owner 'forever' of a wide range of metals and other minerals over the whole area, having the right to mine these on other persons' property. Indeed it was not long before the Lord, Miles Ponsonby, was exercising this right and in 1862 he entered into agreements under which Thomas Carmichael would explore for iron and copper in Lowther Park, north of Wilton, the area that had been awarded to Lord Lowther. There is no further mention of copper, but iron was obviously found, because Thomas Carmichael entered into a lease with Miles Ponsonby in 1864 to mine in the area for a 21 year period, with the right to extract up to 400 tons of iron ore per year. The venture was obviously a success because Thomas Carmichael, now in conjunction with The Parton Haematite Iron Company Limited, took out a further lease in 1876, again for a period of 21 years.

Haile Moor mine. A distant view.

In 1970 the Cumberland Geological Society noted evidence of this mining in the report of a field meeting held in Lowther Park. The accompanying map clearly showed the position of three adits but afforestation, and the construction of forest roads, has now virtually obliterated all traces of these workings.

We now move forward to much more recent times for the first, and last, real commercial mining within the parish, the Haile Moor Mine. This is particularly interesting because it is probably the only large-scale commercial operation, other than farming, to have taken place within the parish. Mining operations in the area had

Haile pit head.

iron-bearing solutions have replaced limestone that has been dissolved away, occurring mainly where the limestone is shattered at faults or where it abuts against other rocks. Drilling revealed a relatively small body of haematite ore on Haile Moor in the same limestone that appears on the surface at Mousegill Quarry. With the distortion and erosion of the land during the last 300 million years, however, the limestone is buried under 800 feet of sandstone at Haile Moor.

Starting in 1939, the company sank the Haile Moor mineshaft about 100 yards to the east of the ore body. The shaft was elliptical in section, measuring 21 feet by 12 feet, divided by a wall to assist ventilation, and was 800 feet deep. From the bottom of the shaft, tunnels gave access to the iron ore workings. In 1942 production commenced and the typical working pattern was a production shift from 6 am to 2 pm, with the remainder of the day being used for maintenance and examination work. The mine was highly mechanized, with ample electricity and compressed air for all

commenced in 1903 with the formation of the Beckermet Mining Company Limited and the sinking of the two Beckermet mine shafts during the next few years.

The Ponsonby family continued to exercise their rights to mineral reserves under the parish and in 1916 entered into a lease with the Beckermet Mining Company for a period of 60 years. In 1920 this company was taken over by the United Steel Companies Limited and later became part of The British Steel Corporation. During the next twenty years there was no mining activity on the surface within the parish, although much was going on underneath. Workings from the Beckermet Number One mine extended under Haile as far as Sheepfields, tunnels having been driven 900 yards from the mineshaft to this area.

By the 1930s exploration for iron ore was much more scientific and a large number of boreholes were drilled in the area by a contractor, Henry Bowes and Sons of Egremont, to locate the haematite, iron-bearing, ore. Haematite is formed in limestone where

Buckets traversing the Kirk Beck valley on the aerial ropeway.

The Beckermet end of the aerial ropeway. Here at Beckermet mine, the ore that had been carried overhead from the mine at Haile was emptied into rail wagons for transporting.

were served by the extensive rail system but the nearest siding was at Beckermet Number One pit. Because of the difficulty of extending the rail system to Haile, it was decided that an overhead aerial ropeway should be constructed to carry the ore to Beckermet Number One railhead, over a mile away. In a straight line this would have passed directly over the village of Haile, so the local authorities insisted that it should pass to the south of the village, turning west through 60° near Town End farm. Tubs, each containing 18 hundredweight of ore, were carried on the ropeway and the system could convey 80 tons per hour.

Mining produces a large amount of waste rock which is dumped, usually as close as possible to the mine shaft, producing the unsightly spoil heaps that scar the landscape of West Cumbria, notably to the west of Haile. At Haile Moor Mine, however, environmental

Drilling at the rock face. A reminder to those of us on the surface of what is under our feet and how the men used to work there.

operations. Large fans also provided ample ventilation, so both diesel and electric locomotives could be operated within the mine as well as air-powered shovels for loading ore into the rail tubs. Miners worked on a bonus system in small 'companies', typically of two or three men each. With the modern facilities it is not surprising that Haile Moor was very efficient, each face worker typically producing 110 hundred weight of haematite per shift, about 40% higher than the output at the Beckermet mines. Many people from Haile and Wilton worked at Haile Moor, as well as other local mines, but there was always a shortage of workers and a large number of Italian miners were recruited to work at Haile Moor from 1951 to the mid-1950s, replacing labourers who had left to work at the Sellafield plant.

Ore was raised to the surface in the same cages that carried men and materials. Two tubs, carrying about two tons, could be carried in the cage and raised to the surface in under two minutes. From there the handling arrangements were unusual. Most mines in Cumbria awareness arrived early and the spoil was progressively levelled, covered with soil and seeded with grass. Flowerbeds and shrubs were added to give a pleasant appearance to the mine.

Eventually production of ore in the Cumbrian mines became uneconomical, having steadily declined since the high point at the end of the 19th century, and cheaper supplies could be obtained abroad. Although Haile Moor Mine was one of the most modern and most efficient in the Cumbrian ore fields, it finally closed in 1973, ending a brief, but significant, period in the history of Haile.

Miner pushing an empty tub.

The aerial ropeway from Haile Moor Mine has now been completely removed, the shaft has been capped and many of the buildings, including the pithead, have been demolished. A few buildings still stand on the site as a reminder of Haile's mining past and the site of the escape shaft can still be found at the edge of the woods, north-east of Haile Hall.

A large amount of high quality ore remains under Haile, so could the mine ever be reopened to extract it? It is highly unlikely that this would ever be economically viable. Quarrying, in any real quantity, has also long been abandoned and so we must assume that the extraction of the parish's abundant mineral resources has finally drawn to a close.

A reunion of some of the early miners who met for a retirement get-together.

CHAUFFEURS, GARDENERS, COOKS AND MAIDS

Information is scarce on early employees at Haile Hall, but in his will Miles Ponsonby, who died in 1893, left to Isaac Lowry, who was obviously a valued member of staff, the sum of £20 which was reduced to £17 10s. 0d. by the time tax had been paid.

Miss Barbara Ponsonby, who died in 1919, left to John Smith, of Haile Moor Cottages, the gun he had used in his work on the estate, and to Polly, his daughter, a travelling clock and two dresses.

When Sir John Ponsonby came to live at Haile Hall, in 1929, after it had been empty for some years, he needed staff. One of the first was Elsie Spedding. She had been working as a housemaid at the

Vicarage for the Rev. Lightfoot. Elizabeth Thirlwell (Lizzie), aged 16, came soon after from Siddick, near Workington. She was to stay almost for the rest of her life, a quiet, faithful member of staff.

Haile Hall kitchen. A cook works in front of the large fireplace in the Hall's kitchen. Only preparation and cooking was done here. Washing up was done in the scullery, and cleaning the cutlery was done in the butler's pantry.

Nora Spedding came to Haile Hall about this time. After a period on Midtown Farm at Ponsonby working for her aunt and a short time at Haile Bank Farm, Beckermet, working for the Barwises, she came to Haile Hall as scullery maid, and eventually became cook. She was to work there for approximately 67 years. She moved into the Gatehouse Cottage, near the Hall on her marriage in 1944. She was a powerhouse of energy, working in the kitchen garden as well as the house, and still swinging a Flymo at the age of 80.

Atbout this time also, Charles Swandle (Charlie) and his wife Barbara went as chauffeur and cook respectively. There was a Frances Jackson, cook, who did not stay very long, and Frances Vickers who was also a cook.

Norman Sherwen moved into the gatehouse cottage with his wife Annie and baby Jim in 1937. He was chauffeur and gardener. He looked after the hens and kept up a good supply of firewood. Norman and Annie received £2 a week, a third share of the eggs and all the wood they needed.

Sir John and Lady Ponsonby were generous employers, occasionally buying baby Jim clothes. Norman got on especially well with Sir John, being able to understand him from the start despite Sir John's speech impediment. While Norman was away in Burma fighting in the war, he received a letter from Sir John telling him that he hoped he would return to the Hall as gardener but life in the army would provide him with a better job and more interesting work. On his return Sir John gave Norman an inscribed Vesta case as a token of his esteem and when Sir John had trees planted to improve a view, he named it Sherwen's Plantation. Norman made the wooden cross for Haile Church which is now carried from parish to parish at Easter.

Working at the Hall also at that time were Billy Gibson, Pike (from Hensingham) and, as well as the two maids in the house, Nora and Lizzie, there was a cook who was from London. Groceries from Peter Leech's were left at the Gatehouse, where the butcher also called, as no delivery vans were allowed on the front.

Sir John Ponsonby chose the uniforms his housemaids wore, a white apron with straps that buttoned on to the

Norman Sherwen. It was Norman who, as well as being chauffeur and handyman at Haile Hall, planted up the bank of azaleas in front of the Hall.

waist band at the back, and a blue dress. Parlour maids wore black with a small white pinafore. Housework had to be completed in the mornings, fires laid, sitting rooms dusted and cleaned before Sir John and Lady Ponsonby came down. A good deal of work was done with a dust pan and brush, and every so often, carpets were taken outside and thrown over a line where they were beaten with a cane beater, but no housework was to be done after mid-day. Parlour maids took over in the afternoon first serving tea and then, in the evening, serving dinner. Hours were flexible as the staff lived in. Lizzie chose to have only one day off a fortnight to visit her family. Later she was happy in her own sitting room with her visitors and her knitting.

Two maids at the Hall. Nora Spedding (L) and Frances Vickers in the uniform chosen by Sir John.

Sir John and Lady Ponsonby dressed for dinner and Lady Ponsonby would come into the kitchen to check on dinner in a long black evening dress. After dinner the silver (now gone, having been stolen in a burglary) was washed in soapy water and polished with jeweller's rouge in the butler's pantry. There was no sink in the kitchen at that time; all dishes were washed in the scullery.

A cold room with a small window and sandstone slabs was where butter, eggs and milk etc. were kept. Apples were stored on wooden racks. The kitchen garden provided a fresh supply of vegetables and soft fruit. Even hay for the horses was made in a small field near the house. At Gatehouse Cottage a meat safe hung on the side of the house near the back door and was the pre-refrigerator way of keeping meat cool and away from flies.

In the summer Sir John and Lady Ponsonby went south to Gilmuire (a house near Ascot which Sir John's mother left to him) taking one or two maids with them. There's a story that Sir John's dog, 'Whisky', ran off down the station platform in London with Lizzie chasing after it, shouting, 'Whisky, Whisky', at the top of her voice. This, not surprisingly, gave rise to some funny looks from other passengers.

THE BLACKSMITHS OF HAILE

If you were to walk around Haile village today looking for evidence of an old smithy you may well find it difficult to decide which building housed the blacksmith's workshop. 'The Smithy' as locals referred to

The Buck's Head. This view of the Buck's Head shows the steps that used to lead up to the small cottage above the smithy.

it, and still do long after it has ceased to work, was the part of the former pub building with the double doors, set back a little from the road, in the centre of the village. There was a cottage above reached by stone steps, no longer there, going up the gable end of Wellbank Cottage next door. This cottage is right on the roadside opposite the telephone kiosk.

There are still rings attached to the wall to which horses could be tied when being shod or when their riders stopped for refreshment at 'The Buck's Head Inn', as it was known in the mid-eighteen hundreds. One ring is beside the double doors of the old smithy while the other is next to what used to be the entrance of the inn. In front, where there is now a concreted area, there were freestone flags and cobbles which formed two circles, possibly for resting cartwheels on when iron bands were being attached to them. Fixed to the wall at the back of the building is an old iron bar which could have been a piece of equipment for the blacksmith's use.

The sandstone outbuilding behind Wellbank Cottage was also referred to as a 'Smithy'. John Mumberson, who has lived all his life in Haile, can remember as a young boy in the early 1930s seeing a fire in there but not a blacksmith working. He and his sister, Mary, remember a Scotsman, John Clark, who was known as the local handyman, living and working there. Haile House next door used to be called 'Anvil House'. From 1871, Census Returns show that a blacksmith lived in Wellbank Cottage – at times referred to as 'Bank Head Cottage' and 'Well Brow Cottage'. However, it seems that the sandstone outbuilding behind was built later than the cottage, which in turn seems to have been built in two stages.

A blacksmith's device. This metal construction, possibly for shaping cart springs, remains on the back wall of what is now part of the Buck's head.

We do not know specific dates of the buildings but it is thought that the The Buck's Head/Smithy building dates from early or mid-Victorian times as did, probably, the smithy that was built behind the already-existing Wellbank Cottage.

Between 1828 and 1912 blacksmiths were resident in Haile village and occasionally there was more than one working here. While Joseph Gainford was the first recorded in a Trade Directory, the name most often mentioned in the records is that of Braithwaite. A John Braithwaite lived at Beck Brow Cottage, across the road from the smithies, with his wife, married daughter, her husband and their three children. John Braithwaite had retired by 1861, becoming 58 years of age that year. For such a large family this cottage of three rooms downstairs and two upstairs seems to us now to be very small, but at some time, perhaps for this family, a living room and a bedroom had been given over from the adjoining farmhouse. At different times later on, these rooms were returned to the farmhouse. The bricked-up connecting doorways are still visible inside the old cottage.

Another John Braithwaite, most probably his son, became a blacksmith in Haile later and lived at Wellbank Cottage for at least twenty years. While he was still there John Braithwaite Pinder, the former John Braithwaite's grandson, followed on in the family tradition and had become a blacksmith in Haile by 1891. Perhaps they worked together. He was still blacksmith in 1912 and may well have been the last blacksmith to work in the village itself, as records show that it is most unlikely that there was a working smithy in Haile village in 1925, and it may have finished even before that.

Other names that appeared as blacksmiths in the village are William Jackson and John Wild, in 1851 and 1861 respectively. Apprentice blacksmiths appear also in the earlier records which suggests there was plenty of work with the large number of farms in the area, each working several horses that needed to be shod, as well as machinery needing repair. In 1894 John Waugh was a blacksmith in Haile at the same time as the John Braithwaite who lived at Wellbank.

There were blacksmiths also at Tail End, the part of the parish which at one time extended as far as and included the Horse and Farrier (now The White Mare) in Beckermet, where the last record of a blacksmith in the parish appeared in a trade directory in 1934.

The brewery who eventually owned The Buck's Head bought the smithy and the cottage above. The cottage was rented out but the smithy became a store and a washhouse for the pub. We are not certain when this happened. But from then on anyone needing the services of a blacksmith would have to go to Tail End, or even further afield. John Fisher would go with his brother, Jim, to Whitehaven Market and while one sold eggs, butter, vegetables etc. on the market the other would take the horse to the blacksmith at Hensingham, returning to the market later in readiness for their return home to Haile.

Now, of course, there are even fewer blacksmiths anywhere at all, and their workshops would probably be unrecognisable to the blacksmiths of old.

WORK AT HOME

CHORES

'But then, I remember us getting a charcoal iron. It had a chimney on. It was a big thing. It was a great thing, in them days, I suppose. It saved us putting the heater in the fire. And you put charcoal into the little cavity, got it alight and then it burned away for ages and kept it hot'.

'If anybody could ask me what was the best thing – labour-saving device in my life – it was a washing machine because when you had to light that fire and boil that water and dolly them clothes and put them through the mangle, rinse them twice, first in cold water and then in the blue, the white . . . Oh, my, what a relief, a washing machine was'.

'. . . just a set pot boiler and dolly tub and dolly legs and a scrubbing brush. There were so many lads with so many shirts and collars all to scrub, I did think we were well off when we got a wooden mangle'.

'Oh, we didn't have a bathroom. You just had a tin bath in front of t'fire, you know, just at weekends. You just got bathed on Friday nights. You just had three vests and three pairs of pants. You wore them a week and we didn't smell. You know, you had one in the wash, and one to wear, but just in case, you had a third'.

Box iron and stand made out of a horse shoe. For ironing, of course, but how did it work?[4]

'And do you know, something else as well with my grandmother – as soon as New Year's Day was over, she used to start talking about spring cleaning. First of all, she would just start talking about it and then if it was quite a mild day she would go upstairs and clean drawers out. That was the start. And I tell you, we'd all feather beds and feather pillows and they were all put over the line and beaten and any bits of carpets we had they were put over the line and beaten. And there was that good dyke, you know, at t'back; things, blankets were thrown over there. Well, when it came spring, we'd blankets then and quilts, homemade quilts, and she used to say that whenever you were put to bed the sheet had to be put over the blanket and the quilt. You didn't have to have that next to you. And so when it came spring, unless there was something dirty on them, the blankets were all shaken out and put on the line all day in the sun. She said you just wash all the goodness out of them, washing these blankets every year. Every other year was the rule but other people would have their own ideas'.

'Every spring any painting and papering was done, and cupboards and drawers cleaned out. A most useful piece of cleaning equipment was the goose wing, which was used for cleaning bed-springs, clearing dust and cobwebs and for cleaning the fire-grate back. Softer goose feathers were used also to stuff mattresses, pillows and cushions. A feather bed was a delight to sleep on'.

Town End Farm, Haile, from the air. We know that this photograph was taken in about May or June because the blankets have had their annual wash as part of the spring clean and can be seen out on the line.

'I couldn't get used to dressin' in black and white of an afternoon, changing out of white an' blue of a morning an' 'avin' to change again of an afternoon before you made afternoon tea, into small, white-lace pinnies, little aprons, and a white band round yer 'ead . . . and stiff cuffs – they used to cut yer 'ands off . . . I couldn't get used wid it'.

COOKING

'We mostly just had the kitchen range. It was a black range, you know, with an oven. My grandmother used to bake the bread in that oven because that was the only oven we had and we just had a swing pulley on the fire which we cooked on but we had a primus stove where we made the chips or fried, you know. They weren't safe, when I think about it today, blowing that wretched primus stove up'.

'Gammy always made the gingerbread with buttermilk and all the boys in the village, they loved Gammy's gingerbread. In fact, little boys would knock at the door for a bit of gingerbread. It had a nice sticky top'.

'Oh, yes, Fridays were baking day – just baked on Fridays. When I got older I would make a fresh cake on a Sunday but with Gammy it was mostly just pastry and rock buns and gingerbread. A special occasion, on a Sunday, you made a sponge cake . . . And the bread was only baked once a week. But it was surprising how long it did keep because there was plenty of lard put in it and the brown bread had treacle put in it so it did keep, you see'.

'Jean was always a good cook. I didn't like her pouring that paraffin in underneath that oven, mind. I used to be at back door. I used to say, 'Well, I don't know, Jean, I'm away out here to this door'. And it would go whoosh! 'Now, she says, it'll cook nice'. Red hot cinders they were, you know. She poured it in. She never had an accident with it, I don't think, like. I was out of that rocking chair, I tell you'.

John Gregg, aged two, helps out with the hens. The buckets on the aerial ropeway can be seen in the distance.

KEEPING A PIG

'1918. A letter read from Rural League urging cottagers to keep pigs. Parish Council replied that most already doing so but would like advice on feeding stuffs'.

'Aye, yes, when you killed a pig, you'd arm up to here in blood. We always kept a pig at Manesty . . . but you were cutting and rendering fat up forever, so you'd basins and basins of fat . . . they tasted gorgeous then, different altogether'.

'Well, we were sitting by the fire at Town End one night and there was a knock on't door so one of us went to the door and there was two men standing there. "Father in?" "Aye". He shouts "Come on in", like he knew who they were. So "Oh, it's you two is it?" "Aye, you haven't a good pig to sell, father?" "Aye, I could hev". So . . . old lamps lit up then and he had a look in the pigsty, like, pig hull. "Oh, that's just what we are looking for. We want a pig to butch". So, next day there was a wagon landed for the pig. They sets off like and away they went, gits to where their destination wus, pig gits butched and one thing and another. Like this was during the war, so they had a licence to butch one, but I think they had butched two that day you see, with this one licence. The next thing, Ministry of Food got to know about this so they sent word they were coming to see this pig.

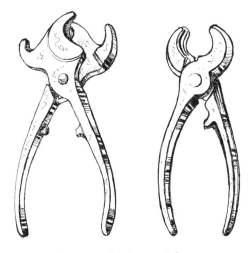

Pig ring pliers. How did these work?[6]

They got it all cut up, salted down int' dairy and covered with salt and one thing and another so when the inspector was coming Missus of the house said "What are we going to do with that pig?" "Oh, we'll do summat". So the food man was coming next day. So he said to the Missus "You just go and git in bed and", he says, "I'll bring the pig up and put it in bed beside you". So that got done. It wusn't long till there was a ran-tan ont' door. He went to see who it was and it was the food man. "I've come to see your licence about this pig". So he

produced a certificate like, to search the house, and then he says "I'd like to see it". "Aye, come on in like", says the farmer. He goes int' house and Ministry man says "I've got to search your house". So he started, underneath the table, and settee and such like and he says to the man "Don't put thi hand under theer. Cat was under theer yesterday". Next thing he goes through into the dairy and this pig was lying, salted up like. So he says, "What's these in these dishes here?" "Oh" he says "Missus was only mekking some gingerbread yesterday and she burnt it a laal bit". "So" he says "I'll hev to go upstairs". So he goes upstairs, looks int' bedrooms, under the beds and such like and t'farmer's saying "Noo, be careful, noo, where the cat ga's". Gits to one bedroom and the door was shut so he started to open the bedroom door and the farmer says "Noo here, dooant ga in theer". He says "My Missus is damn badly. I dooant want you in theer with her". "Oh, well" he says, "I'll just bypass that room. Any more rooms?" "No, thoose seen aw there is".

That was it, and t'pig was in bed beside of her'.

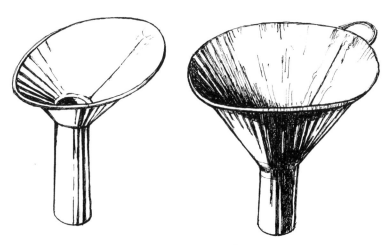

Sausage funnels. Which was the easier one to use?[7]

WAYS OF LIFE

THE HAILE MANOR COURT

Manor courts were important in our area until into the 19th century. Manors had their own by-laws and the manor courts enforced these, settled disputes and small claims and dealt with minor offences and misdemeanours. The courts also had a sort of 'planning permission' role. Their other main function was to confirm tenancy changes, and payment of the admission 'fines' that new tenants had to pay, which were quite an important part of the Lord's income.

There was a court for the Ponsonbys' Haile and Wilton manor, and we have records of it in a Court Book dated from 1690, and from a few separate court 'verdict' documents in the archives.

The court met yearly, usually in November, for a number of years, but then less frequently. The permanent officials were the Steward and Bailiff, the Steward presiding over the court in the Lord's absence. There were 12 co-opted jurors, who were tenants or freeholders from the manor.

Each court appointed 'officials' which, for the Haile and Wilton court, included the Constable, and two 'Hedge Lookers', and, sometimes, two so-called 'Afeerors', whose job was to assess the fines awarded by the court, and to reduce them if they thought them too harsh. Hedges and gates loomed large in the court's business, and failure to maintain them was the most common cause of people being fined.

COMMON HAWTHORN

Everyone took an oath, to say that they would do their duty fairly and without favour.

Records were taken at the meeting and signed by the jurors, and written up later in the court book.

The 1709 court record gives a list of 25 by-laws 'within this mannor'. With other court orders issued from time to time, they show the concerns of a rural community. Many relate to the control of livestock, and use of the commons and of common resources such as peat, wood, bracken, stone, water etc.

Hedges between the commons and the 'inn fields' (the better, enclosed lands used for haymaking and crops and from which livestock was excluded during the growing season) had to be kept in repair between 'Lady day in Lent' (25 March) and Michaelmas Day (29th September). The fine for disobeying was 6s. 8d.

Related to this would be bye-law 6:

'that none do suffer their sheep to go on the inn commons of this mannor (except such sheep be langled – meaning fettered-

Bringing home the peats. Peat was still used for burning well into the twentieth century. Nora Spedding is here bringing peat down from Cold Fell for the fire at Simon Kell.

91

or hirded) between May Day and Michaelmas on penalty of 13s. 4d. for every 24 hours'.

Evidently a serious matter! Likewise a November 1700 order says that no tenant is to put any cattle 'upon any of the In Moores unlangled except the same be under an Herd'.

Co-operation between farmers was expected, as we can see from a by-law that no tenant or freeholder was allowed to refuse 'to help drive the commons', 'on notice given them'.

Resources regulated include bracken, often used for thatching; 'that none shall pull before our Lady day commonly called Crabb faire', and 'that none shall mow any brackens before Michaelmas day';
and 'spelkes' (sticks/branches, also used for thatching) which 'shall not be cut before 30 September' or cut with a 'toothed sickle'; penalties 3s. 4d. However, for selling or giving spelkes 'out of this mannor' the fine was 6s. 8d. 'a time or hundred'. This last phrase seems to suggest that if you tried to sell more than a hundred branches you could be fined again for each hundred. So it wasn't worth risking selling a lot on the grounds that you 'might as well be hanged for a sheep as a lamb'.

Peat was not to be dug before May day, or left 'unpotted' beyond St Johnmas day (24th June) in the following year (fines 3s. 4d.). Also no-one was to burn 'peats or turphes' on the fell (fine 6s. 8d.).

A couple of laws about lime say that nobody was to use anyone else's 'lyme kilne' without their permission, and that 'none presume to burn any lyme within this mannor without the Lord's lycence first obtained'.

Water courses and drainage were a perennial concern. There are several general orders in the court records about drainage of the Syke and Kells commons (areas roughly south-west of Sheepfields and near Kells quarry respectively, later enclosed by the 1810 'Haile enclosures' Act of Parliament). An example from the November 1721 court says that anyone with a right of Turbary (digging for peat) on the 'Sike or Kells' has to 'drain or gutter such places as is likely to become prejudiciall to the whole neighbourhood'. All had to meet and finish the job on the first Monday after the next Lady Day, 'on penalty of one shilling on each tenant or freeholder refusing or neglecting'.

At the same meeting three 'Inhabitants of Blackbeck' were fined for 'not keeping the water in its ancient course'. ('Putting water out of its proper course so as to annoy a neighbour' was one of the by-law offences.)

An amusing case from 1692 was when the court fined Thomas Wilson, a tenant at Hole of Haile, the present day Woodlands,
'for emptying and washing his chamber potts and other filthy vessels in the well streame, to the damage and annoyance of his neighbours, by corrupting their water which they should have to use for their houses, 6s. 8d., affeared to 6s.'.
This same Thomas was a bit of a 'bad un' having been fined only the previous year 'for keeping his horses and mares on the common being infected with the scab'.

Relations between neighbours was a common theme. One by-law offence was to speak 'scandalous words' so as to 'harm the reputacion' of someone else, for which the fine was a hefty 13s. 4d. We don't know if this happened in Haile, although one chap from Black Beck was fined 2s. 4d. in 1703 for 'scandalous words tending to sedition', evidently not such a serious offence!

Complaints to the court often related to trespass. An example from the 1723 court concerned one John Ponsonby a tenant at Orchard Brow, not the Lord of the Manor but doubtless related to him, who was in trouble on several counts. First he was fined 1s. 6d. for three offences of putting his 'horses and other cattle into the Low and High Lonnings contrary to a bylaw'; then 9d. for 'suffering the gate between the Low Lonning and Hardgate to lie down'. He was then 'presented at the prosecution of Richard Thompson', his neighbour at Orchard Brow, for going over one of Thompson's fields 'with his horses cattle and carriages'. For this the court fined him 1s., which was reduced to 9d. by the Afeerors, one of whom was Thompson himself!

Use of the commons was jealously guarded, and there are several cases of outsiders being fined; for example in 1733 John James of Low Broadleys took one John Williamson to the court 'for bringing his goods unto Haile common which he should keep upon Calder Abbey'. The court fined Williamson 3s. 4d., but this was reduced to 1s. 6d. – 'paid'. However, some outsider access was allowed, as we read from a 1714 entry that five 'tenants of The Thwaites' were each to pay 2d. yearly for the access they needed. The access was referred to as 'an overleap', possibly meaning a right of way. (The Thwaites here may be the fell farms such as Simon Kell, but might have been Near Thwaites farms such as Lagget, Sillathwaite and Standing Stones; we know that people there had rights of way over common land at 'Uldale Bottom' from the claims made to the Haile Enclosures Commissioners early in the next century.)

OTHER BUSINESS

The court sometimes got involved in settling inheritances, as for example in 1703 when the court ruled that the son of 'widdow' Thompson of Hole of Haile should pay her 5s. a year for the rest of her life as her share of his half 'tenement', in addition to the third of her late husband's half tenement that was her common law entitlement.

An example of a court authorisation, similar to our 'planning permission', comes from a 1755 'verdict'. This says that the court met at 'Haile Scool House' and that the jurors had viewed a wall built at Beckbrow and heard Henry Walker's plan to build a cart house where his midding shed adjoins his stable end. The jurors agreed that this 'will be no detriment to any person' as there will be 'sufficient way' for John Herd, his neighbour at Beck Brow, between the cart house and Henry Walker's bridge. The bridge here was presumably over the beck in the village. This verdict was not in the court book, as after about 1750 court business other than tenancy changes seems not to have been written up in the book.

The record is interesting in the mention of a school at such an early date. Perhaps related to this is the fact that of the 12 jurors, only one couldn't sign his own name.

One of the Constable's jobs seems to have been tax collection. Constables were appointed on a 'Buggins turn' basis and were usually unpaid, making it an unpopular job, although the November 1733 appointment of John Herd, of Beck Brow, gave him the title 'Constable and Overseer' at 6s. per year for three years. Constables had to arrest felons, 'pursuant to Hues and Cries', and apprehend 'rogues vagabonds and sturdy beggars', according to the Egremont Court records. However, references to them in our manor record relate only to tax collecting. A 1707 entry says:

'Wee doe order that the inhabitants of the townshipp of Haile (and it is so agreed on amongst the said inhabitants) that the Constable of the said townshipp shall collect and receive all taxes and assessments whatsoever laid upon the said townshipp dureing the time he is in office and to beare his own proper charges in and about collecting the same'

A later 1723 entry orders 'the present constable', Richard Thompson of Orchard Brow, mentioned earlier,

'to gather within this township four purveys to defray certain charges, and to be accountable for what is over and above to the succeeding Constable'.

(The 'purvey' was a sort of unit of taxation used for raising local, county or national taxes.)

We have a breakdown dated from 1709 of people's payments of a 6s. purvey for Haile. The payments agreed were mostly 1 pence to 3 pence, given to the nearest half farthing! but 'My Lady Lonsdale, for the Rectory' and 'Madam Ponsonby for her lands in Hale', were to contribute 6 pence and 1 shilling respectively.

Occasionally the court got involved in collecting money for the poor, as in a 1692 entry that 'Henry Ffleming the elder, John Herd and Henry Viccars' (from Head of Haile, Moorhouse and Weddingshaw respectively),

'do compute and charge every tennant within this manor with the maintenance of Clare Hudson and other poore people being resident therein according to every man's ability, and we do order that every person doe pay their severall rates according to such computacion'.

TENANCIES

The court book tells us who were the freeholders and tenants in the manor, and the place names of some of the freeholdings and all of the tenancies. The places named include everywhere in Haile, from Haile Bank, now in Beckermet, in the South, to Brayshaw in the North. Wilton tenancies were at Brackenthwaite, High House, Weddingshaw (Weeding Shaw in the book) and Uldale. (Other parts of Wilton mostly belonged to the Lord of Egremont.) Haile village was centred around Hole of Haile, where there were seven tenancies, with three tenancies described as being at Orchard Brow, one at Manesty and two at Beck Brow.

The freeholders paid a nominal 'free rent' of a few pence per year and had to attend court when required, on pain of a fine if they didn't (of which several cases are recorded in the court book), serve on the court jury, and obey manor laws.

However, most people, at least until the later 1700s, had 'customary' tenancies (a type of secure tenure) which were inheritable, and, with the Lord's permission, could be bought and sold, or mortgaged by the tenants, subject to the payment of so-called admittance fines. These 'fines' were payable when a new tenant was admitted to a tenancy, and also after the death of the Lord (when all tenants had to be readmitted to their tenancies by the new Lord).

Customary rents were small and never changed, being typically a shilling or less for a plot of land or a cottage and garden, and up to a few shillings for the average 'farm'. Admittance fines were larger and increased as time went on, this being the main way that the Lord could get more 'income' from such tenants. For example, for the largest Orchard Brow tenancy, the rent was always 6s. 4d., but the admittance fine, of £9 in 1709 after a Lord's death, had increased to £30 by 1776. To put this amount into context; around the middle of the century a skilled farm worker probably earned in the order of up to about £10 per year, subject to whether food and lodging was provided. (Only larger estates could have afforded to employ such full time labour, not the family-run farms in our area.)

New tenants also paid court charges for their admittance and 'enrolment'. The charge (in a tariffs note at the front of the book) was 3s. 6d. for admittance of an heir after a tenant's death, but for a so-called 'purchase' admission, involving provision of a purchase deed for the buyer, the total charge was 16s. 10d. Provision of a mortgage deed cost £1 4s. and the Court Records detail the mortgage repayments agreed to.

The overall impression we have from these records is of a paternalistic but interdependent community, who had their own laws which they mostly obeyed (the court often had few or no offences to deal with), who paid their taxes, reluctantly, and who took care of their poor.

Lady day. There are several feasts celebrating the Blessed Virgin Mary only one of which, on March 25th, has been referred to for many years now, as Lady Day. The feast of Our Lady on 8th September celebrated her nativity. The fact that Crab Fair is now around the 18th September rather than the 8th has to do with the introduction of the Gregorian calendar.

A Dispute between Haile and Wilton

In the early 17th century the inhabitants of Wilton complained to the Earl of Northumberland, the then Lord of Egremont, that Haile people were using 'their' fell.

In a petition to the Earl's Steward in 1618 they pointed out that there were two fells, one belonging to Wilton and the other to Haile. Henry Ponsonby pays free rent for Haile Fell, but since his father enclosed some of this, Haile people now 'commonly drive their goods to the said Wilton Fell, alleging they have as good rights' as the Wilton people to use it. Henry Ponsonby claims to be chief Lord 'thereof', but they disagree. The Earl is the chief Lord.

They go on to say that Haile people are getting brackens and peat and taking limestone, and that the said Henry Ponsonby, claiming to be chief Lord of their fell, is saying that they can't burn lime there without his 'licence' and must pay him 'he says' for the lime.

HAZEL OR COBNUT

A note added to the petition document records that Haile tenants were fined (amerced) for using the fell, 'Payment to' the 'Baron Sergeant' in Egremont. 'Verdict given at Cockermouth Castle.'

In a later, 1628, petition to the Earl's Steward, they complained that a Wilton tenant of the Earl's had been fined by Dorothy Ponsonby (widow of Henry and mother of the Sir John who went to Ireland with Cromwell), 'by jury of her own tenants' (the Ponsonbys'

Haile and Wilton Manor Court) for building a Peat House. Others had been amerced for burning lime. Also Haile people were still 'taking brackens to thatch their houses'.

They agreed that the Ponsonbys had some Lord's rights over Wilton Fell, such as 'Chattels of Felons', but argued that Wilton Fell and other places 'including Mousegill', to which they had always had rights, properly belonged to the Earl of Northumberland as overlord. Amercements etc. were matters for Egremont, and had been nothing to do with Haile 'till lately'.

We don't know the outcome of the 1628 petition, but it seems clear that there must have been many legal disputes over use of the fell, between the two townships and, presumably, between the Ponsonbys and Northumberland.

The last we hear of this is in an entertaining 'Agreement' from 1666 between the inhabitants of Wilton and Sir John and his Haile tenants. This starts:

'Whereas there have been several suits and controversies of late . . . concerning a certain common of pasture called Haile Fell alias Wilton Fell' within the Manor of Haile and Wilton 'belonging unto the aforesaid Sir John Ponsonby Knight. . .'

It then goes on to say that 'the said differences' chiefly arose,

'through the evil advice of one Abraham Ponsonby, one of the inhabitants within the township of Wilton, who of late pretending that he had at sometimes seen, and at other times he had only heard some old men say, a boundary to have been gone upon the aforesaid common of pasture . . . thereby animating and encouraging the said inhabitants of Wilton to debar the inhabitants of the township of Haile'

and to stop them from getting bracken and peat, and all such 'appurtenances' necessary for their tenements, from the Wilton side of the 'afforesaid' 'pretended' boundary.

'Which said pretences and cunning devices have occasioned very many debates, quarrels, contentions and suits' between the two townships 'to the great impoverishment of the inhabitants thereof'.

The outcome was the agreement, 'signed' by eight Wilton inhabitants (only John Vickars and Henry Walker could actually sign

their own names, the others giving their 'marks') vouching that inhabitants of Haile and Wilton had equal rights to get their 'necessaries' from Haile alias Wilton Fell. The boundary of this is described as going from Cold Fell 'Yeat', via boundary markers ('merestones') to the 'rivulet called Kirkbeck, Uldalebeck alias Ulverdalebecke', and so along the west side of the common above the township of Wilton to the Demesne lands of Haile (i.e. via Dyke Nook and Brackenthwaite to Quicksand Gill).

Binder with four horses. Four horses were needed because of the slope of the field here above Quicksand Gill. 1940.

Wilton inhabitants would still keep their 'ancient' shepherds' 'properties', but would pay compensation for past costs to John Ponsonby Esquire (son of Sir John), and a bond of £10 'a piece . . . for the true keeping' of the agreement in future.

The agreement doesn't specifically mention lime, but it seems fairly clear that the Ponsonbys had control of the Mousegill quarry, and of lime burning, at least until the quarry was assigned for public use in 1814, under the Haile enclosures Act. Notwithstanding the earlier disputes, it was evidently established that the Ponsonby Manor of Haile and Wilton (for which Egremont Lordship rent records show they paid free rent of nine shillings a year) did contain all the unenclosed land in the Parish, including all the quarries.

A Tale of Courtship Amongst the Gentry

In searching for historical references to Haile we found that by far the most occurred in an early diary for 1684/5 (published in 1901 in the *Transactions* of the CWAAS) of William Nicolson, Bishop of Carlisle 1702-1718. Nicolson is well known to historians as 'Bishop Nicolson', an eminent scholar and churchman of the period, and for his diaries, which are a mine of information on many subjects.

SWEET WOODRUFF

The diaries mostly date from his time as a bishop, but the earliest diary is particularly interesting to us because, amongst many other things, it contains a poignant account of a courtship involving local families which was ultimately unsuccessful, despite the willingness of both parties, and which tells us something about how life was lived amongst the better-off classes in our area in those times.

The story of the courtship is retold here, based on William's diary entries. Many of these are in German, which he used a lot in this earliest diary, especially for entries on more private matters, with bits of Latin, which we have had translated. (The diary entries are often brief or abbreviated, with archaic wording and spelling, and therefore sometimes a bit obscure, although the bare bones of the story are clear enough.) As the story shows, courtship amongst the 'gentry' was then a formal business, often involving families from different parts of the county, and subject, at the very least, to parental agreement.

The background to the tale, and William's connection with Haile (he always spells it Hail), is that he was first cousin to John Ponsonby of Haile Hall, his mother, née Briscoe, being the sister of Dorothy, wife of Sir John Ponsonby. His cousin was about 20 years older than he was. At the start of the diary in January 1684, William

was 28, and was evidently a man of great promise, having been appointed Archdeacon at Carlisle in 1682, a post which included the rectory of Great Salkeld, which was his home during the period of the diary. He also still held the vicarage of Torpenhow, to which he had been appointed in 1681 whilst a Fellow at Oxford University.

He was also wanting to marry, and the girl he had in mind was one Barbara Copley of Gosforth, younger sister of his cousin's wife Ann. Barbara and Ann were daughters of the Robert Copley, died 1675, who built Gosforth Hall, and his wife Isabella, an heiress of the Gosforth Tubman family.

The first diary mention of Haile was at the beginning of January, when he spent an evening of 'Christmas' celebrations with the Patricksons at Calder Abbey, returning to Haile with his cousin, and lodging with Thomas Morland, Rector of Gosforth, the following night. Barbara, referred to as BC in the diary, is not referred to then but is first mentioned a couple of weeks later, when he discussed the propriety of wanting to marry her with Bishop Rainbow at Rose Castle, the Bishop's residence. The Bishop's response, given in English in the diary, was:

'I see ye many Inconveniences yt (that) attend it on both sides; am very well satisfy'd it should be broke of (broken off), without any unkindness on either side'.

(The suggestion here seems to be that Barbara already had a suitor, but that the Bishop didn't think this was an insurmountable difficulty.)

Two days later he went to the Sessions at Cockermouth, and spent the next two nights in Haile, after visiting St Bees ('St Beghs') and Whitehaven, and speaking 'somewhat too much' about BC. (He was accompanied on this trip by Thomas Tullie, a church 'Chancellor', or legal officer, at the time.)

The next mention of Barbara is in April when he goes to Haile from Torpenhow and stays four nights, visits 'Egremond' and Calder ('Cawder'), christens his cousin's third son William (with Barbara's brother William as one of the witnesses), and talks to his cousin about 'BC', 'but not much'.

Later in April and in May he writes to his cousin and his cousin's 'sister' (here meaning Barbara, his cousin's wife's sister) and on the

30th May travels to Haile from Salkeld in the morning and has his first talk with Barbara the following day. On the next day he preached twice at Haile, and saw 'B' again the day after, noting that he was well received by her mother. Barbara was 'modest', but finally conceded 'perhaps you may'! He records on the 3rd June that it is his 29th birthday, and that he left Haile at 3 a.m. and arrived at Penrith at 11 a.m., before church business in Appleby the same day! (William was an indefatigable traveller during all the period of this diary, on horseback, mostly on church business, often covering prodigious distances and at all hours of the day.)

There is then a gap in the courtship story, as from the 20th June to the 21st July he was away on church business, travelling firstly to Durham and then to London for the consecration of the Bishop of Durham. There is just one cryptic mention of 'B' during his trip south when he seems to have asked for some legal advice, which concludes: 'Advice to Marry'.

His journey back is worth mentioning. He set off back from London on the evening of the 21st July, arriving in Ravenglass on the 28th, where he was met by 'old Mrs C', and 'thence to Gosforth'. His entry for the 27th July, when he travelled from Lancaster, reads 'Over ye three Sands to Bootle. A long Sabbath's journey'. The day after he got to Gosforth he writes that 'B' has consented – (but) her mother was absent. The mention of the mother's absence is the first warning note of the events to come. The next day he went to 'Sea-Scale' and spent the night at Haile before travelling to his father's at Plumbland (his father was rector there).

The next event in the tale was in the middle of August when he went to Gosforth. Old Mrs 'C' wouldn't be seen – 'quite discourteous'; Barbara was quite different, confirming that she had made her own decision to consent. A further comment is added in Latin, the gist of which is that he had gone early to avoid spending time with the old lady who is 'irascente' (becoming angrier?). There is no entry for the next day, and he returned to Salkeld the day after.

A week later he sent letters to Gosforth, which the mother wouldn't receive. A further week later, he sent to Haile with a letter to his cousin and one to Barbara, and got a 'sehr lieblich' (very lovely) reply from Barbara by return.

In early September he went himself to Haile with a letter from his father for Barbara's mother, which was taken to Gosforth by 'Mr Sherwin'. He notes, in Latin, that the mother gave a dignified reply. Early the next day he went to see 'B' and was given a 'sehr lieblich' reception, Barbara assuring him she 'was not a turncoat etc'.

Not long after, he notes that his father went to Haile, and then to Gosforth with 'Mr Tubman', presumably as arranged following his father's letter. An obscure bit of Latin follows, the gist of which is that his father was not successful in his mission, presumably to persuade the 'old lady', who was even 'madder' than usual, to change her mind. It seems that his father must have agreed, or at least accepted, that relations between William and Barbara should be broken off.

Nothing daunted, William went back to Haile at the beginning of October and saw Barbara the next day when her mother wasn't around. Initially they had a bit of a tiff, and Barbara was in a 'huff', perhaps as a result of his father's unsuccessful visit, but they then made up. A week later he sent his boy to Haile with letters, and a gold present for Barbara. The boy returned with news that Barbara was now with her sister in Haile, having been thrown out by her mother (!), presumably for continuing to see him against her wishes.

SNOWDROP

As a last desperate effort he went back to Haile on the 14th October, leaving Rose Castle a 4 p.m., where he had dined with the Bishop. The next day he did some hunting with his cousin Ponsonby, and another cousin, and discussed how Barbara's mother, and his father, might be persuaded to change their minds. The following day he went to Gosforth, but was refused admittance, and was rebuked by Mr Morland for persisting with his attentions. He then went to visit Mr Senhouse in Seascale. He stayed another day, doing some more hunting 'near Egremond', and acted as Umpire in an Arbitration for his cousin, finally returning to Salkeld on the 18th.

His final meeting with Barbara was in early November, when she pressed him to take back his letters. 'Finally, and very late, we agreed to separate'. He received his letters back on 17th December, and sent a reply the next day, together with letters to his cousin and his cousin's wife, writing 'And so Adieu' in the diary.

This was the end of the matter but there are a few post-scripts.

At the beginning of June 1685 he went to Haile again and stayed in the area for three days, but doesn't mention Barbara or visiting Gosforth. On his return there was an 'angry' letter from his father awaiting him, reproving him for, as his father called it, this 'Scandalous Ramble'. Presumably his father thought William still had some idea of renewing the courtship. Also, at the time, Barbara's mother was probably very ill, which perhaps his father knew. In fact Barbara's mother died soon afterwards. In the Gosforth parish burial record for 24th June, Isabella Copley is recorded as 'Gentlewoman', 'buried in linnen' (as befitted someone of her dignity).

William records hearing of Mrs Copley's death a few days later, and getting news the next month that Barbara, now orphaned, is in a low way. In the last entry in the diary, on 20th July, he writes that he has sent letters to Haile for his cousin and Morland and, separately, to 'BC'.

Whether Barbara replied we don't know, but we do know that she got married some years later to a Mr Richard Trotter of Dent, as recorded in the Gosforth parish records on 19th May 1692. Nicolson himself got married on his 31st birthday in 1686.

The final post-script is from his diary entry, now as Bishop Nicolson, living at Rose Castle, for 7th June 1708, in which he records that his visitors included 'Cous. J. Ponsonby and his sister and their little cousin Trotter'. The J. Ponsonby here would be the son of his first cousin, and the little cousin Trotter would be a child of Barbara's, a pleasant ending to the tale.

One thing we don't know is why Barbara's mother objected so much to the match. It seems clear that William didn't like her much, and presumably the feeling was mutual. It may also have been that she didn't want her remaining daughter to leave the area, or preferred another suitor, preferably with some personal wealth and property or land. At the time of the courtship William would probably not have had much personal wealth, although he had a reasonable income, which we know to have been £55.12s. 0d. in 1684 (of which £33 was from Great Salkeld corn tithe).

Haile church.

THE PARISH AWARD

A big event in the history of the Parish was the enclosure of the commons, following the 'Haile Inclosures' Act of Parliament in 1810.

The outcome was our Parish 'Award', presented at a 'Special General Meeting' in Calder Bridge on the 16th November 1814, by the three Commissioners who had been appointed to carry out the requirements of the Act. The original Parish copy of the Award document produced by the Commissioners still exists.

In all there were something over 800 acres of commons to divide up and enclose, nearly 700 of which were in Wilton, called 'Haile Fell also known as Wilton Fell', in the document. The remainder was split between five areas in Haile called Kells Moor, Syke, Herd Moor, Haile Moor and Brayshaw Moor.

The main requirements of the Act were, firstly, to divide the commons into allotments to be given, as freehold, to people with 'rights of common', which included everyone with freehold or customary tenant land and property in the Parish, 'according to their respective properties', and, secondly, to abolish tithes and ecclesiastical dues – 'Easter offerings, Mortuaries and Surplice fees' excepted.

Further important requirements were the allocation of parts of the commons for new roads, quarries and gravel pits, and for cattle watering places.

Lastly about 100 acres was kept aside by the Commissioners and sold to cover expenses.

The tithes being abolished were owned at that time by the Earl of Lonsdale, as 'Lay Rector Impropriate' of Haile. In consequence, in compensation for his loss, Lonsdale was awarded much the largest (313 acres) area of commons (corresponding to the present day Lowther Park of the Forestry Commission). A few acres of this was also for rights of common in respect of the 'property' and 25 acres of glebe land he owned in Haile.

The next largest allocation, after Lonsdale's, was 166 acres, most of it on Wilton Fell, awarded to the Ponsonby family. Much of this was for rights of common with respect to their demesne and other land, and part in relation to 'Lord of the Manor' rights. The Lord of the Manor nevertheless retained many rights and privileges, including mining and game rights, although he would in future have to pay compensation to other allotment recipients if he wanted to mine on their lands.

This left only about 210 acres to be divided up between the remaining claimants, after allowing for the roads and 'public' places and the land to be sold to cover expenses.

In the event, after some selling, with the Commissioners' permission, of entitlements by people who didn't want to take up their allocation, around 70 plots, of widely varying sizes, were awarded to 33 people. On average about one acre of commons was awarded for about every six acres of land held by those with rights of commons, but with appreciable variations between recipients.

A typical larger farm example would be that of John Smith, who farmed 65 acres of partly freehold land at Head of Haile, and who was awarded three plots on Kells and Haile Moors totalling nearly 10 acres. Less generously, Daniel Jackson, with an average sized farm of 43 acres at Stockbridge, only got three acres on Wilton Fell. In contrast Joe Thompson, with 45 acres at Town End in Haile, got 11 acres, most of it on Wilton Fell which he sold to Henry Mossop of Calderbridge, who didn't have an entitlement of his own.

The Ponsonbys' allocation of 121 acres on account of 480 acres of Demesne and other land, may partly have been so large because Miles Ponsonby, who died shortly before the awards were finalised, had separate arrangements for payments to Lonsdale in lieu of tithes, and, it seems, was therefore not benefiting from their abolition. (The claims people made, including Miles' lengthy submission, are mostly given in an 1811 summary of 'claims made to the Commissioners'. People's land acreages quoted here are taken from the 1811 summary.)

WILD CHERRY

A few cottage owners in Haile got awards of less than a rood (a quarter acre), which some sold, though what Moses Haile, with a cottage and garden in Haile, wanted with 10 perches (a sixteenth of an acre) on Wilton Fell, can only be guessed at! (Moses' tiny allocation was evidently the last to be made as one can see from the allotment numbering system. His entry in the 'Schedule of Allotments' Table in the award document seems to have been squeezed in as an afterthought. Perhaps he didn't have time to sell it before the awards were announced.)

In return for their awards, recipients had to make hedges or 'fences' – either of earth planted with good 'quicksets' or of stone – around their allotments, and the award specifies who had to do which parts for each allotment. They also had to make, and to maintain in future, all the private roads, or 'occupation ways' specified by the Commissioners, although the lion's share of this road-making fell to Lonsdale and the Ponsonby family, as the largest recipients of commons land. All this work had to be completed by the '15th of February next', i.e. 1815, before payment of tithes could be abolished. Those liable to tithes also had to pay the costs of 'ring fencing' Lonsdale's allotment, with a wall six feet high 'including coping stone', which the Commissioners had to get made.

The private roads included 'Winder Road' down to Uldale bottom, mostly to be made by Lonsdale, and 'Wilton Private Road'

from Dyke Nook to Brackenthwaite, which 13 people had to make parts of, specified in yards. Others included 'Limekiln Road' and 'Beck Coat Road' leading to the limestone quarry at Mousegill and the freestone Kells quarry respectively, these being the two public quarries specified in the award.

The award also specified a 'Public Gravel Pit' near the Winder Road turn off, and a 'Sand and Gravel Pit' near Cold Fell Gate.

All stone and gravel was to be strictly for the use of parishioners, within the parish.

The expenses to be covered included the costs of the Act of Parliament, the assessment of claims and associated surveying, and the surveying and staking out of the commons. The Commissioners also undertook the construction of new public roads, covering most of the length of the roads to Cold Fell Gate from both Haile and Wilton, and the Calderbridge road between Robertgate Bridge and Sheepfields.

To cover these costs 10 plots of land on Wilton Fell were sold for a total of £2959. Most of the plots were sold to Wilton farmers who were adding to the allotments they had been given. The prices paid, of around £30 an acre, give an indication of the value of the land that people were given, even though the majority only got a few acres.

The award document ends with some final instructions. The sand and gravel quarry pits are to be supervised by the Highways Surveyors of Haile and Wilton, who will control when and how they can be worked, and rubbish arising disposed of. Cattle or any other livestock must not be allowed to 'remain and be at liberty' on any of the roads or 'other Public Grounds', but must be led or driven along 'without unnecessary delay'. Everyone given allotments must 'from time to time and at all times hereafter' make sufficient drains in their hedges to allow water to drain from adjoining roads and allotments, and must keep all such drains and water courses scoured and in repair. All in all, the usual country concerns!

Uldale farm.

THE BUCK'S HEAD

Buck's Head.

As we were setting out on our research in January 2003 a newspaper cutting under the heading '100 Years Ago' came our way from *The Dumfries and Galloway Standard*. The entry was entitled 'A Clergyman Wants a Pub kept open for School Children'. Mr. Hail, landlord of 'The Buck Inn', Haile, was applying for an extension of two hours in connection with a concert and ball to be given in the school. His application, sent to the Chairman of the Licensing Committee, Whitehaven, was supported by Mr. A. H. Cooper, vicar of the parish, who wrote:

'Dear Sir: As we have our annual entertainment on Friday in aid of our school, Mr. Hail will be glad if you will allow him to supply refreshments beyond the usual closing hours. I seldom take any intoxicating drink of any kind, and have brought up all my children total abstainers, but as The Buck Inn is reputably conducted and I have heard no complaint during the past six years, I think his request should be granted. He tells me that his is a very poor business, and hardly worth carrying on, and I believe I am sure the people of the parish – with one or two

exceptions – are very much more temperate than when I came here sixteen years ago. I am, yours faithfully, A. H. Cooper'.

At the hearing, in answer to a remark that 'the extension seems to be more to help your business than for the convenience of the entertainment', Mr Hail explained to the committee that the application for extension had always been successful. When asked if it was a Sunday school, he replied that 'it was a day school entertainment in the schoolroom'. The chairman said a majority of the bench declined to grant the application, an announcement 'which appeared to surprise the applicant very much'.

No longer a pub, the former 'Buck's Head Inn' is the lovely sandstone building standing a little off the road in the centre of the village with a small concreted area in front. It is believed to date from early to mid Victorian times. It began as a single cottage and spread to cover three cottages and a smithy, all under the one roof. There are still rings attached to the front wall, suitable for tying horses to while their riders took refreshment in the inn. At one time there were two stone mounting steps beside the doorway to help riders mount their horses.

An advertisement for the letting of an Inn at Hail appeared in *The Cumberland Pacquet* in October 1834.

BUCK'S HEAD INN, HAIL.

TO be LET, and may be Entered upon at Martinmas next,

All that commodious and well-established I N N, with the Conveniences thereunto attached, situate in H A I L, and now in the Occupation of Mr. Fletcher Nicholson, as Tenant.

The Premises are in good Repair, and fitted up with every Accommodation for carrying on a respectable Business both in Spirit and Ale.

For further Particulars apply to Mr. JOSEPH GAINFORD, Calder Bridge.

Calder Bridge, Oct. 11th, 1834.

** (Not to be repeated.)

The Buck's Head To Let. An advertisement from the Cumberland Pacquet. *October, 1834.*

The inn was a converted cottage and probably not as 'commodious' as the advertisement suggests. The phrase 'well-established' indicates a business that had been running for some time. Since the advertisement was submitted by a private individual it would appear that the inn was at that time a 'free house'. Did this Joseph Gainford start the business, and was he the same gentleman of that name who was a blacksmith in Haile between 1828 and 1847? Some time between 1881 and 1891 it appears that the middle cottage was taken over and became part of the inn. Presumably the smithy, the last part to be taken over as an extension to the pub, was bought by the brewery only when the smithy ceased to function. This became a washhouse and store for barrels of beer etc. The cottage above, reached by stone steps going up the gable end of Wellbank Cottage next door, was still rented out for a while but then became a store for table tops and trestles used for village functions. Eventually in 1976 it was included in the major alterations and became part of the flat that was created above the pub for the landlord and his family.

'The Licence Registration Book', in which 'Extensions Granted' were recorded from 1903-1968, describes The Buck's Head as follows:-

Description	Full Licensed House
No. Rooms	9
No. used Bedrooms	5
No. Drinking Rooms	3
No. Licensed by Excise	4
No. Refreshment Bars	4
No. Drink Cellars	4

Stabling Accommodation For 4 horses

(Some of these figures suggest more space than was actually there, but official figures must mean something to somebody!)

Conditions of Tenancy   Quarterly

Tied to Cleator Moor Brewing Co. Ltd. For all liquors.

Owner – Cleator Moor Brewing Co. Ltd.

1926. Matthew Brown and Company Ltd, Preston.

There follows a list of tenants and dates of extensions granted, with a note of the occasions. They were mainly Christmas, New Year, a supper and ball and Coronation Day and for VE Day the extension allowed the pub to open from 10.00 a.m. until midnight!

At first it must have been one of the smallest inns ever when it was just the one cottage with only two rooms downstairs. Even when the second cottage was included none of the downstairs rooms was used as a private sitting room by the landlord and his family. They lived in the kitchen or sat in one of the drinking rooms. In 1976 when the major alterations took place, most of the ground floor was opened up to create one large public room and The Buck's Head finally got its bar! New toilets were put inside. Upstairs a large flat was created bringing into use the old cottage above the smithy for the landlord and his family. The outside steps up to the cottage and the stone mounting steps had already disappeared.

The first publican to be recorded in a census, in 1841, was a gentleman by the appropriate name of Moses Haile. Wilson Cook had taken over by 1847 and ran The Buck's Head for forty years or more. During his time there, apart from being landlord, he was also a grocer and farmer. It looks as though innkeeping in Haile was never a very lucrative job and that it was necessary to earn extra income from other jobs as well. By 1891 Wilson Cook had been replaced and there followed three licensees, including a lady, before John Hail, mentioned at the beginning, who remained in the post for about ten years in spite of its being a 'very poor business'. Henry and Elizabeth Bowe became tenants in 1913 and the family remained at The Buck's Head until 1966. After Henry died the tenancy was transferred to Elizabeth in 1939. When she retired she stayed with the family and Wilfred, her son, took on the tenancy in 1951. It is from this family we begin to learn about the running of the pub and what it was like to live there in the first half of the twentieth century.

There were official opening hours, much the same as they are now, but the doors at 'The Buck' were generally open most of the day so that they could sell tobacco, cigarettes and paraffin. The policeman from Thornhill would warn them of a likely police raid and usually have a drink at the same time! There seemed to be quite a relaxed attitude to the regulations then. Drinks had to be carried through from the kitchen where the beer barrel, crates and bottles were kept. They had a set of pewter tankards of differing sizes for measuring but mostly they used jugs for carrying beer through to the drinking rooms to be poured into pint and half-pint glasses. The barrels delivered to the pub in those days were the traditional wooden barrels with cork stoppers which were replaced by a brass tap when required for use. Optics were only introduced to 'The Buck' just before the Bowe family moved out in 1966. All three rooms downstairs, apart from the kitchen, were drinking rooms.

In the early days of the Bowes' reign, the young son, Wilfred, would collect newspapers from Beckermet on his bike before he went to school in Haile. The papers were placed in a rack on the door for the villagers to collect and this service for the village continued while the Bowes remained tenants.

It was to be hoped that you did not have to use the toilets often, especially on a dark, wet night for they were out the back at the end of the garden and could only be reached by thirteen steps. However, you would have been provided, free of charge, with a torch and an umbrella!

The pub's year was marked by some important occasions. There were the Hunt weeks in February and November at the end of which tatie pot suppers, cooked all day by the landlady and one or two other ladies of the parish, were provided for the huntsmen. The mutton for these feasts was given by the Mumbersons of Town End Farm. The huntsmen would gather at The Buck's Head at the start of each hunt and would be sure to end up there on the Saturday night for the tatie pot supper.

New Year's Eve was a great occasion then too, when all customers were given Christmas Dinner in relays in the kitchen. Betty Spedding would make sure everyone had a good dollop of trifle to follow.

Cards, dominoes and darts were regular pastimes as well as having a 'crack'. It was even possible to play cards on a Sunday.

'I went up one Sunday and I went into the drinking room and there was one or two in. "Bring us t'cards will you love?" I said "Oh yes." And then Wilf's mother said, "Do you know what you've done?" "No, what have I done?" "You took cards in to them. We don't play cards on Sundays, not in pubs". I said, "Oh heck. They can do many a worse thing than play cards, can't they?" So after that, they played cards on a Sunday'.

Business was good in the summer but not in the winter – 'Summer

was great. They were coming and going all night'. People would go on rides around the countryside, calling at pubs here and there. But it was necessary for the publican still to have some other form of income as well.

Living in The Buck's Head must have been very difficult for tenants, especially when they had young families. They had very little privacy and not much space. Everything was done in the kitchen – cooking, eating, washing-up, keeping the drinks for the pub and washing the clothes – until the smithy was taken over. The kitchen doubled up as a bathroom too. The floors were red sandstone flags which might have looked nice but were difficult to clean. The clothes of crawling babies must have been forever red!

Because there was no bar the landlord would have to keep an eye on the drinking rooms to ask if any customers were ready for any drinks. At times it could be frustrating when they would tidy themselves up for evening opening time and maybe no one would come in until ten minutes before closing, and then sit till 11.30 p.m!

Much later, after Ida had joined the family in 1948, the brewery at different times made a back kitchen, a bathroom out of one of the bedrooms and replaced the sandstone flags with asphalt. Periodically magistrates had been to inspect the property but it was a long time before pressure was brought to bear on the brewery to make these improvements. When the bathroom was being put in Elizabeth Bowe, a particularly fastidious lady, was heard to say, 'I've never had a bath for fifty year'! There were also improvements made to the kitchen.

'We got a Carlyle grate at one stage . . . You could put a rice pudding in them. you see, and cook it slowly . . . Wilf's mother used to knit socks for ever, you know. Wilf had loads of socks. And I thought – I said to her one day, "You know, this wee oven thing at top'll be great to air clothes as well, won't it?" We put a lot of socks in one day. Well, they were like cinders when they come out!'

The oven wasn't as slow as they thought.

It was not until 1953, however, that they could stop taking candles to bed when electricity was put in upstairs although it had been put in downstairs earlier. With these improvements life did become a lot easier.

The family was blessed with good, helpful, regular customers who were always ready, when Wilf was at work, to put coal on the fire, bring beer crates through from the smithy and happy to wait on the village green after closing time until the lights went out in 'The Buck'. Amongst their regulars was one who liked six raw eggs in his pint, a huntsman who liked to 'entertain' with his singing and blowing of the hunting horn and one who liked pickled onions and once ate a bowlful, not knowing they had been on the shelf for rather a long time. One Sunday lunchtime a neighbour appeared with her baby, spotted her husband and said, 'If you're going to sit in 'ere, you can sit nursing this'. And she plonked the baby on his knee. Mostly their customers were well behaved and not many over-indulged. Elizabeth Bowe was noted for being a good landlady. She knew how to deal with people. They had customers from all walks of life, from elsewhere in the locality and a number of holidaymakers who all enjoyed a 'crack' over a pint in the The Buck's Head.

A regular visitor to the pub from round about the 1920s was Mary Spedding who came not for a drink but to see her sister, Elizabeth. She never left much before 11 p.m. when she had a long, dark, lonely walk up the road, down the track behind Haile Hall, across the beck by Mill House and up the steps back to her home, the Pigeon House, in the wood. She was a tall, gaunt lady, normally dressed in black and all she had to light her way was a candle! 'I'd say it would go out a lot.'

A difficult rule for tenants involved the changeover of the tenancy. Those moving out had to be out by 11 a.m. and those moving in had to be in by 11 a.m., in readiness for opening time. Ida Bowe remembers when they were moving out in 1966 they had all the furniture on the concrete outside. Fortunately, the weather was fine.

By 1968 when Elsie and Ronnie Farren took over the tenancy, the two drinking rooms on the left had been made into one long room while the third room on the right became a private sitting room for the tenants and their family. During their stay they had, on loan, above the fireplace, a stag's head, the stag having been shot by Sir John Ponsonby himself. Still there was no bar, or beer pump, just a tap room. At this time the pub witnessed a different kind of event – a wedding celebration at The Buck's Head with the wedding breakfast set out in the village hall. But afterwards, celebrations continued in the pub. A regular event, though, was the arrival on Sunday lunchtimes of a customer on horseback. Children had rides and a nearby garden benefited from the manure! On the journey home from the pub, the horse had been known, on more than one occasion, to have arrived home without its rider, though they had definitely left together.

Perhaps the most important change in The Buck's Head history was in 1976 when the bar was finally installed. Three years after Bill

Hunting Mural. Painted on a wall inside the 'Buck's Head'.

and Freda Relph had taken over, the major alterations to both the ground and upper floors were made, complete with a hunting scene mural next to the bar. There were ten weeks of builders' confusion during which the pub had to stay open as usual. Each day there had to be frantic cleaning up, dusting and washing floors, before the pub was ready for opening.

Hunt weeks continued as usual. The pub would be full all week. Pie and pea suppers were served every night until Saturday when tatie pot suppers were provided by Freda and several other ladies who were warned in advance as to when theirs would be collected. New competitions for this night were devised – Best Bowler Hat, Best Singer and Best Lamplugh Boot (similar to a clog, turning up at the front with studs in the sole like a horseshoe). Hound trailers would return to 'The Buck' after an outing but not on Fridays. Friday night was still card and dominoes night with card players on the fire side of the room and dominoes players on the other side.

Sadly, in spite of the licensees' efforts over the years, the brewery decided that it was no longer a viable business and closed The Buck's Head doors in 1987. Happily though, it has gained a new lease of life as a family home.

THE COMMUNITY

'The people in Haile are quite special, I think'.

'. . . because people were so – they could have watched me make mistakes but they never did'.

'. . . and in farming you seem to get groups of families or farms who worked together . . . I think there were about six occasions (during the year) where people worked together and so that makes community. It brings it together'.

'And in the church of course there was more community spirit then because at – of course, weddings and funerals are still the same – at funerals you'll get a whole farming community, as you know, and the churchyard is very often full. In fact, people tend to stand out in the churchyard until the family have come in and then they knock out their pipes and squeeze in at the back'.

'Well, the Hunt Ball was the first autumn we were there – it must have been 1957 – and to my amazement, I was asked to judge the Beauty Queen at the Hunt Ball and I was obviously asked because I was new and didn't know anybody so I wouldn't be biased in any way, but I must say I did feel a bit nervous about it. I didn't know anybody really. Well, I did a bit. I can't remember now who asked me . . . But for some reason or other – I think I must have just met Thai in the village road or something; he must have brought the subject up and I said to him, "Thai, how am I going to judge this Hunt Queen?" And he said, "Mrs. Barns, choose a gay lass with nay clart on her face". And that was it.'

'. . . so as I wouldn't be on my own in the evening. She would ask me up and I would be marvellously looked after. Lizzie had to bring me the same sort of breakfast as I imagine she brought Molly which was, I mean, Victorian standards – great big tray with this wonderful white linen on it and everything, everything, cooked breakfast, everything there, you know, with lids on the top to keep the bacon and so on hot and everything there. I was just so incredibly lucky. Just to meet with such kindness you could never, ever forget, never'.

RANSOMS
WOOD
GARLIC

'I would have hated to have missed the years I had up there. Oh, it was, it was lovely. One happy family, it was. It was in them days, wasn't it? If Wilf went night shift to Sellafield any time, (*and I was looking after the pub on my own*) I always used to say to all t'lads, "Now don't go off that school green till I get to bed. Make sure you see that I'm in bed". It was great. "Right, we'll do that now. We won't leave you". And, you know, they'd fetch you a case of beer in, or owt at all. Put some coal on fire. It was real, typical old fashioned, wasn't it. It was, it was nice, though'.

'Lady always come through, sat and had a chat. She was an exceptional woman, was Lady Ponsonby, really. She wasn't a bit snobbish or owt. Really nice. She never seemed to mind. You could just go up and go round gardens and everything'.

'T'door was always open at Nora's. You were always welcome at Nora's. It was great. To me it was really living, you know, not like down here at other spots. It's 'good evening', 'goodnight' and that's yer lot sort of thing'.

GOOSEY TYSON

If you go up Limekiln Lonning, north of Wilton, passing the old limekiln and turning right across the fields, you will shortly come to Goosey Tyson's Cave. Here a small stream disappears into an underground passage in the limestone, known technically as a 'swallow hole'. A small cave lies behind the entrance and older residents in the area can remember playing in it as children. The cave has now largely collapsed and, unless you are an experienced caver, you are definitely not advised to try to get into it these days.

This is know locally as Goosey Tyson's Cave and is the focus of one of the few local legends. The story varies according to who tells it, but most will say that Goosey Tyson stole geese and hid them in the cave, later selling them in neighbouring villages. Some will even remember seeing photographs of pots and pans hanging up in the cave, suggesting that Goosey Tyson actually lived there, but no one can tell you when these events actually took place.

Byron wrote '. . . truth is always strange; stranger than fiction.' and this was never more so than in the case of Goosey Tyson. There was a real life 'Goosey' Tyson and *The Cumberland Pacquet*, in October 1840, recorded the events that gave rise to the legend in great detail. The story is indeed strange, starting with an anonymous letter and detective work at dead of night, followed by a high-profile trial and sprinkled with innuendo and even high farce. Read on and be amazed.

In earlier times geese were widely kept, although they are seen less often today. Most farms would have had a flock and it was the usual practice to put them out on common land during the summer, where they became heafed to a particular area in the same way that sheep are grazed on the fells today. During the winter months they would be brought down to the farm, many to be fattened up for Christmas.

John Mossop farmed at Carleton Lodge and had a flock of forty

geese. On the morning of Wednesday 7th October 1840 he went to feed them but found that twenty-nine were missing. He sent two of his farm servants to look for the missing geese and they eventually discovered twelve some distance away but, of the other seventeen there was no trace. Assuming that the remainder had been stolen he placed the following notice that appeared in *The Cumberland Pacquet* on the following Tuesday:

FIVE POUNDS REWARD.

WHEREAS on Tuesday Night the 6th Instant, Seventeen Geese were Stolen from a Field belonging to Carleton Lodge Farm, near Egremont, the Property of Mr. John Mossop ;

Notice is hereby given

That the above Reward will be paid by the Association for the Prosecution of Felons in the Parish of St. John's, Beckermont, to any Person who may give such Information as may lead to the Conviction of the Offenders.

T. J. SCALES, Solicitor.
49, Roper Street, Whitehaven, Oct. 10, 1840.

At this point a mysterious, anonymous letter was put under Mr Mossop's door and, because of the information it contained, he went straight to the magistrates at Whitehaven and got a search warrant, which he put in the hands of the constable, John Douglas. Late in the evening of 13th October Douglas, accompanied by Henry Bragg and William Barnes, went to Henry Tyson's farm at Wilton, which was known at the time as Town End but is now renamed Dentside, and heard geese in an out-house. Returning the following morning, when it was just light, they found eight geese in the out-house and nine in a stable. Mr Mossop identified the geese as part of his flock and consequently the constable took Henry Tyson into custody and conveyed him to Whitehaven police station.

On Friday 16th October Henry Tyson was brought before the magistrates, accused by John Mossop of stealing his geese. On the basis of the evidence presented by Mr Mossop and Douglas, the police officer, the magistrates agreed that there was a case against Henry Tyson and he was committed for trial at the next Quarter Sessions.

Now Henry Tyson was a 'yeoman', meaning a farmer who owned the land that he farmed, and was also regarded as a 'statesman', which showed that he owned an estate. He farmed seventy or eighty acres, of which he owned about thirty or forty, and his father and grandfather had farmed there before him. It was almost unprecedented for a person of such standing in the community to be accused of theft, so the case aroused great interest when it came to court at Cockermouth on Wednesday 21st October 1840.

This meeting of the Quarter Sessions was particularly important because a new chairman had to be elected. Consequently the magistrates turned out in force; all the great families and great houses of the area were represented, the names including Lowther, Curzon, Irton, Stanley and Spedding from Lowther Castle, Armathwaite Hall, Irton Hall, Corby Castle, Greystoke Castle, and Dovenby Hall. E. W. Hasell of Dalemain was elected chairman and the trials commenced.

By the time Henry Tyson's trial started the Court was packed with members of the public who wanted to hear this unusual case, to the extent that witnesses had great difficulty in getting through the crowd when they were called. Both parties were represented by counsel, Mr Fawcett prosecuting for John Mossop and Mr Ramshay defending on behalf of Henry Tyson, who was referred to throughout the proceedings as 'the prisoner'.

One goose looks much like another, so identification of the stolen geese became an important matter. John Mossop explained that his geese were unusual in the area because they were crossbred with a Chinese goose. Moreover, when the missing birds were put back in their field, they 'showed great fondness' for the others in the flock and, geese being naturally quarrelsome, would not have behaved in this way if they were strangers.

William Barnes, a servant of Mr Mossop, said that he had brought six of the geese to Cockermouth. 'Produce them', demanded Mr Ramshay. What a mistake; obviously he had not considered the effect of a crowded courtroom on the composure, not to mention the bowels, of six geese. They were brought through the crowd to the front of the courtroom in a shower of feathers and

'. . . the table was considerably soiled, and many books and hats thereon shared a similar fate, as did also the garments of one or two individuals'.

The Court quickly decided that they could manage without the geese, which were taken away, and, after the courtroom had been mucked out and mopped up, the case continued. However, John Mossop, together with William Barnes and Betsy Speight, his servants, confirmed that these were some of the missing geese.

Much was made of the fact that the geese were found in buildings, several witnesses saying that it was unusual to house geese at that time of the year. Henry Tyson's son, also Henry, and his daughter Hannah explained that they were housed because it was so wet and also to teach the young geese to feed inside. Elizabeth Jackson of Stockbridge and her son, Richard, both confirmed that they had seen geese in Henry Tyson's buildings before John Mossop had lost his.

Mr Ramshay then presented his case to the Court in great detail, speaking for an hour before calling a stream of character witnesses in support of Henry Tyson. His case largely depended on the good character of Henry Tyson and his standing in the community, together with his extensive property, and how improbable it was that he would jeopardize all this for the sake of a few geese.

The case continued with both counsel questioning the character of some of the female witnesses, with obvious male chauvinism. Hannah Tyson had to admit that she had the 'misfortune' to have a child, although she was not married. Betsy Speight was asked whether she took a glass of spirits with her master; perhaps the counsel was rather envious, because John Mossop was seventy-five and she was only forty. Well, those two were no better than they ought to be then . . .

The counsel even tried to discredit each other; Mr Ramshay interrupted Mr Fawcett, accusing him of misrepresenting the testimony of a witness. Mr Fawcett was incensed; this implied he was guilty of disreputable, unprofessional conduct, 'My temper will not bear it', he protested and asked the Chairman to intervene. However the Chairman wisely declined to become involved and left Mr Fawcett to come to terms with the insult and his temper.

Finally the Chairman summed up the evidence and asked the jury to consider their verdict. Unable to reach an immediate decision, the jury decided to retire and, accompanied by a bailiff, they were locked up in a room at the Globe Inn to consider the evidence that had been presented to them. It was now four o'clock in the afternoon and the case had started at eleven in the morning. The jury was evenly divided, so it took another three hours before they finally reached a verdict. No doubt spurred on by the pangs of hunger, and the knowledge that the magistrates were already wining and dining elsewhere in the inn, they came out and the foreman announced their verdict. Guilty. However they recommended that Henry Tyson should be shown mercy on account of his previous good character.

Goosey Tyson's Cave.

Henry Tyson was sentenced to six months imprisonment with hard labour, one month to be spent in solitary confinement, the court indictment book recording that he stole geese to the value of sixty shillings, or three pounds . . .

Well, ladies and gentlemen of the twenty-first century jury, how do you find the defendant, Henry Tyson? Guilty or not guilty? Was this a respectable member of society who had suffered a moment of madness? Was it a feud between the newly-arrived John Mossop and the long-established resident Henry Tyson? Or was there more to this case than came out in Court? Were Henry Tyson's activities well known in the area, perhaps? Wherever the truth lies, it is unlikely that a court would pass such a harsh sentence today. And then what about Goosey Tyson's cave? There was no mention of this in the case, so was there really any connection with Henry Tyson? Or is this just an embellishment that the legend has gathered over the years?

Some twenty-eight years later, we find many of the people involved in this case, including three of Henry Tyson's sons and a later John Mossop, acting as a local coroner's jury, all described as 'Good and lawful Men of the Liberty of the Lordship of Egremont'. So later generations of the families were not touched by the stigma of the case and many Tysons and Mossops still live in the area. No harm was done, Wilton had its moment of infamy and gained the legend of Goosey Tyson, which is still going strong after a hundred and sixty years. Indeed the truth is stranger than fiction.

WILLS

Copies of wills from this parish can be viewed at the Records Office in Whitehaven. The Cumbria Family History Society has recorded an index to all the wills in Copeland.

The wills for Haile and Wilton date back to 1585 and, as with all wills, they follow similar formats. The older wills sometimes also contained an inventory of the deceased's property and belongings together with a list of debts owing. An example of this is the last will and testament of Robert Dickinson of Wilton in the parish of Haile in 1677.

In this will he left 'to his natural daughter Elizabeth Dickinson one shilling by legacy' and likewise left one shilling each to Mathew, Jane, John, Robert and Henry Dickinson. The rest of his goods he left to his beloved wife Anne Dickinson. All of his goods were assessed by Henry Viccars, Henry Ponsonby, Michael Walker and John Jackson. These were itemised and contained among other items:

	£	s	d
Brass	0	4	0
Wooden vessels	0	5	0
Earthen Potts	0	0	6
Hemp and yarns	0	3	0
Husbandry geare	1	2	0
Corn and Hay	1	14	6
Sheep	2	16	0
Horses	4	10	6
Poultry	0	3	3

There then followed a list of debts owing to various persons. This sort of will that has an inventory attached to it is very useful in putting together a picture of life at that time particularly in terms of the goods and the values placed on them.

The Will and Testaments can also be very prescriptive in what was to be done. All this was left in the hands of the executors appointed in the will. These could often have very long-term consequences, resulting in the heirs of the executors having to carry them out. A typical example is that of Isaac Viccars of Weddingshaw, Wilton, in 1783.

His last will and testament states:

'First of all I give and bequeath unto my loving wife Frances all my personal estate and also the sum of thirty pounds in money to be paid her by my trustees herein named one year after my decease, like wise the sum of eight pounds yearly and every year during her natural life'.

It went on to list a number of payments to a variety of persons for monies owed. It then adds,

'Also to pay to each of my three daughters Sarah, Mary and Frances one year after my decease the sum of Ten pounds apiece – Also my will and desire is that my eldest son Willm be brought up a scholar and supported 'till he is fitt for holy Orders. And my son John to be put to a trade or Business such as by them my trustees and he shall be most agreeable to'.

Finally, as his estate is in trust to pay for all these items, he ensures that after the death of his wife,

'that as soon as convenient after the death of my said wife, the remaining part of my said estate after my just debts be duely paid, shall be equally divided amongst my children share and share alike'.

In order to pay for all these requests out of the estate, the trustees and their heirs are given the power to administer the estate. The money raised from renting the farm was presumably not sufficient to cover these costs as part of the estate had to be mortgaged to William Irwin in 1791.

A third type of Will not only lists a set of bequests but also details the relationship of each name. This is particularly useful to family historians in tracing their ancestors. An example of this is in the will of William Steele of Uldale dated 1824. A transcript of this was sent to Mr and Mrs Johnson (Yewcroft) from a person in Canada, researching the same Steele family tree, and it established that the ancestors they were struggling to find in the Harrington area of the county were in fact from this parish. In this will it states,

HOLLY

'I William Steele of Uldale in the parish of Haile in the county of Cumberland Yeoman being of sound and disposing mind and body . . . I give and bequeath unto my sons John Steel and Gerard Steel the sum of five pounds a piece . . . and bequeath to my Daughter Elizabeth wife of William Bewsher the sum of five pounds . . . I bequeath to my two grandchildren John Archer and William Archer . . .'.

The list continued and so from this one document three generations of the Steele family could be worked out.

THE SCHOOL

HAILE SCHOOL

If you visit our Village Hall you will see where the children of Haile and Wilton were educated between 1880 and 1955. The main hall was the schoolroom where often 30 to 40 children between the ages of 4 and 14 were taught all together in the early years by one Master or Mistress. By 1910 a partition was put up to meet with the regulations that infants must be taught in a separate room from the older pupils and an assistant teacher was employed. At this time there were 67 children in the school, 37 upper class and 30 infants.

A NEW BEGINNING

The present Village Hall in Haile began life in 1880 as Haile and Wilton School. The vicar had received a letter from the Education Department about the necessity of providing adequate school accommodation in response to Forster's Education Act. At this time there were growing numbers of children for whom parents were demanding an education, and Britain's industrial expansion needed growing numbers of educated employees. Decent schools for all children became a government priority. Voluntary schools were no longer adequate and existing schools were asked to elect a board to build and staff a school financed by an educational rate on the inhabitants. Because the church did not want a 'board school forced upon us' the vicar of Haile called a meeting of all parishioners and it was agreed that they would be willing to pay a voluntary rate towards providing a suitable school.

'Those who had canvassed the Parish since the last committee meeting had found that forty-four ratepayers had signed in favour of a voluntary rate and none in favour of a school board'.

Before this time education was mainly a private enterprise, many schools being run by the Church of England as was the case in Haile and Wilton. We know that there was a schoolroom on this site in 1859 from an original document on the *Rules and regulations for the better running of Hail School*. The Trustees were the vicar and churchwardens of

Schoolroom. A very accurate impression, drawn with the help of the memories of old pupils, of what it was like in the old village school.

Haile and Wilton and parishioners who had subscribed 'not less than 10 shillings annually'. Pupils paid fees dependent on what they wanted to learn. It was 7s. 6d. per quarter for reading, writing and arithmetic, or 4s. for reading only.

However, an even earlier reference to a school at Haile can be found in the manor records where one entry is headed;

'The Court Baron of John Ponsonby Esquire Lord of the Manor holden at Haile School House within the said manor on Tuesday 26th August 1755 before suitors of the said court'.

A statement of account from December 1807 mentions 'Straw for school £1.0.0. Thatching 5.0d'. Again, in December 1812 Jacob Dickinson was paid 6 shillings for further thatching work on the school.

A school had existed at Wilton on the site of the Gravel Pit and the Wilton reservoir. This was 'Built by Subscription A.D. 1806' as stated on the only remaining stone which is built into the perimeter wall of 'Greenfield' Wilton. In 1880 Wilton children began the long walk to the new school at Haile. An extract from the School Managers' Minutes Book says that Wilton school was advertised in the *Whitehaven News* and sold at public auction in 1881 to Dr Syme for £10 15s. As the ownership of the school could not be established by the trustees the advertisement included the warning phrase: 'Purchaser does so at his own risk'.

The new school at Haile was planned and built within a year and opened on 4th September 1880 by the vicar, the Rev. Robert Webster. The school was run by a management committee of the vicar and churchwardens and four ex officio members from Haile and Wilton elected annually. Payment for the Master and upkeep of the school was provided by subscriptions from the parish, pupils' fees and a small annual grant from the County which depended on attendance and good reports from school inspections.

Originally there were three fireplaces, one of which remains today at the far end of the room. The fires had to be lit each morning by the teacher or caretaker. Sticks for the fire, often donated by the Ponsonby family, were stored at the back of the school and coal was also used. Many children, having walked long distances to the school, would often arrive cold and wet and so had to dry their clothes by the

Haile school management rules and regulations. These rules applied to the older school which existed in 1859. Similar rules still applied at the new school which opened in 1880.

fire. Mary Gregg, who was at the school from 1925 to 1934, remembers the fires having a sturdy fireguard around each fire with three horizontal rods which would have been useful to dry clothes on. Where the present kitchen is was then the children's cloakroom with one entrance for the boys and one for the girls. The children's toilets, or 'offices' as they were called, were originally outside on the low part of the grounds next to the road through the village.

TEACHERS

The first master was a Mr Doughty appointed after answering an advertisement in the *Whitehaven News:*

> 'Wanted for new elementary school at Haile and Wilton, a certificated master for the school capable of accommodating 60 children. One able to take charge of the harmonium in church preferred'.

Mr Doughty was assisted by Agnes Brown who taught the girls sewing and knitting and was also the school cleaner. By the June of 1881, 43 children were attending aged between 5 and 14 years. The first year seemed to run smoothly. Mr Doughty reported to the school managers; 'I find the children very regular in attendance, painstaking in their work and altogether very docile'. He also commented that he had not yet had to resort to corporal punishment but would not hesitate to use it 'if absolutely necessary'! A year later he reports 'Order improved though whispering is not quite cured'.

The school hours were 9-12 in the morning and 2-4 in the afternoon with a 15 minute playtime morning and afternoon, during which the children played such games as netball, football, marbles, conkers, whip and top, skittles or hoop and stick. The boys' and girls' play areas were separate as were their entrances to the school. There is a note of some concern in the head teacher's comment of September 4th 1883:

> 'Boys' door lock out of order today. Am compelled to admit boys and girls at the same door until the lock is repaired.'

Homework was given for all.

Mr Doughty admits that keeping the children employed was somewhat difficult. His first purchase was a hand bell bought with money raised from the parishioners. Later a map of Cumberland and a globe were purchased as a result of the first HMI inspection. Another practical improvement was lighting and ventilation for the toilets and provision of a urinal for the boys.

Despite these gradual improvements it is clear that the conditions in and around the school were not up to the standards we would expect today. An early injury which was reported was a child cutting his head 'on one of the large boulders that cover our playground'.

Mr Doughty also started a night school, the purpose of which is not known; it was perhaps for the adult parishioners to learn the three 'R's.

Soon Mr Doughty warns of his intention to improve discipline;

> 'They (the pupils) must rise from their seats when answering a question, pay attention to their posture when sitting and whispering is now strictly forbidden'.

In January of the following year, 1881, an evening concert was held in the school which meant that the children had to assemble at 8 a.m so that they could be dismissed for the day at 12.15 to prepare for the concert. Imagine the cold, sleepy children walking maybe one or two miles to school on that dark January morning!

After three years Mr Doughty handed in his resignation. Twelve

Haile school. We have no date and no names suggested for this early photograph.

teachers followed him over the next 15 years, nine masters and three mistresses, some lasting less than a year. During this time the managers struggled to keep the school going. Masters and mistresses were chosen not because they were most suitable but because they were asking the least salary! Materials were very basic.

> 'The work of the children suffers through the use of cracked and badly ruled slates and of short, blunt pencils'.

This resulted in poor teaching and damning inspectors' reports. Masters and Mistresses were either dismissed because of incompetence or they handed in their notice because they were unable to cope with the difficult conditions. Nor were the parents always satisfied. A note from the school record, July 1897, states:

> 'Tom Harrington is reported left, because a mistress is to be appointed and his mother says "He wants a master to thrash him"'.

LEARNING

The school curriculum in the early days of Haile School was firmly based on the three Rs with perhaps some history and geography and visits by the vicar to teach scripture. At Haile school we know that sewing and knitting were taught, with the vicar's wife and the school cleaner both recorded as sewing mistresses. Also in 1892 the teaching of drawing was introduced with drawing schedules and an examination. The development of the school library service in 1909 was a great help to both teachers and pupils and reading books were delivered regularly from Carlisle.

In 1902 detailed schemes of work began to appear in the teacher's log book. The scheme of work of Miss Turner, who took over the school in 1904, shows that Haile and Wilton children would be learning: Arithmetic, English (grammar), History (places of interest in the district – by silent reading and stories for the younger ones), Geography, Physical drill ('simple exercises with dumb bells and wands') and Object lessons (e.g. 'a rivers journey', 'common trees', 'the earthworm – the farmer's friend'). It also included time for recitation, sewing, singing ('songs learnt by ear') and drawing.

The Education Act of 1918 made schooling compulsory, pupils no longer had to pay fees and schools were encouraged to provide a wider

Haile school. 1894(?) It is difficult to find the names of the children of so long ago but these few have been suggested. Front row, 4th from left – *Mary Logan.* Second row, from left, 4th – *Jack Mumberson,* 5th – *Joe Noble,* 6th – *Thai Mumberson.*

curriculum. The Local Education Authorities began to provide P.E. and games and establish schools or classes for practical subjects. For 2-3 years government money was spent on new developments in education, but then came the post-war slump and for the next 15 years there was very little money to put these plans into action.

For smaller schools like Haile School delivering the wider curriculum was a problem. Past pupils remember doing drill in their clogs in the school yard and in 1927 there is mention of 'the field nearest the school' being used for physical education. Netball posts were received from the County and netball matches against Beckermet, Gosforth and Drigg are mentioned. By 1935 the girls were taking domestic science, including cookery and washing, at the Gosforth Centre, opposite Gosforth village hall above what is now the hobby shop. The boys attended woodwork in Egremont. The girls went by bus, having to walk to the road end to catch it and the boys walked to Egremont. Not that these arrangements were without their difficulties as the following quotations from the teacher's log book show.

> 'Four boys set off for woodwork class but returned because they had left the register and pass on the porch window.'

> 'Post card arrived for girls to attend cookery at Gosforth but arrived too late for the morning session, so girls went for afternoon session and teacher had gone. They walked back to Calderbridge, then caught the bus and then walked to Haile'.

Some of them would then have a good walk home!

INSPECTIONS

Inspections were a regular part of school life. The following excerpts from Inspectors reports clearly show the ups and downs of Haile School. In 1891

> 'The children were listless and show little interest in their work. The attainments have seriously fallen off. Grammar and geography are almost worthless and the infants appear to have been neglected'.

Again in 1901 we learn that

> 'The discipline, tone and organisation are at present defective. A firmer discipline, including much greater smartness, must first be established. This must be accomplished by systematic training and not by harsh methods of compulsion . . . The desks almost fell to pieces when moved'.

A further report in 1904 found the school with

> '. . . Much to be desired. Floor worn/uneven. Inadequate cleaning. Boys yard littered with iron desk legs, iron weights, roof slates and wire'.

However, after 1904 and the arrival of

Miss Turner, who took charge for the next 38½ years, standards saw a gradual improvement.

So it was that in 1912 it is reported that:

> 'The pupils are alert and well behaved. They apply themselves to work with a cheerful vigour, and not only answer questions correctly, but at times volunteer sensible remarks of their own'.

The following year the teacher is congratulated on

> '. . . a very well conducted school. The premises are conspicuously clean and well kept, and the behaviour of the children and their attitude towards their work are equally satisfactory'.

The children are again praised in 1914:

> 'The written work of the children is particularly well done and supervised, and the children are ready to discuss their work orally, even in the Babies' class'.

The inspectors' reports also give us some insight into characteristics of

Haile school. 1924. Among the few names suggested here are: Back row, left to right. *Miss Turner, standing.* 4. Robert Bowe. 6. John Coles. 8. Walt Logan. *Miss Patrickson standing.* Second row down. *2. Annie Coles. 12. Grace Noble.* Third row down. *1. Annie Holywell. 3. Esther Cole. 5. Molly Spedding. 9. Enid Bowe. 11. Alice Harrington.* Front row. *3. Isaac Bowe. 5. Arthur Poole. 6. Frank Spedding.*

the Haile and Wilton scholars and the isolated nature of their life in the village.

'The children have little knowledge of things outside their village and the teaching of English is consequently difficult' (1913).

'An unusual feature in this school is the natural way in which children ask for information' (1919).

'There are one or two here who would undoubtedly benefit from a secondary education, but Whitehaven is very inaccessible and attendance there necessitates ten hours away from home' (1919).

NOT AT SCHOOL BECAUSE . . .

From the beginning school registers were completed every day and had to be inspected regularly by the managers. Attendance at the school was important, not just for the children's learning but because the annual grant depended on good attendance. It was a great worry to all the teachers, especially when there were many good excuses for absence, for example storms, wet weather, snow, haymaking, harvest, threshing, potato picking and helping at home. Even if you arrived at school but were late you could not be given a mark, which maybe explains the teachers' determination to encourage punctuality. The experience in the early 1940s of a boy who lived at Grange, about two miles from the school, illustrates the effectiveness of this incentive:

'We used to run it because we had to do our work (at home) in the mornings, and if we were five minutes late we used to get the stick. Roger Bannister used to – what is it? – the four minute mile. We did it years ago!'.

The pupils had annual holidays for church feast days, Empire Day, Trafalgar Day and, later, Armistice day. There were other official closures of the school, usually for half a day, and the reasons for these were many and varied. They included: farm sales, the annual hunt, induction of the vicar, vicarage garden fête, funerals of local dignitaries, Gosforth show, circus in Egremont, children's gala in Egremont and Royal marriages, funerals, coronations and visits. A holiday was recorded in 1908 for a 'Boundary perambulation of the Manor of Beckermet by Sir Humphrey le Fleming, Lord of the Manor'. In 1939 an unusual event occasioned a loss of a holiday as a result of the official school year beginning on April 1st.

'Today school closed for Whitsuntide holiday – two days instead of the customary three – because of two Easters falling in one school year'.

Other half days were earned: an attendance of above 94% for four consecutive weeks entitled the children to another half-day holiday.

Illness was a common reason given for absence. The first closure of the school was due to an outbreak of measles in May 1891 and lasted one week. Over the following years the school was closed because of the very contagious diseases mumps, whooping cough and diphtheria. Not that parents always attached the same importance to such illnesses; in about 1932, Harold Wilson recalls:

'They sent me back from school with mumps. When I got back home my Dad sent me out with two horses and the old wooden plough, to plough'.

It seems, then, that attendance was a problem from the start. During his first year Mr Doughty reported the attendance to be 'desultory' and later in the year attendance was 'wretchedly uneven'. Attempts were made to improve attendance but seemingly with little success. In 1884 Mr Dalby, the Master, records that the local 'School Attendance Committee' are,

'altogether a dead letter as far as the school is concerned. The children come to school or stay away as they or their parents choose'.

Every effort was made by County to keep attendance at a high level and a challenge shield inscribed: 'With head, with heart, with hand we work for Cumberland' was presented to the school with the best attendance record. There is no record of Haile school ever receiving this accolade!

It may be surprising to us today, when transport to school can be by bus or car, how much the weather could affect attendance. The distances that children had to walk – sometimes up to three miles – to get to school had a noticeable effect on attendance when the weather was bad. The occasional problem with heavy snow, such as in January 1940 when the snow was 'level with the hedges', resulted, as it would now, in much absence. On that occasion only three children managed to get to school. Not even the home-knitted socks and extra straw put in the clogs were any protection against such severe conditions. But rain, often described as stormy, even in mid-summer, often resulted in low attendance. Attendance affected by storms and heavy rain is mentioned dozens of times throughout the school's history. Because of a storm in June 1939 the girls were unable to get to the bus to go for cookery lessons and attended school instead. The boys were unable to attend woodwork at Egremont for the same reason, but decided not to attend school either!

There is a story that Frank Spedding, who as a lad attended Haile School in about 1930 and who lived then at Simon Kell, about two and a half miles away, was told by his mother that if it began to rain he was to turn back. There were reputed to be occasions when Frank had already walked all but the last hundred yards before it began to

rain, but that didn't stop him turning tail and going back home.

Nevertheless there were periods when attendance was good and these were celebrated. The school log book records that prizes were first awarded to the pupils in August 1881 for good attendance. Later, medals were distributed to all pupils with perfect attendance. In 1912 excellent attendance was rewarded with a special presentation of a picture of King George V. How the children must have appreciated that!

War time

The two world wars had their impact on the school, as they had on all aspects of society. The children at Haile School were very much part of the 'war effort' during both world wars, though there seems to have been much more active involvement in helping the war effort during the first war. In that first war the log book relates that the children were knitting socks for the soldiers on the front. They also had a collection for the Overseas club in order to 'send comfort and happiness to soldiers and sailors'. It is told how the children brought in eggs for wounded soldiers. On another occasion the children picked and despatched 145 lbs of blackberries towards the war effort. The school was used for a whist drive and dance on behalf of the military hospital at Moresby and later on there was entertainment in the school on behalf of the YMCA Army huts.

Perhaps the major contribution of the school in the second world war was to take in, as many country schools did, evacuees from the towns under threat from bombing. The log book during the second war relates a good deal about the arrival of refugees, mainly from the North East. In September 1939 at the start of the new term sixteen evacuees, mainly from Newcastle, were admitted with their teacher, Miss Herdman. They were taught mainly by their own teacher though three of the older children and some mid-aged children were taught by the Haile teacher, Miss Turner, 'to facilitate matters of instruction'. The school roll became 27 local pupils and 16 evacuees, including one private evacuee from Bedford. We can imagine the buzz of excitement in that small school as these extra children and their teacher adjusted to the routines and life of the school. In the following year there was more coming and going with evacuees, some

Haile school. 1928. Back row, left to right. *1. Colin Campbell. 2. Sam Bowness. 3. Walter Logan. 4. Arthur Poole. 5. Arthur Powe. 6. Billy Tyson. 7. Robert Bowe.* Second row down, left to right. *1. Rene Moffat. 2. Annie Coles. 3. Eleanor Wallace. 4. Jean Moffat. 5. Molly Spedding. 6. Alice Harrington. 7. Betty Bowes. 8. Nora Spedding. 9. Isobel Tyson. 10. Agnes Wallace. 11. Dorothy Logan* Third row down, left to right. *1. Bobby Moffatt. 2. Nora Bell. 3. Sarah Wallace. 4. Mary Harrington. 5. Hilda Clark. 6 .Mary Mumberson. 7.? Bell. 8. Mary Mounsey. 9. Esther Coles. 10. Florrie Logan.* Front row, left to right. *1. Frank Spedding. 2. Gilbert Bowness. 3. Wilf Bowe. 4. John Coles. 5. Harold Wilson. 6. Eddie Raven. 7. Jack Raven.*

arriving from Leeds, others moving on to Egremont and others returning home.

There was still the 'war effort'. There was a collection in 1941 of Christmas gifts for soldiers, and during a weapons week in 1942 the school collected £160 5s.

CHURCH AND SCHOOL

Because the school was a church school, the vicar was usually the Chairman of the School Managers' committee, and the two churchwardens were also on the committee. The committee was a powerful body responsible for appointment of the schoolteachers and the upkeep of the building. What is more, the teachers were required to defer to the committee for all aspects relating to the running of the school and any materials needed. There was no doubt, also, that the vicar had a great influence on the school. It was usual for the vicar to go into school each week to give religious instruction to the scholars and the school was inspected regularly on scripture by the church dioceses. In 1910 a report on religious instruction by the Diocesan Inspector states:

> 'The lower classes have been carefully and suitably taught. The right method had been adopted to render the children free and responsive. The higher division showed pleasing interest and reverence'.

This influence of the church is reflected in the fact that the children were given time off school for church feast days or to attend parishioners' funerals. The church also had the right to the use of the building any time when the school was not open. Sunday school was held each week in the school room. Not that the children necessarily shared the enthusiasm of the church for its involvement in their education. While a woman, who was a girl in the 1930s, praised it rather faintly thus:

> 'You had morning service, Sunday school and evening service, which we didn't miss. It was our only way out wasn't it? Unless you were going somewhere, which wasn't often',

a man, who was a boy at about the same time, commented rather more assertively:

> 'I did go to Sunday school but not very much, I didn't. I couldn't

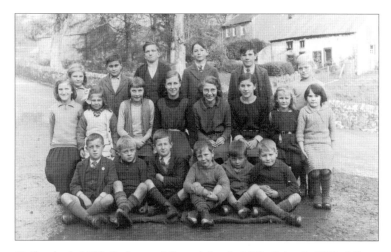

Haile school. 1932. Back row, left to right. *1. Milly Coles. 2. Wilfred Bowe. 3. John Coles. 4. Harold Wilson. 5. William Walker. 6. Sarah Wightman.* Second row down, left to right. *1. Esther Coles. 2. Violet Newby. 3. Rene Moffatt. 4. Dorothy Logan. 5. Hilda Clark. 6. Mary Mumberson. 7. Florrie Logan. 8. Connie Walker.* Front row, left to right. *1. Joe Mumberson. 2. Sam Wightman. 3. William Sherwen. 4. James Coles. 5. Robert Moffatt. 6. Jack Wightman.*

git away with it . . . ordinary day school, five days a week, was plenty'.

Another found a different way of passing the time when in church:

> 'I can remember having monkey nuts. We sat behind Grandda in church and we would peel these monkey nuts, eat them and put the shells in his pocket and when he came out he used to stand at the door and just empty them'.

Nor was the church's involvement always stern and forbidding. In January 1892 the *Whitehaven News* reported:

> **'Haile Sunday School treat** – The annual tea and treat to the Sunday School Children was held in the above schoolroom, on Thursday evening. With one exception all the scholars attended and evidently enjoyed the good things provided, which were served out by Mrs Cooper, who had the able assistance of Miss Braithwaite and Miss Wilson. After tea Miss Ethel Cooper recited "Cinderella and the glass slippers", subsequently the

children had games. The vicar, Rev. A. H. Cooper distributed the presents which consisted of knives, balls, dolls and bound copies of *Home Words*. Each child also received from Mrs Cooper a packet of sweets and an orange, a handful of nuts and a Christmas card'.

During its existence many people and organisations had an influence on the school: the people who paid to send their children in the early days; the teachers; inspectors; the management committee; local dignitaries and the church. It was a vicar who wrote of a rather less-than-successful teacher:

'Especially would I warn them (teachers) against occupying themselves in Parish concerns outside their own Scholastic responsibilities and Ecclesiastical duties . . . Had our late master

Haile school. 1937. Back row, left to right. *1. Jimmy Coles. 2. Joe Mumberson. 3. Sam Wightman. 4. William Trohear. 5. Eddie Raven. 6. Jack (?) Raven. 7. John Poole.* Second row down, left to right. *1. Milly Coles. 2. Elsie Wightman. 3. Dorothy Harrison 4. Dorothy Taylor. 5. Annie Wallace. 6. Connie Walker. 7. Violet Newby. 8. Florrie Harrison. 9. Florrie Logan. 10. Jean Fisher. 11. Vera Graham. 12. Sarah Wightman.* Third row down, left to right. *1. Walter Newby. 2. Jessie Coles. 3. Rhoda Harrison. 4. Eleanor Sanderson. 5. Dorothy Crank. 6. Harold Graham.* Front row, left to right. *1. Edward Poole. 2. John Mumberson. 3. John Roper. 4. Jack Wightman. 5. George Coles. 6. Harold Poole.*

minded his own business more, and forsaking an absurd mock championship of imaginary popular wrongs left others to mind theirs, there would not be remaining in Haile so many violent letters in his handwriting as well as unpleasant recollections which I will do him the justice to believe he must now and henceforward think of with a burning and ever deepening regret'. So there!

By 1955 the school was declared too small to meet the demands of modern educational thinking and was closed on 22nd July that year. From the early years of the twentieth century until its closure, despite further financial problems, the depression and two world wars, the school enjoyed a long period of stability, thanks mainly to the efforts of their longest-serving headmistress, Miss Turner.

MISS TURNER

5th April 1904 – 'I Elizabeth Turner took charge of the school this morning with 34 scholars present. The work of the school is not able to be done properly, owing to lack of materials; those ordered having not arrived yet but are expected daily'.

Miss Turner, a young certificated teacher, 24 years old, with little teaching experience was appointed as headmistress of Haile School by the school managers at a low time for the school, after a run of poor teachers, severe criticisms by school inspectors, a lack of basic materials and with the school fabric in poor condition. There was, for instance, no proper lavatory accommodation and it was only in 1910 that, because the Education Committee objected to the cesspit in the playground, it was decided to apply for a water supply to the school. It was 1912 before the new toilets were installed. Other improvements that were introduced at the beginning of the twentieth century were the installation, in 1910, of a glass and wood folding partition required to separate the older class from the younger, and, in 1913, the replacement of the decayed joists and floor.

At first Miss Turner cycled to school from her home in Gosforth until she moved with her parents to a new house in Haile which they called 'Ellerslie' after the row of cottages where they had lived in Gosforth. We were told by a one-time scholar how the children had gardening lessons, which consisted of going down the road to Ellerslie to dig out the weeds and tidy the garden. On one occasion a mischievous child decided that he would pull out the carrots instead!

Pupils who were at the school in the late 1930s remember that playtime was supervised by Miss Turner, described by them as an excellent teacher, firm and fair but with very little sense of humour. Supervision involved walking about with stick in hand! By then the lunch break lasted only 60 minutes during which those pupils who lived too far away had their sandwiches and were provided with a cup of tea for a penny per week. Mary Gregg remembers having the job of collecting the milk for this from Orchard Brow every morning on her way to school.

Sampler made at Haile school. This sampler was made in 1863 by Anne Walton who then lived at Brayshaw.

Much of what we know of Miss Turner comes from her entries in the school log book; comments from school inspections; her correspondence with the school managers; and from memories of some of those who were children under her care in her later years. We are presented with a picture of a tall slim woman with a quite stern expression and clothed from head to toe in black. She would always have her cane at hand 'around a yard long with a curved hook at one end'. When she went out into the yard with her cane and blew the whistle for the children to come in, they soon had their coats off and were back at their desks! Some claim that the cane was not used frequently; it was enough to have it there as a warning – 'You did what you were told in those days'. Other ex-pupils have vivid memories of that cane causing red marks across their hands or pain across their shoulders, sometimes for what the pupils, at least, thought were minor misdemeanors!

Anne Walton.

There is no doubt that Miss Turner was a dedicated teacher throughout all those years who must have performed what seemed to be a Herculean task in the early years. There is frequent mention in the school managers' minute book of her letters pointing out much-needed repairs and requesting improvements to the fabric of the school and for essential materials for teaching the children. It was not long before new desks were being delivered, detailed schemes of work appeared in the log book, and quarterly examinations of the whole school were initiated. Glowing reports on religious instruction in 1916/17 tell us that,

'Miss Turner is clearly doing excellent work in the school. The tone, atmosphere, and discipline are worthy of the highest praise . . . The school easily retains its excellent standard of tone and scholarship and it is impossible to praise too highly, the indefatigable labours of the Headmistress, Miss Turner'. It is noted how she 'invariably overcomes difficulties'.

Was Miss Turner liked by the children? Personal memories of her in her later years show her to be strict and unapproachable, 'firm but fair'. However from school reports over the years it seems that the children were enjoying their schooling. There are references to 'enthusiastic' children, infants showing a 'highly responsive manner with no trace of shyness or reserve'. On other occasions it was said that the children 'expressed themselves in the happiest spirit'. There was 'evident enjoyment' and 'lively interest'.

Haile school. 1939/40. Back row, left to right. *1. Harold Poole. 2. Jack Wightman. 3. Jimmy (?) Coles. 4. John Poole. 5. James Wightman. 6. John Roper. 7. Sam Wightman.* Second row down, left to right. *1. Eleanor Sanderson. 2. Jean Fisher. 3. Dorothy Harrison. 4. Violet Newby. 5. Florrie Logan. 6. Elsie Wightman. 7. Vera Graham. 8. Jessie Coles.* Third row down, left to right. *1. Edward Poole. 2. Mary Wightman. 3. Dorothy Crank. 4. Mary Jackson. 5. Walter Newby. 6. Lawrence Graham.* Front row, left to right. *1. Tom Poole. 2. John Mumberson. 3. Derek Taylor. 4. Harold Graham.*

After 38 years of a career dedicated to teaching the children of Haile and Wilton Miss Turner resigned her post. She wanted no fuss when she finished, but a house to house collection raised £22. 13s. 0d. which was presented to her to

'serve as a reminder, from the parents, scholars past and present, parishioners of Haile and friends, of their appreciation of your long and valuable service'.

She enjoyed a lengthy retirement before she died in March 1963, aged 83 years. Her grave stone can clearly be seen in Haile Churchyard.

FROM SCHOOL TO VILLAGE HALL

When the school finally closed in 1955 Haile Church became the responsible authority for maintenance and repair of the building. As the church was already struggling with its own finances and upkeep, the school became an extra burden.

Until 1970 the building was referred to as 'the school' in Haile Church minutes and the charge for hiring the premises was £1. 10 shillings. It was used by the hunt committee for whist drives and dances to fund the annual children's outing and party, and the occasional slide show was arranged. The 'School Restoration Fund' was referred to in the minutes.

Later in that year Archdeacon Hardie was licensed at Haile Church followed by a buffet in what had now become the 'Church Hall'. It was a grand occasion with all parishioners invited as was a coach full of people from Rev. Hardie's previous parish in Hexham. A very embarrassing episode, still remembered, was after the refreshments, when the visitors asked for the whereabouts of the toilet facilities. There was no 'powder room' available in our Church Hall but the helpful locals gave them two options: to visit the bramble bushes at the rear of the hall; or to walk through the pub (The Buck's Head) into the rear garden, pass the open urinal and ascend the steps to the top of the garden whereupon they would find a small 'privy', although one without electric light. We can only wonder which was the preferred option!

The Archdeacon called for urgent action to provide decent kitchen and toilet facilities and volunteers were sought to help with painting and repairs. Fundraising began and the availability of grants was explored, though with little success. In March 1973 a meeting was held to discuss the school's future. The decorating had been done but more work was needed. The care of the school grounds was discussed as was the need for tables and chairs, which were eventually purchased.

In August 1974 the school became the Village Hall after the Carlisle Diocesan Board conveyed the land and building to be held in trust for the inhabitants of the parish, 'including use for meetings lectures and classes and for other forms of recreation and leisure time occupation, with the object of improving the condition of life for the said inhabitants'.

The Board would no doubt be delighted to see the changes and improvement that have taken place over the last 30 years and that the 'said inhabitants' of all ages do indeed enjoy many forms of recreation, leisure time, meetings and lectures in the same school building.

DOG'S MERCURY

In 1979 the Village Hall became a registered charity and in October 1998 the land was vested in the Official Custodian for Charities.

The first Haile Village Hall Committee meeting was held on 17th September 1974 and over the next 30 years a gradual transformation has occurred. First the school cloakroom and boys' and girls' entrances became the kitchen, and a small extension provided the much needed toilets. An opening party was held in May 1976 with the committee providing a buffet.

Over the following years many events and activities were enjoyed. There were whist drives, cookery demonstrations, slide shows, handicrafts and wine making, youth clubs, Haile Homemakers and a gardening club to name but a few. For a number of years an annual bonfire, Christmas parties and the summer barbecues took place. The competitive nature of the parish came to a head in the Wilton v Haile rounders and football matches!

The Mother and Toddler Group first met in 1979 and has run continuously since then. Haile Playgroup followed in 1980 as the children 'graduated' from the toddlers group and, remarkably, it has been available to and enjoyed by the children of the parish and many children from outside the parish without a break for the last 23 years. The group continues to flourish.

Storage of equipment became a problem and in 1981 a wooden hut was built at the back of the hall, an extension to the hall having been considered but proving to be too costly. In the early 1990s the building was deteriorating and badly in need of repair and improvements. The income was not sufficient to cover such expenses. Support was sought from local companies and Copeland Council which resulted in repairs to the roof, new windows and central heating.

In 1997 the committee was encouraged to think again about a much needed extension to the building and to make it a millennium project. Invaluable help from Voluntary Action Cumbria was received and applications to the National Lotteries, the Countryside Agency and other charitable trusts were made. Fund raising began in earnest. Building work took place over July and August 1999 providing new storage space and an entrance hall and toilets with full disabled access.

More advice from V.A.C. led the committee to embark on phase two; replacing the old floor and removing the suspended ceiling to reveal the original roof beams, now cleaned and treated for woodworm. The kitchen was refurbished and new chairs and tables were purchased. Finally the car park was newly surfaced.

The first newsletter for Haile Village Hall was printed in May 1999 and continues to be produced by volunteers and distributed to all households in the parish two or three times a year.

The grand relaunch of Haile Village Hall was held on 20th January 2001 – people of the two villages packed the hall to see what had been done and to enjoy the buffet and wine. Everyone who had contributed with advice, help and financing was invited.

Unfortunately events were soon suspended as the outbreak of 'foot and mouth' took a hold, devastating Cumbria and much of the rest of the country.

Commencing again in September 2001 the Rural Touring Scheme was embraced by the committee. Sponsored by Copeland Borough Council and the Arts Council the scheme offers the opportunity for professional entertainment in rural village halls. The parish and beyond is now treated to a varied programme of theatre and music which attracts all age groups and has been an astounding success.

The biggest recent event to take place was in June 2002 when Haile and Wilton celebrated the Queen's Jubilee with sports for the children, cream teas and afterwards a grand barbecue. The village hall was bedecked with red, white and blue and people sat outside listening to Egremont Town Band playing in the sunshine.

The village hall continues to be well patronised for all events and is used by several groups including playgroup and mother and toddler groups, young farmers, the local history group and private parties. Haile and Wilton now has its own website.

Haile village hall was described in 'Egremont Today' as 'a stylish base for a thriving village community' which sums up the now modernised building which still retains much of its original character and sense of history.

The Queen's Golden Jubilee Celebrations at Haile Village Hall, June 2002.

MORE WAYS OF LIFE

ADJUSTING TO TWENTIETH CENTURY LIFE

'It was the only house with no electricity and old Mrs. Walker didn't want electricity because she thought the house was so draughty that the lights would blow out – the electric light'.

'Albert had been a genius with horses but it took some getting used to when the milk started being collected with lorries. When he was driving the lorry, there's many a time when he's ended up off the road because it didn't stop when he said "Whoa"'.

'Who used to shut their eyes when they got their photograph taken? Yan of 'em did.

Tell me why she shut her eyes.

'It was Mary.

You think it was Mary?

'Yan o' 'em shut their eyes an' then she thought she wouldn't be on it'.

Turnip snagger. When did a turnip need snagging?[8.]

HAILE AND WILTON MOTHERS' UNION

Our Mothers' Union was founded in 1938 and the vicar at the time was a Mr Berry. Among the founder members were Lady Mary Ponsonby of Haile Hall and Mrs Ruth Lace of Calderbridge, the local butcher's wife.

For many years, Mrs Lace and Mrs Jenkinson, another founding member, walked from Calderbridge to Haile for the meetings once a month, there being no transport in those early days. Mrs Lace was ninety-four when she died, and to my knowledge never missed a meeting. Her stamina was reflected again in the fact that she was both Secretary and Treasurer for 45 years, from the founding of our Mothers' Union until 1983.

Our membership never seemed to go much above twenty, but that did not stop us from following the normal pattern of meetings that were associated with the Mothers' Union – a short prayer meeting led by the vicar, followed, usually, by a talk by a visiting speaker. And then a Haile home-made tea!

'We all had our little thing, you see, that we took. We always had a tea afterwards. I took drop scones . . . Mrs Raven from Blackbeck – she was a stalwart – she used to make a big fruit cake.'

Visiting members from other parishes always raved about the food provided. Haile, seemingly at all its events, has a reputation for its teas.

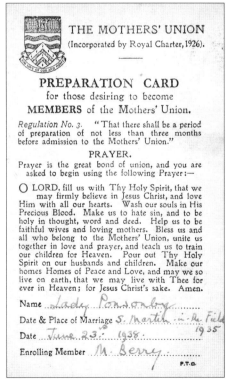

THE MOTHERS' UNION
(Incorporated by Royal Charter, 1926).

PREPARATION CARD
for those desiring to become
MEMBERS of the Mothers' Union.

Regulation No. 3. "That there shall be a period of preparation of not less than three months before admission to the Mothers' Union."

PRAYER.
Prayer is the great bond of union, and you are asked to begin using the following Prayer:—

O LORD, fill us with Thy Holy Spirit, that we may firmly believe in Jesus Christ, and love Him with all our hearts. Wash our souls in His Precious Blood. Make us to hate sin, and to be holy in thought, word and deed. Help us to be faithful wives and loving mothers. Bless us and all who belong to the Mothers' Union, unite us together in love and prayer, and teach us to train our children for Heaven. Pour out Thy Holy Spirit on our husbands and children. Make our homes Homes of Peace and Love, and may we so live on earth, that we may live with Thee for ever in Heaven; for Jesus Christ's sake. Amen.

Name *Lady Ponsonby*
Date & Place of Marriage *S. Martin in the Field 1935*
Date *June 23: 1938:*
Enrolling Member *M. Berry.*

P.T.O.

Lady Ponsonby's preparation card.

The Mothers' Union meet at Haile Hall. This was an annual and much-looked-forward-to event.

Afternoon tea. Tea was always an occasion at the Hall.

In the library. The business meeting took place in the library of Haile Hall.

Part of the Hall gardens. The meeting at the Hall always ended with a walk round the gardens.

The highlight of the year's meetings was always the June meeting held at Haile Hall because of two things especially; the tea, of course, which was a feast, and the walk afterwards around the beautiful gardens.

We arranged other events and visits to places like Muncaster Castle, Wordsworth House and Hutton-in-the-Forest. Our other activities included the annual charity effort and, meeting the needs of the time, the Sewing Party efforts during the last war.

1988 was the year we celebrated our Golden Jubilee. On 5th July

---

HAILE MOTHERS' UNION SEWING PARTY.

Affiliated to Central Hospital Supply Service,
Red Cross and St. John War Organization.

Sept. 3rd, 1939, to Sept., 1945.

———

The following is a list of work done for the Red Cross Hospital Supply Service by Mothers' Union members and friends in Haile :—Shirts, 216 ; Pyjamas, 86 pairs ; Bedjackets, 77 ; Vests and Knickers, 10 sets ; Dorothy Bags, 400 ; Operation Blankets, 6 ; Blouses, 120 ; Mattress, 1 ; Patchwork Quilt, 1.

Scarves, 105 ; Gloves, 133 pairs ; Helmets, 77 ; Socks, 52 pairs ; Vests (knitted), 55 ; Bedsocks, 65 pairs ; Pullovers, 58 ; Hot Water Bottle Covers, 20. Children's Knitted Garments, 90.

Also 52 Garments for children, made from pieces.

Total Articles made—978 Sewn Garments.
635 Knitted Garments.
———
TOTAL. ... 1,613
———

N.B.—Total number of Garments made to order and sent to C.H.S.S. from six Working Parties in West Cumberland, 8,878.

Sewing party. This document illustrates what was done as part of the 'war effort' by members of the Mother's Union.

we invited two members from each parish Mothers' Union in the district and two members from our link Mothers' Union in Holme, to a commemorative service in the church, attended by Mrs Joan Stannard, Diocesan President and her husband, Rev. Stannard. Afterwards they were our guests at a buffet lunch in the village hall, when Egremont parish presented us with a cut-glass crystal vase and Holme Mothers' Union presented us with a photo album, in which to keep a record of our mementos.

It was quite an occasion and we were lucky to have three of the founder members still with us to help celebrate. Perhaps such longevity results from the Haile teas!

We Take Water For Granted

This parish is one of those places where you can trace your water supply, if you really want to, by going for a walk. Manchester folk would have a much longer journey to make.

You can even see elements of the history of the provision of water in the parish without looking too far. Of course both Haile and Wilton relied for generations on spring and well water and if you ask around you will be shown where the old wells and springs were.

The beginning of the twentieth century saw the demands for water in the surrounding area, such as Beckermet and Egremont, increasing. Egremont, as early as the 1880s, had a desperate water supply problem, so much so that the 'Skirting Beck' which runs round the castle mound was nicknamed 'Skitter Beck'. The properties in Haile and Wilton, however, with a few exceptions, had an adequate water supply. Some properties in Wilton had their own supply and others were supplied by an old reservoir fed by springs at Castley Hill. In Haile seven houses were within 60 yards of the parish well and four were within 20 yards. So that was no great inconvenience then. Thus, when it was suggested that Haile ought to be part of the proposed Southern District Water Supply getting mains water from Gosforth, the idea was rejected. Anyway, it was too expensive.

The springs at Castley Hill, by Cold Fell gate, which were within the Haile Hall estate, already supplied water to Brayshaw, Head of

Haile and even across the valley to Whitehow Head. It was suggested that if three or four gathering wells were sunk there it could also be used to supplement the supply to the people of Beckermet. Negotiations with Haile Hall resulted in the scheme going ahead. The Hall itself, which up till now had drawn its water from the Parks above the Hall, decided that it needed more water, and so benefited from free taps and fittings and free water. It also received an annual rent of £30.

The demand for water continued to increase and in about 1910 navvies could be seen digging trenches for a water supply from Worm Gill where the surrounding fells could provide water in plenty. You can still see the take-off point if you walk up Worm Gill heading up

Worm Gill. The inlet for the Haile and Wilton water supply.

towards Lank Rigg. The iron pipes ran to a service reservoir at Wilton on the site of the demolished Wilton school, though only after some years of wrangling about how much the parish council should be paid for the site. From this reservoir at Wilton the water was piped through Grange to Egremont and through Haile to Beckermet. So at last Haile joined those people who could get water from a convenient tap. You may notice something missing in this arrangement: Wilton, perhaps because it consisted only of eight farms and a smallholding, was not included. So the folk of Wilton had to manage with their old supply of spring water for a little longer; well, up to the 1950s actually. (Or was it that they were still not prepared to pay?)

Now we all have mains water which in recent years seems to have come from Worm Gill (not the most hygienic sounding name when you think of it), Ennerdale and possibly elsewhere for all we know. A new plastic main has been laid, the iron pipes have been lined with plastic, the water complies with the hygiene health standards laid down by the E.E.C. (who else?) and we are plunged, so to speak, into the twenty-first century.

Butching knife. Why is the knife tapered?[9.]

MONEY

'We had a penny a week pocket money. We had a halfpenny on Mondays and a halfpenny on Thursdays and the things that we could buy with that halfpenny. We could get four golden charms, which were chocolate-coated caramels, or five silver links which were just plain toffee, and Mrs. Hale must have had the patience of Job because we had this halfpenny and we would be there making our minds up what to have. And if anybody gave you sixpence, well, I mean, that was great, you were as rich as Croesus. It was great'.

'But I used to collect this hospital money. I don't know if I went once every month or once every three months. That was a lightener in the day, you know, going round to other people's houses and having the crack. I've forgotten how much it was, tuppence a week or something but it did entitle the people in that household to have free hospital care. But of course they still had to pay for their doctors'.

'But I remember Joe Noble telling me that he used to go to Egremont and he had threepence, a penny for the pictures and a penny for fish and chips and a penny for a drink of some sort. I mean he would get his fish and chips and a drink for tuppence and it was a penny for the pictures'.

'Butter was med on about Tuesday or Wednesday ready for Thursday morning to go to Whitehaven market. We used to stand in the market at Whitehaven on and off for about sixpence a pound, tenpence and a shilling that's about what price butter was. Eggs the same, you know, tenpence a dozen. That was how they made their living.'

'Well, lambs went to the auction. They'd be taken to the auction with horse and spring cart for a few shillings each – not pounds, a few

Haile church interior. Before the days of the car people would always walk to church, and thought nothing of walking from Blackbeck or from even further afield.

shillings. Same way with a cow. A good fat cow would mek about twelve pound, like a butcher's cow. Twelve pound each maybe, summat like that. That's going back in the early 50s.'

WALKING EVERYWHERE

'We would walk to Ennerdale – it was quite a way (six miles). We must have been off soon on a Sunday morning because when we got to Aunty Mary's at Lane Foot she would be just having her breakfast. We would have had ours, but anyway we'd have some more. And then we would walk on to Aunty Sarah's which was another mile further on up by the lake, and then we'd walk back at night, likely'.

'All the stock was walked – we set off in the morning and walked to Whitehaven auction (about seven miles)'.

Alice Logan demonstrates her control of the hound. Alice, together with her husband, did occasional work at Town End in the 1930s. As with so many others who had lost their jobs in the Depression, the Logans were happy to come to work on the farm whenever they could, to help make ends meet.

'On Good Friday Jean and friends used to walk (about three miles) to Stakes Bridge, over the Calder above Calderbridge, for a picnic and to collect daffodils and watercress'.

'Ghyll Farm. *(About 3 miles)* 'E used to come up on to t'road and walk all t'way alang road till Cold Fell gate, round and down there, an' 'e was seven year old when 'e come t'Gyhll . . . 'Is father fetched 'im in t'oss and cart two mornins . . . Very seldom, 'e got a lift an' 'e walked it back at night. An' many a time, 'e said, at winter it was black dark when 'e got yam. Aye, it was a lang way to ga. If it was a wet mornin' 'e walked round bi t'road and if it was a real dry time 'e just cut across field.'

Clearing the snow just outside the village. 1940. 'I can remember going to school – it was at Whicham then – in 1940 when it snowed, and the snow was that high we had to git hod of the telephone wires as a hand-rail, like.'

William Dawson of Egremont was head gardener at Irton Hall and he cycled daily from Egremont to work. During the snow of 1940, however, there was no way he could make it, but his employers insisted that he could have got there if he'd tried. So it was that he handed in his notice and bought the three greenhouses which had been built four years before within the parish at Blackbeck, at what is still known as Nursery Corner. Later his nephew, Mr Jenkinson of Egremont, bought the greenhouses to produce flowers and vegetables for his shop.

WORLD WAR TWO

'The Potato Marketing Board was formed during these war years and each farm was given a stipulated acreage to plant with potatoes'.

'When the war . . . everything was blacked out. We used to carry a lamp about on the farm. We had to put it in a little box. It had little holes in to let you see where you were going'.

'Yes in them days everything was home-made. Until the war started and they had the coupons, and for what you were getting your bread for off the Co-op shop car, you couldn't get sufficient flour to make it. So that's why you bought the bread in them days. It was taking more coupons to get the flour than what you had for bread'.

'War was there looking at you and it was a seven day week wukking on the farm 'cos there wus all that much extra ploughing and ivvery day life come and you had to do, and it kept you going all the time. There's a lot of lads round here had to do just the same. You daren't set off of a night anywhere 'cos it was all blacked out. If you had a bicycle with a light on it, it only hed to be about half a crown size.'

'Maybe you were harvesting away through the day and it would git to night and you were still working out on top of a corn stack, int' dark like. You'd maybe be lucky if the moon was shining summat like that.'

THE EVACUEE

On the first day of September, 1939 Wilfred and Ethel Trohear went to Gosforth Agricultural Show. When they returned home they found two little boys sitting on the settee in their kitchen. During August

Norman Sherwen and an evacuee family. As did others, the Sherwens took in evacuees at the beginning of the war. These two children and their mother stayed with the Sherwens in the gatehouse of Haile Hall.

Council officials had gone round the area deciding how many evacuees could be billeted on people.

That morning my brother Norman and I had gone with my mother and sister, Audrey, to Newcastle railway station. I had my gas-mask slung round my neck and a brown luggage label through the buttonhole in my overcoat. My emergency rations (6 Oxo cubes) were in my coat pocket.

The previous week we went to our local school where we were fitted out with our gas-masks and were given strict instructions to take them everywhere. I even wore mine on the earth closet at High House and announced their lack of efficiency to all and sundry. We were also taught how to deal with incendiary bombs. Cover them with sand (no water!) using a long-handled shovel etc. etc.

We eventually arrived at Egremont Town Hall and were allocated to our single-decker coach. We were told our first stop was to be in Hail, Hale or Haile depending on which signpost one looked at. After we turned off the main road at Glasshouses Corner at Blackbeck I

was struck by the fact that bramble (or blackites, as I learned to call them) canes were scraping down each side of the bus. We were used to roads in Newcastle where even double-decker buses could pass each other easily. We were dropped off at High House, Wilton, near Egremont. We soon settled in and started school in Haile. First we had to learn a new vocabulary – yan, styan (we scopped these), lonnin, yat, laik, beck, thee, thou, etc. We wore clogs on our feet and corduroy britches with pockets at the front. You were nothing if you didn't have corduroy britches! At break and lunchtime we indulged in Cumberland-style wrestling, cricket or pushing each other into the beck which was part of the playground. On the other side of the road there was a gas indicator. It looked a bit like a bird table and was painted with special paint that changed colour if the Germans decided Haile School was a worthwhile target for a gas attack.

One day the beck ran red instead of its usual clearness. There were dozens of dead eels lying about. The iron ore mine at Head of Haile was in business.

June feeds the sheep. June, an evacuee at Town End farm in the early 1940s, takes on one of the more pleasant jobs on the farm. Beckermet mine can be seen in the background.

The contrast in life-styles was enormous. In Newcastle we had gas, electricity and mains water. In Wilton we had a coal fire, paraffin lamps, an earth closet and water came from a spring on the hillside on the other side of the road. It ran into a set pot and thence into a pipe to the house. About once a fortnight we would lift the wooden cover and remove any dead mice, frogs etc. which had fallen into the set pot and drowned. (I'm convinced that the resistance to germs we built up in those days stayed with us for life. On a holiday in the Soviet Union I was the only person in the party not to suffer from Leningrad Tummy!)

We didn't have a bull at High House and so our cows used to make the trip to Brackenthwaite to visit the bull. One day I was allowed to take a cow there on my own. I felt very proud to be entrusted with this task. My mother was horrified at what her little boy had been exposed to.

My mother and sister, Audrey, were billeted with Mr. and Mrs. Davies in Wilton. My mother was there as a helper – mending socks etc. for the evacuees.

It wasn't very long before evacuees started to return to Newcastle. When the number of evacuees fell below a certain level my mother went to an hotel in St Bees as a cook. My sister went to Whitehaven hospital to train as a nurse.

Early in 1940 West Cumberland had a very heavy snowfall and some children were off school for two weeks or so. Hedges were completely covered by drifts. My brother Norman took the 11+ early in 1940 and passed for Rutherford College which had been evacuated to Carlisle. He attended that school for about three years before transferring to Whitehaven Grammar in Catherine Street.

I was as happy as a sandboy. On my way home I had to cross two becks and frequently tickled fish and had them for supper or breakfast. Tony Trohear was like a big brother to me. We had some good fishing trips together.

When I first arrived at High House the milk was separated using an Alfa-Laval separator and churned into butter which was sold in Whitehaven market. Then the great day came when the Milk Marketing Board set up in business in Egremont. L.M.S. (London Midland and Scottish) wagons called each day and collected the milk

The two evacuees try riding one of the horses. The evacuees, Rita and June, watched over by Thai Mumberson, have a ride on one of the work horses.

in metal churns. At the end of the month a cheque would arrive. Milk producers got more money for less work. Sometimes I would beg a lift with the milk lorry. Eventually, Big Ike would stand on the back of the wagon while I released the hand-brake and drove down the hill stopping to pick up the full churns and leave the empties. The farmers had to fill in a label with their name and the amount of milk in the churn. One farmer consistently claimed his churns held more than the amount as measured by the M.M.B. He said the road from his farm to the milk stand was very bumpy and his milk 'shook down'.

Eventually my mother remarried and I had to leave High House and live in Whitehaven. (My father died in Newcastle.)

When I left school aged 16, I worked in the Meteorological Office at Silloth airfield, did my National Service at Aldergrove, worked at Eskmeals gun range and then trained as a teacher. I married, had two children, took my Private Pilot's Licence and retired from teaching.

Life in this parish, and Haile School obviously did me no harm at all and certainly didn't hold me back from eventually getting a degree.

Some Sayings

Referring to sheep's gestation period of 19 to 21 weeks, and to shepherds' limitations in forecasting:

'The best shepherd that ever ran, didn't know whether a sheep went nineteen, twenty or twenty yan'.

Sheep cameral. What was it used for? Clue: similar to a milkmaid's yoke on which buckets were hung.[10]

'Look at corn (oats) in May, you'll go weeping away. Look at corn in June you'll be hummin' a tune.'

'If thoo sees crows building in a fella's yard, you knew 'e wus on 'is way oot '(financially, one presumes).

Considering a horse with white legs: 'One, buy it. Two, try it. Three, think about it. Four, let it alone'.

Most sayings in a farming community were, of course, to do with the weather.

'March dust is worth a guinea an ounce.'

'For grass in May you need a shower a day, and a shower of muck every other day.' (Thai Mumberson)

'You can guarantee rain if t'mist 'as cum doon on Dint or there's a cap on Black Combe.'

'If there's a blue skee and t'new moon stands street up an' you couldn't see no sign of t'old moon, you'd 'ave a good month. But if t'new moon were inside o' t'old moon, that's a sign of a bad month.'

'Floods in May are soon away, but floods in June, becks nivver go doon.'

'If Carolmass day (Candlemas – 2nd February) be bright and clear, there'll be two winters in t'one year.'

'When t'wind meets thi feet, there'll be rain afore neet.'

'Git a frost in November that'll bear a duck, and there'll be nowt else but slush an' muck.'

'If thoo saw mowdies scamperin' aboot above t'grund at plooin' time in May, it were a sign of hot weather to cum.'

Not all farmers, however, took notice of such sayings. Sam Wightman was one such who, when he heard such sayings being trotted out, had one of his own: 'What's a sign of hot weather is a sign of wet'.

Mowdie spade. Why is the size of this spade important?[11]

LEISURE

CHILDREN'S GAMES AND PASTIMES

'I tell you what we used to like, mind, when it was frosty, what skating we had on that school yard down that bank where all the trees are now'.

Cold Fell gate. Two boys, obviously well organised for a long stay, watch over the gate at Cold Fell. A small fee would encourage them to open it for any passing motorist. This source of income dried up when a cattle grid was installed. Just think what an income could be derived from the present-day Sellafield traffic!

'We used to sew, we used to make our own clothes. A matter of needs must, I suppose. But we were never bored. We had a good life really. I feel sorry for the young people nowadays . . . they don't seem to have the same fun that we had, going for a picnic with your bike, you know. We used to go for picnics to Ennerdale . . .'

'They were happy days and we used to open the gate, the fell gate,

Harold Wilson, Jessie and foal. Jessie was bought at the Lamplugh sale and she was in foal at the time. Later in the year young Harold walked her with her foal to Gosforth show where they won first prize. The previous owner had only ever won second prize with Jessie and her foals. 'Funny that', he was heard to comment. Jessie went on to win first for two or three years after that, so Harold must have been doing something right.

for the cars going through and get a penny. And on Cold Fell there was this big mossy patch. We used to make all sorts of things out of this moss, you know . . . It was lovely'.

'Mrs Harvey introduced us to shinty and we played it in the field behind Manesty. The boys played shinty as well, I think. We had these sticks like a hockey stick but they were just more like a rough walking stick thing, you know. Anyway, we always enjoyed it. And we played rounders. Oh we had great fun'.

'Hoppy beds we used to play. You marked out the squares and had a piece of flat stone and you used to scud it like that and then scuddle into which hoppy bed you were going to set off from. If the stone landed on a line you were out'.

'. . . they used to fish for minnows. Well they used to grapple like this, you see, and I had the jam jar with water in and they used to catch these little things and put them in the jam jar. I don't know what they were going to do with them and then they'd go back to the river. They thought I had a jam jar full. I just kept my arms round it, ran up the river and put them back in . . . All they did was they kept on catching these'.

Harold Wilson and Jessie at Gosforth show. About 1930.

ESKDALE AND ENNERDALE FOXHOUNDS

Haile, along with many other villages, has a long-standing connection with the Eskdale and Ennerdale Foxhounds. The hunt covered an area from St Bees in the North and Broughton in the South, to the Langdales in the East and the Irish Sea coast in the West. It aimed to cover the whole of this area once in the season and then twice in the season during the second world war, when, because of the need to produce as much home-grown food as possible, it was felt that there was a more urgent need to control foxes.

In the 1920s the hounds were hunted by Mr W. C. Porter and stayed at Head of Haile, but in 1928 they moved to Town End Farm from where they hunted the Haile district in November each year.

When it was the turn of Haile to host the hunt, the hounds would be walked from their kennels in the Eskdale valley, the twenty or so miles to the Mumbersons at Town End farm with Mr Porter, the

Master, at the front on his bicycle, and the Whipper-in, appropriately, bringing up the rear. They would arrive on the Friday ready to hunt on the Saturday and the Monday. In those days there was no hunting, you notice, on the Sunday.

In the meantime at Town End farm the Friday afternoon was spent cooking enough Indian Meal and Flaked Maize to last the time the hounds would be staying. The meal would have been brought from Egremont Mill by horse and cart a day or two before. Then, as now, the meal, boiled up in the set pot, was known to have been cooked for a sufficient time when the stirring stick stood up in it. Any less and the meal would go off too quickly. Friday evening was the time for the Whist Drive and Hunt Ball, and, no doubt, The Bucks Head did a good trade. It was at the pub that the hunt would assemble the next day for the stirrup cup and the start.

While hunting in the Haile 'district' the hounds, the huntsmen and the spectators, all of whom walked, would find themselves following the fox as far as Dent, Cold Fell, Braystones and even Wasdale Head; that was in the days before the woods were planted in

Foxhounds collecting at Town End. W. C. Porter, grandfather of the present master and huntsman, Thai Mumberson and Jack Porter, son of W. C. Porter assembling the hounds.

The stirrup cup.

summer months when they were not working. In many cases it was the same place where the hound had been sent to be reared from the time it was weaned at its kennels in Eskdale until it was eighteen months old. By then it was ready to join the pack. Because at the beginning of the summer, the hounds had been walked to their summer home, it was not unknown for some to disappear if they weren't happy with the way they were treated while 'on holiday'. 'If one went missing, they'd have to go out and look for it and they'd find it back at the kennels.' This happens less today, even if the hound is unhappy, because they are transported both to the hunt and to their 'Summer Walk'.

Throughout this time, which must now be about eighty years, the Porter family have been Masters of the hunt. When Mr W. C. Porter died the pack was hunted by his son, Jack Porter and then by Mr Edmund Porter who has now hunted the pack for forty years.

Edmund Porter leads the hounds up from Town End before the hunt begins. 1974. The hounds are accompanied by a few of the more energetic followers who will walk the hunt after, that is, they have called at the 'Buck's Head' for the stirrup cup.

places like Blengdale. Not surprisingly, it often happened that the hunt did not return to base until ten at night by which time the hounds had to be led home. As there weren't always enough leads available they would arrive back held with belts, binder twine and sometimes garters. The latter no doubt held the hounds in check but did little for the tidiness of one's socks.

The hunt in those days was a very special occasion and, at a time when there were no football matches you could go to, it was an entertainment that was widely enjoyed.

Out of season the hounds went to their 'Summer Walks'. These were farms and other places where they were looked after for the

Today, the cost of running the pack – still a thing to be taken into account – is met by Whist Drives, Dances, subscriptions and social events. When Haile pub was still going, these social evenings were held there (in fact for its last few years it was redesigned with a hunting theme) and the hunting folk enjoyed the usual tatie pot supper and a good sing-song. The hounds work as hard as ever but the spectators at least, often prefer cars and binoculars to a pair of boots.

Mr Edmund Porter, the present master and huntsman.

THE 1981 FLOWER FESTIVAL

It wasn't just to follow any trend that Haile in May 1981 held a flower festival in the church. Until 1981 the church had been fortunate in having as its resident vicar Archdeacon Hardie. At this time the church did not have to pay a large stipend to the Diocese, but on the retirement of the Archdeacon, the church was required to pay such a stipend or risk losing its independence – not a thought that goes down well with the parishioners of Haile. This, and the fact that the church organ was in dire need of repair, meant that money had to be found. The flower festival was the outcome.

Just about everyone in this small community was involved in the various activities: in the arranging of the displays in the church; or in the organising and running of the arts and craft exhibition and sale held in the village hall; or in the preparation and sale of teas, also in the village hall. All this activity was largely overseen by Margaret Smith who then lived in the parish.

The theme of the display was 'All Things Bright and Beautiful'. While the font, windows, screen, and altar each portrayed a particular

The church entrance.

verse or couplet from the hymn, many other parts of the church were decorated to reflect the idea of simplicity and natural beauty. In keeping with this idea, many of the flowers and much of the foliage used were from the wild or garden-grown. The church porch was a particularly striking example of the use of natural features, with driftwood, moss, primroses and other early summer flowers arranged as if growing naturally.

The art and craft fair provided a rich mixture of paintings, wood carvings, soft toys, pottery and furnishings to mention only some. Many of these were made by the talented people of the parish.

The exhibition of crafts.

And, of course, there were the famous Haile teas available.

It was remarked by many how wonderful it was that such a small community could present such a fascinating and comprehensive show. It was no surprise, though a great delight, that the efforts of all those parishioners raised £1,000.

Music in the church, provided by the Lynwood Ensemble, added further to the rich experience that arose from a financial need and exploded into a joyous occasion for the thousand or so visitors and all those who, in its preparation, had given up so much time and shown so much talent.

Some extracts from the summary given to the Parochial Church Council by Margaret Smith may best describe the excitement and intensity of the activities of the festival.

'. . . the distress at first as Mrs Nixon, then Mr Hall and then Mrs Barns went into hospital – at one stage it looked as though our Festival should be held in the West Cumberland! Of the willingness of others to "fill the breaches"; of the activity around the church as grass was cut, gravestones cleaned, walls built and piano installed . . . exhibition to mount, flowers to arrange, church to prepare, programmes to collect, last minute details to see to – of which there were hundreds! . . . wonderful exhibits being mounted in the Craft Exhibition, representing hours and hours of labour and skill; masses and masses of beautiful flowers being arranged, in church, by extremely talented ladies; cakes, scones and biscuits – in quantity and quality sufficient for a royal banquet. Then, suddenly Tuesday night arrived. All was ready. "All Things Bright and Beautiful" had been achieved. The church – quiet, dignified, magnificent; the hall – pretty, bright, light and professional-looking. Memories of the contrast, during

'Purple headed mountains.'

Rose Queen. 1920. Florrie Logan, Haile carnival rose queen, prepares to set off round the village.

Carnival at Haile. The popular fancy dress on the school green.

the Festival, between the peacefulness of the church and the hustle and bustle in the village hall; of the look of pleasure on everyone's faces as they saw the flowers, ate their tea and viewed the exhibition; of the concert – beautiful music in equally beautiful surroundings; of the car parks at both church and hall full of cars and, occasionally, coaches! and of the weather – the best week's weather in May!'

LEISURE TIME

'Well, you had to entertain yourselves really. There was quite a lot my age then in the village and everybody went to church on Sunday night and sort of walked to the road end in them days and back again at night'.

'We always had a good bonfire on the green. We first of all set off doing the potatoes in their jackets on the bonfire. But then, you see, Hubert would come across with some diesel or summat to get it a good start. So the taties didn't taste so good'.

'All the young men played quoits. It was up by the top. By the road sign. They used to have a little thing with sand in,

Jubilee clowns. Part of the fancy dress celebrating the Queen's Silver Jubilee in 1977.

like a sort of cold frame, and they used to throw the quoits in there'.

'In the field by the junction where the two bungalows are now they used to do Cumberland and Westmorland wrestling'.

'Dancing was a great thing and, of course, a live band. But a great thing was to go the Empress ballroom at Whitehaven . . . we had good bands at Whitehaven, Harry Gold and his Pieces of Eight and a band called The Blue Jacks'.

WRESTLING

Cumberland and Westmorland wrestling has played a significant part in the life of this parish. During the summer months the young men of the parish would get together on a Friday evening to practise their sport in a field just by the road junction in Haile village.

Joe Noble was one such young man. He was born and lived just about all of his life in Haile; in fact he used to say that he had lived in nearly every house in the village. We think he first learned wrestling

Joe Noble. 1923. Joe, on the right, with the cup he won at Grasmere.

The Noble family outside 'Beechwood'. 1919. Joe is standing at the centre back, with his father to the right.

with Jack Mumberson around the turn of the twentieth century. He certainly learned well for he won the lightweight competition in 1923 at Grasmere, the centre of Cumberland and Westmorland competition. The photograph of him with his trophy shows him in his vest embroidered by his wife, Annie, who was a skilled dressmaker. When he could no longer participate he became a referee for the sport and officiated at Grasmere every August until he was in his eighties. Such was his enthusiasm for and dedication to the local sport.

Joe was one of the referees when Hubert Nanson, who was now living and farming in Haile and who belonged to Gosforth Wrestling

Academy, was matched in a new, 12-stone class, even though he was a lightweight. *The Whitehaven News* reported: 'J Bland of Clitheroe got the better of H. Nanson . . . who is a lightweight and displayed remarkable cleverness in winning against so many heavier men'. The photograph from *The Yorkshire Post* shows Hubert Nanson, the nearer of the two wrestlers, and Joe Noble wearing a trilby hat, as referee standing in the background on this occasion in 1955.

'There were wrestling academies, towards the end of the war, I suppose. There was Gosforth, Bootle, Kirkbride, Egremont, Carlisle and Gilsland. Wrestling was just a summer sport, you see, at the Sports. So, during the winter they had these academies as they called them. So they did that inside in the winter time. And they used to do it in like a boxing ring, you know, with cord round'.

'These lads used to wrestle best of three and you had the team . . . they had the three weights, you see, the lightweight, middleweight and heavyweight and they had to be weighed in and all done properly and of course the highlight was Grasmere Sports'.

'Well, Hubert was light and the first championship he won was just after the war, in 1948, and there wasn't any medals to be had. So, he didn't get a medal for that. But, the second one that he won was later on . . . he got a medal. All the Kirkbys were big on wrestling, Henry and Bill and John, they were all good wrestlers'.

Hubert Nanson at Grasmere. Hubert, on the right, competes in the final at Grasmere. Joe Noble is the referee standing to the left.

THE PARISH COUNCIL

NOTES FROM THE PARISH COUNCIL

These notes extracted from the Parish Council minutes show how the Council's deliberations reflected both what was going on in the parish and some of the events and changes in the world beyond.

BOOK 1

December 1894. A meeting of the Electors of Haile and Wilton was held in the School Room, Haile, to vote for the motion 'That we apply for a Parish Council'

January 1895. This first meeting was to nominate and elect seven Parish Councillors. Fourteen were nominated and the following elected as the councillors – Isaac Benson, farmer (Far) Head of Haile, John Hail, farmer Beck Brow, John Moffat, joiner Blackbeck, John Storey, farmer Head of Haile, Edward Sumpton, farmer Brackenthwaite, John Shepherd, Darcy Thompson, vet practitioner/farmer Isle House, Black Beck.

1895 continued. Clerk's Salary £10 to £12. (Stephen Nicholson). Precept £5.

Repairs to the village well.

London Bridge, Wilton. Poor condition and a hand rail needed.

State of roads from Black Beck.

Each council has 2 overseers (auditors?).

Maintenance of roads one of the few duties of the Parish Council.

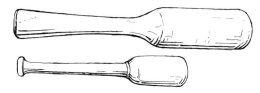

Bleeder. Made of wood but how was it used? [12]

1900. Meeting called by the overseers to appoint a new council, the previous one not having acted according to the Parish Council Act. County Council order needed for approval.

1901. Special meeting of the largest ratepayers of the parish to discuss the Southern District Water Scheme – the parish to oppose the scheme, already an abundant water supply.

Bad state of the Parish Lime Kiln. Also complaints against District Council taking stone from the kiln for road repairs when the lime was needed by farmers.

Water scheme from Friars Well.

1904. Appointment of School Manager.

State of road to Brackenthwaite – property owners responsible for road repairs.

Stretch of road to Brackenthwaite belonging to Hole of Haile (owner requested to arrange repairs).

A new footbridge be erected over river at Hole of Haile.

1911. Coronation meal for Haile Children.

Council give assent to Egremont Water Scheme and the use of Wilton School Green for this.

1912. Jas. Mumberson and George W. Thompson be reappointed Charity Trustees.

Agreed to ask 2s. 6d. per yard for Wilton School Green.

1913. Further correspondence with Brown, Auld & Brown asking them to 'enquire what Egremont Council would be prepared to offer for the land required for their Reservoir at Wilton'

Special meeting – the contractors seek permission to have possession of the land. No possession until the price is agreed.

Egremont Urban Council offer £50. Haile Parish offer to sell for £100. Professional advice is then sought and the land is valued officially. An arbitrator is appointed and conveyances drawn up and exchanged. Trustees appointed to receive the money from Egremont Council.

1914. Parish Council asked to contribute to new fire engine at Whitehaven – No, too far away to be of use to the Parish. Discuss possibility of purchasing standpipe and hose.

Seek advice on investment of money from the sale of Wilton School Green.

Sale of Parish Gravel Pit. How shall money be invested?

1915. Letter from Mr. Chapman re recruiting (for the war). Mr. Adair was asked to canvas the Parish for recruits.

District Council to be asked 'What authority had they for taking gravel from the Parish Gravel Quarry for the benefit of another Parish?'

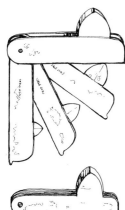

Fleams. What was the therapeutic use? [13]

Mr. Hodgson should desist from taking gravel until he could prove his right to do so and what remuneration he was prepared to pay for what had been taken.

A claim of £12 to be made. Met with Mr Hodgson who offered £7, which was accepted.

Monies from sale of Wilton land for reservoir to be invested in Government Stock.

1917. Concern for bad state of Church Brow and London (foot) Bridge.

Letter received concerning National Service. No public meeting called 'as all had received their papers if they wished to volunteer' but the council were willing to assist.

1918. A letter read from Rural League urging cottagers to keep pigs. Replied that most already doing so but would like advice on feeding stuffs.

New Polling District to be considered, made up of the Parishes of St. John's, St. Bridget's, Lowside Quarter and Haile.

Poor state of road to Brackenthwaite – several owners to be contacted. Alterations at Stockbridge Brow – District Council to be contacted.

1919. Public meeting called to consider the question of celebrating Peace.

Parish wall in Haile in bad state of repair.

Letting of allotments – no action as no requests.

1920. Housing Scheme – District Council dealing with this but no application was made.

'Haile Poor Money' balance £5. 8. 6d.

Letters read from Ministry of Health in regard to Beckermet

Sewage Scheme and that an enquiry would be held.

1926. A notice to be placed in the village warning people not to deposit rubbish over the wall on the Parish Ground.

1927. Letter to Haile Hall Solicitors regarding dangerous state of road leading to Manesty Cottage caused by recent flood.

Letter to Whitehaven Union concerning 'dirty water for consumption' from the mains supply.

1928. Decided to notify trustees of Haile Hall Estate of the dangerous conditions adjoining their property.

Thanks be given to Miss Turner in regards to Further Education Classes.

1930. Question of village lighting discussed but decided to oppose the scheme as benefits would not be to the Parish in general. 'Well I don't see any reason for street lights, because anybody that went out in the dark at Haile, they weren't *wanting* a light.'

1931. Oppose the proposal to take a portion of Haile Parish and add it to St Bridget's – all land and houses known as Haile End lying south of road to Calderbridge.

Haile's Victorian letter box.

Query as to how many Managers required to serve on the Haile Elementary School Board.

1932. Question of altering Parish Boundary was again raised and Mr. Black from the District Council attended the meeting and advised the

Council not to oppose the scheme, which they agreed to. The Parish would not incur serious loss but had been put to much expense on account of sewering and lighting as this part of the Parish was in St Bridget's District.

1933. Motion to install Public Telephone in village but Council decided to query the expenses.

Sir John Ponsonby wrote to the Council asking if they would support the electric lighting system and have the village and surrounding houses supplied as he was prepared to take it to the Hall. Enquiries to be made.

Complaint about the dangerous state of Church Hill.

1934. Asked Post Office if a collecting box could be installed at Blackbeck (18 dwellings) and Wilton.

Rev. Woof wrote to the Council pointing out that the Parish would benefit from having a Public Telephone.

Problems with various roads in the Parish being in poor state of repair.

Refuse causing a problem having been dumped in the beck bottom.

Noted the shortage of houses in the Parish and that other parishes had workmen's houses erected.

Letter received from the Ministry regarding boundary changes and they had to say why they proposed to keep Haile End as part of the Parish. The clerk to attend the meeting in Carlisle. Received expenses of £1. 1s. 0d.

1935. Letter received from the Ministry regarding Jubilee Celebrations. All parishes expected to make some entertainment. Decided to give all children a mug and afternoon tea.

1936. Question of collection of ashes discussed as there was difficulty in disposing of them. Sanitary inspector to be informed about dumping of ashes and rubbish in the beck.

London Bridge in poor state of repair and dangerous for children to cross when walking to school. Bridge at Godderthwaite to be repaired.

1937. Letter received from Head Postmaster asking for council's consent to alteration of half day closing at Beckermet Post Office from Tuesday to Thursday. Haile Council agreeable.

1938. Question of Public Telephone again raised. Letter read on behalf of Haile Nursing Association (presumably supporting the idea) and the matter was to be put to Rural District Council seeking their advice.

1939. Question of collection of house rubbish discussed especially as sewerage scheme for village nearly completed.

Application made to Rural District Council for several new houses in the Parish as many of the existing ones are unsuitable for habitation. Application refused as the Parish was not in a slum clearance area.

1941. 'Spitfire Appeal' set up. Attempt to visit every household. Letter to Sir John Ponsonby asking if Banqueting Hall could be used in an appeal.

Enrolment of fire fighting volunteers to the Parish.

Rev. Berry pointed out dangers of crossing the road from school and the excessive motor traffic through the village.

1946. The VJ & VE celebrations were left over to a later meeting again and forgotten.

1947. Cost of Public Telephone in Haile and Wilton to be £4 per annum for 5 years. Ennerdale Rural District Council consulted about precept regarding this. Further application about installation and also a letter box in Wilton.

Transporting of Wilton children to school – Vicar and School Managers to deal with this.

Problems of finding housing for agricultural workers in the area.

1950. Council to assist County Council Survey of Footpaths and Byeways for National Survey.

1954. Complaint about sewer on roadside at Low Broadleys.

Letter sent to Rural District Council asking if Haile and Blackbeck could have street lighting and if ashes and house refuse could be collected from Wilton.

1955. Application for lighting the telephone kiosk in Haile showed it to be too expensive.

BOOK 2

1960. Noted the growth of brushwood on road from Brayshaw to Cold Fell Gate.

Reported that drinking water supply was dirty at times and had a bad smell.

1963. Letter read from Ennerdale Rural District Council about closing of railway between Barrow and Whitehaven.

1964. Decided not to enter competition for best kept village.

Blackbeck to get a street light.

Clerk instructed to write to Cumberland Motor Services asking that 'Haile Moor' be shown on bus indicators because parishioners have been left standing in Egremont. CMS replied that they were governed by the work at the mines. (It was, strictly speaking, a works bus.)

1966. £16 raised from door to door collection for the Winston Churchill Memorial Fund.

Council confirmed there were no allotments in the Parish.

Following plots to be registered as common land – Around Haile Church and Haile School.

1967. In answer to a letter from HMI of Taxes asking whether income tax had been paid, council replied that 'It was hardly paying its way!'

1969. A complaint was received about water constantly running down the road past Haile Moor Cottages.

Council perturbed that no light in the telephone kiosk (Complaints about this for at least 30 years). Installed New Year's Day 1970.

Plan for building sites to be drawn up after several enquiries.

Bull holder. Still in use today, but how does it work?[14]

Agreed that Haile Parish Council should join the Cumberland Parish Councils Association. (CALC) after much deliberation for several years.

1971. Possibility of clean up programme for Ullcoats Mine.

Special Meeting on Housing – proposed plan for a few bungalows would be acceptable.

1972. Council agreed to precept for one penny rate.

A car had been dumped at Cold Fell Gate.

Church Hall in need of care and attention but the Parish Council could only help if it was made over to a Village Hall/Community Centre.

County Planning Officer discourages a village plan as we would be commercialised. Some small infill development could take place without spoiling the charm of the village.

1973. Future re-organisation of Local Government. Joint meeting to discuss and consider amalgamation with Ponsonby and/or St Bridget's.

Radio Carlisle to start broadcasting in November and Parish Councils could publicise their work.

Sites of Archaeological interest – Aerial Ropeway, Haile Mill Quarry-freestone, Lime Kiln-Wilton, Matty Benn's Bridge, Kells Quarry-freestone (Broadleys Bottoms) Grange Quarry-freestone.

Licence of Buck's Head Inn transferred to H. Hellen.

Planning Application for 10 dwellings in Haile. Did not fit in the proposed Village Plan.

1975. Public Rights of Way Listed.

Survey for Recreational Facilities needed for children since the Haile Park Development.

1976. Enquiry about 30 mph speed restrictions through Haile Village but it was not allowable.

Parishioners to be informed if they were on the route of any motor rallies through the villages.

1977. Mines and Quarries Act 1969 – Haile Moor Mine was to be listed as it was now abandoned.

Silver Jubilee Mugs to be purchased.

1978. Open meeting to discuss how to provide play facilities and what would be required.

1979. Jubilee Seat made by Pelham House School sited on the Village Green.

Parish Boundary/Parish Review – 'Residents of Oxenriggs, Whitehow Head and Grange centre their activities on Haile and should more properly be part of Haile Parish.'

Centenary Celebrations Haile Village Hall (School) – Old scholars and partners. Birthday cake to be provided.

Playing Field – grant of £1,000 awarded but no land at present available in village and it was not enough to purchase land at present prices. Equipment to be installed on village green – wendy house and climbing frame. Table tennis for indoors.

BOOK 3

1980. Ramblers Association would like all Parishes to have their footpaths accessible and marked.

Parish Council to pay £50 towards insulation and false ceiling in Village Hall to cut fuel costs and make the hall warmer to use.

Outline Planning Application for 20 executive dwellings at Haile Moor Mine site – felt to be inappropriate to agreed development plan.

Activities for Parishioners – survey of Parishioners to find out their choices. Clubs set up.

Recycling of waste – Cumbria Countryside Conference. Parish Council suggested skip in Egremont for glass and paper but Copeland Borough Council said it was too costly and Friends of the Earth recycled glass.

Removal of pit banks – reported that British Steel had a duty to do this.

1981. Pit bank sold and would be transported to British Nuclear Fuels Ltd.

Ongoing problems of fly tipping throughout the Parish.

Proposed roundabout at Blackbeck and concerns that there would be increased traffic from Sellafield through Haile to Cold Fell.

Best Kept Village Competition. Village clean up. Came second.

Wedding of Charles and Diana – the Parish children to get another mug.

Wilton to get weekly dustbin collection.

1982. Road problems – blocked drains, culverts, gratings – no longer cleaned out regularly. Continually reported throughout the minutes.

1983. Redrawing of Parish Boundaries – the Parish had not gained Oxenriggs, Grange or Whitehow Head but Tail End had gone to St Bridget's Beckermet.

Won the Best Kept Small Village Competition.

1984. Ullcoats Trading Estate – concern over inadequacy of access road in light of increased heavy industrial traffic. The matter had been with Cumbria County Council for 12 months. But no action

taken. To be taken up again.

1985. Parish Council information to be published in Parish News Letter.

Bulbs planted outside churchyard after winning a prize in the Best Kept Small Village Competition.

Traffic in Haile – between 06.45 and 08.15 approx. 60 cars passing through village causing distress and danger to residents due to excessive speed and the narrowness of roads.

Boundaries Review – St John's Parish Council thought that Oxenriggs naturally fell into their boundary along with Scurgill and

Bridge and trees.

144

Carleton but that Grange and Whitehow Head were more aligned with Haile Parish.

Grass cutting equipment stolen from shed in churchyard grounds. Haile Parochial Church Council decided not to replace equipment but to pay for grass cutting. Parish Council agreed to pay £100 and review the amount annually.

1987. Mayor-Making Meeting – a representative was chosen to attend this meeting. Sherry reception and buffet dance to follow.

Drinking water – concerns about the amount of chlorine in the water. Meeting with the Water Board.

1988. Haile Poor Money – £62 was paid to the Parish Council for them to use suitably.

Ennerdale Parish Council conducting a survey – 'Whether the Local Authority takes note of Parish Council views?' Haile Parish Council said they thought No.

Sellafield Emergency Planning – several meetings attended over past years. Copeland Borough Council wanted information regarding size of Village Hall in case it was needed as an Emergency Shelter.

1991. West Cumbria Motor Club gave notice that a rally was to pass through the Parish.

Six Parish Councils – The Parish Council was asked 'Why is it not on this Committee because of the concern about Nirex?' Contact was made and by 1993 a representative was attending meetings.

Planning Application. For Travel Lodge at Blackbeck roundabout – was not seen to be advantageous at this time.

Haile Moor Mine being used as a storage dump which was not in keeping with Village Plan.

1992. Beckermet mine – unsightly tipping on the pit bank.

Request for Notice Board at Blackbeck was seen to be too expensive.

Gas will be brought to Haile very soon.

1994 to 1998. Inter County Waste – skips of rubbish being tipped and buried plus rubbish burning at Haile Moor Mine – not a licensed tip. This issue caused great concern for 4 years, as did the site at Hardheads which had been overfilled, and was run by the same people.

Public Meeting was called to discuss the matter as it was felt that this was inappropriate use of the site and also concern over the adequacy of the company proposing to run the site. (Site is now privately owned by local farmers.)

1996 to 1997. Beckermet Mine (St John's Parish). Considerable activity and removal of pit bank. Concerns over noise and dust pollution as Haile Park is overlooked by the mine. Proper Rules and Regulations eventually enforced so that there was a satisfactory outcome.

Further concern about application for 'extended time' on Landfill site at Hardheads. Petition signed by Wilton residents opposing this application.

1997. Suggest Neighbourhood Forum Grant be applied for to help with plan for storage room at Village Hall.

1998. Low Winder Lane Wilton – Parish Council recommended to claim this as parish land.

1999. Parish Council bi-monthly meeting to be set out in advance due to increased work load and many changes taking place.

Millennium mugs for the children.

2000. Wilton Reservoir – Copeland Borough Council enquire 'Who owns Reservoir as NWW would like to have deeds transferred to them'. The land had been sold to Egremont Town Council.

2001. Meetings curtailed due to Foot and Mouth Outbreak.

Wilton – road closed due to installation of new water main but the Parish Council was not informed.

Roads – concerns about amount of traffic passing through village to and from Sellafield. Usual problems due to lack of regular maintenance.

Government issues Rural White Paper – many changes to take place in the near future. Training for Councillors and the Clerk.

Play equipment now in dangerous state and needs to be removed and replaced.

2002. Beginning of Parish Council's programme to draw attention to the poor state of the Parish drains and its effect on the roads. Meeting with engineer so that proposals can be made for funding.

2003. Public Meeting to discuss how the Parishioners would like the Parish to go forward. A Parish Plan Committee is formed and the work progresses.

ENDING

A Thought to End with

Rev. Simpson ended his historical notes about Haile and its church with a suitable ending for our book:

'Sufficient has been written, or so we hope, to stir up your interest and awaken a desire to walk in the steps of those who have left us such a goodly heritage'.

Thai Mumberson.

APPENDIX

Answers to 'What was this used for'

1. **Medicine chest.** (Why 'universal'?)
The regular container for animal medicines supplied to the farmer, either containing medicines that had been ordered or containing a 'universal' collection of medicines that would most likely come in useful.

2. **The Cowhorn.** (Obviously, but why was it cut to this shape?)
A horn with the larger end cut diagonally to make a container for giving medicines to animals. The medicine was poured into the horn and then the large end of the horn inserted into the animal's open mouth. A smaller horn was used for calves.

3. **Milk measures.** (Self-explanatory, but how was the law involved?)
These were stamped every year with a lead stamp in the presence of the 'Weights and Measures' to authenticate their accuracy. These particular ones were taken to the 'White Mare' pub in Beckermet where a store room was used on these occasions. Other portable devices that farmers used for weighing, such as potato scales, were taken along for authentication at the same time.

4. **Box iron and stand made out of a horse shoe.** (For ironing, of course, but how did it work?)
Iron inserts were heated in the fire, and when hot enough they were put into the iron through a hole in the back of the iron which was revealed when the spindle was lifted. This particular, small, iron was for collars and cuffs.

5. **Jam pan, bread tin and moulds**.

6. **Pig ringing pliers.** (How did these work?)
First catch your pig. Stroke it to calm it because there will be enough fuss soon. Loop the end of a rope and place this behind the pig's front teeth. Put the rope over a door in order to lift up the pig's head. (The squealing now will be quite something.) Place the U-shaped pig ring, which has sharp ends, in the pliers and place the ring in the pig's nose. Closing the pliers secures the ring in the nose.

7. **Sausage funnels**. (Which was the easier one to use?)
First the intestine had to be cleaned in salt and water, and then turned inside out and cleaned again. As much as you could, or as much as you wanted, was wrinkled up the funnel shaft and a knot tied in the end. You then used your fingers to push the meat down into the skin. The shallower one was easier to use because you could push your finger further down the spout with this one.

8. **Turnip snagger.** (When did a turnip need snagging?)
The snagger was used to put under the root and pull up the turnip if there was too little top to get hold of. The blade was to trim the top and root.

9. **Butching knife.** (Why is the knife tapered?)
This knife was used for cutting the animal's throat. It was tapered for skinning the animal. This particular knife was made at the local New Mill smithy.

10. **Sheep cameral.** (What was it used for?)
Used for hanging the butchered sheep by the back legs while you 'dressed it up, skinning it and suchlike'.

11. **Mowdie spade.** (Why is the size of this spade important?)
A spade, still used, when setting mole traps. It is six inches square, in order to cut a hole just the right width for the trap.

12. **Bleeder.** (Made of wood, but how was it used?)
For 'bleeding' animals, a process once considered to be an aid to health. Its 'truncheon' shape might give a clue. See 'Fleams' for more details of this procedure.

13. **Fleams.** (What was the therapeutic use?)

For 'bleeding' animals. The fleam, according to 'The Modern Farrier' published in the 1830s, was used to help reduce any local or general inflammation, such as a fever or pneumonia. A rope was placed round the animal's neck as a tourniquet. The fleam was placed transversely on the jugular vein which was thus raised and the 'bleeder' was used to give a sharp tap to the end of the fleam in order to penetrate the vein. Once the rope was released, the bleeding stopped within seconds. It was important in all this that the animal remained still, so the man holding the animal's head had quite an important role to play in this operation.

14. **Bull holder.** (Still in use, but how does it work?)

Still sometimes used, for controlling an animal. The slightly bulbous end of the device was placed in the animal's nose and tightened with the screw. Some types have a sprung slide to tighten them. The rope for leading the animal was tied to the other end of the holder.

BIBLIOGRAPHY

Baldwin, J. R. and Whyte, I. D. *The Scandinavians in Cumbria*. University of Edinburgh. 1985.

Bouch, C. M. L. and Jones G. P. *A Short Economic and Social History of the Lakes Counties 1500-1830*. Manchester University Press. 1961.

Brunskill, R. W. *Traditional Buildings of Cumbria*. Cassell. 2002.

Brunskill, R. W. *Vernacular Building Tradition in the Lake District*. Faber. 1974.

Bulmer, *Bulmer's History and Directory of West Cumberland. 1829*. Bulmer and Co.

Burkett, M. E. and Sloss, D. *Read's Point of View*. Skiddaw Press. 1995.

Caine, C. The Manor Court of Egremont. *CWAAS Transactions*, Vol. XV (New Series), ART III.

Denyer, S. *Traditional Buildings and Life in the Lake District*. National Trust. 1991.

Fell, C. *Early Settlement in the Lake Counties*. Dalesman. 1972.

Jackson, P. J. *Jackson's Directory of Carlisle and Towns of Cumberland and Westmorland. 1880*. Jackson and Co.

Jollie, F. *Jollie's Cumberland Guide and Directory of 1811*. Michael Moon. 1995.

Jones, R. A. *Arthur Ponsonby – The Politics of Life*. Christopher Helm. 1989.

Kelly, *Kelly's Directory of Cumberland and Westmorland 1894, 1910, 1914, 1921, 1925, 1929, 1934*, Kelly and Co.

Kelly, D. *The Red Hills*. Red Earth Publications. 1994.

Kuhn, W. H. *Henry and Mary Ponsonby*. Duckworth. 2002.

Loftie, Canon A. G. *Great Salkeld, Its Rectors and History*. Chapter XIV, 'Archdeacon Nicolson'. Bemrose and Sons Ltd. 1900.

Loftie, Canon A. G. *Rural Deanery of Gosforth*. Titus Wilson, Kendal. 1889.

Mannix and Whellan, *History, Gazetteer and Directory of Cumberland. 1847*. Michael Moon. 1974.

Millward, R. and Robinson A. *The Lake District*. Methuen. 1974.

Morris, Harrison and Co., *Directory and Gazeteer of Cumberland. 1861*. Michael Moon. 2000.

Neville, St. B. *Life at the Court of Queen Victoria – Selections from the Journals of Queen Victoria*. Sutton Publishing. 1984.

Nicolson, Bishop W. Diaries. *Transactions CWAAS New Series*, Vol. 1, ART 1, pp. 1-32.

Nicolson, Bishop W. Diaries. Part IV, *Transactions CWAAS New Series*, Vol. IV, pp. 1-10.

Parker, Dr C. A. *The Gosforth District*. Titus Wilson, Kendal. 1904. Reprinted Michael Moon. 1986.

Parson and White, *History, Directory and Gazetteer of Cumberland and Westmorland with Furness and Cartmel. 1829*. Michael Moon. 1984.

Perriam, D. R. and Robinson, J. *The Medieval Fortified Buildings of Cumbria*. CWAAS. 1998.

Pevsner, N. *Cumberland and Westmorland*. Penguin 1967.

Ponsonby, Sir Charles. *The Ponsonby Family, 1929-1970*.

Ponsonby, Sir John, *The Ponsonby Family*. The Medici Society. 1929.

Robinson, J. M. *A Guide to the Country Houses of the North West*. Constable. 1991.

Rollinson, W. *A History of Man in the Lake District*. Dent. 1967.

Slater, I. *Slater's Directory of Cumberland and Westmorland. 1879*.

Slater, M. *Old Parish Churches of Cumbria*. Poly publications.

Trevelyan, G. M. *English Social History*. Longmans. 1946. 3rd edition

Webster. *The Life of a Country Clergyman*.

A fuller record of the books, documents and papers used or referred to in the text is listed along with the resources lodged at Reference YDX 430 with the Cumbria Record Office and Local Studies Library (Whitehaven). Those resources represent some of the information drawn on by the writers of the book in their researches and are available to members of the public.

WILTON